'*Human Trafficking, Structural Violence, and Resilience* is a beautifully written piece; deep yet breezy, colloquial yet academic. This text is a must read for anyone interested in understanding the nuances of human trafficking experiences beyond notions of victim, particularly in light of those who rarely get to have voice.'

Associate Professor Rochelle Stewart-Withers,
Massey University, New Zealand

'With careful attention to Mindanao migrants' agency and the social ties that can both be a source of personal resilience while also being coercive, this powerful volume makes a significant contribution to the ethnographic literature on Philippine labour migration by troubling the simplified dichotomy that separates literatures on migration from those on human trafficking. The author's detailing of individual migration histories illuminates the compounding social conditions and rural social disparities that compel migrants into risk-prone irregular international migration channels in a nation where historically produced structural violence limits local livelihood options and state-sponsored labour brokerage has normalized migration for several generations of global travellers.'

Professor Pauline Gardiner Barber,
Dalhousie University, Canada

'In *Human Trafficking, Structural Violence, and Resilience*, Dr Lennox considers the first-person narratives of Filipino trafficking survivors and situates them within a framework of compounding structural violence. Understood this way, trafficking becomes not only a possible, but normalised and tolerable option for these survivors.'

Dr. Jesse Hession Grayman,
University of Auckland, New Zealand

Human Trafficking, Structural Violence, and Resilience

This book explores and examines human trafficking in Eastern Mindanao in the Philippines, and the social conditions which facilitate and maintain this exploitation.

Through a combination of ethnographic research and life-narrative interviews, the book tells the stories of those who have experienced exploitation, and analyses the social conditions which form the context for these experiences. This book places the trafficking of migrants in context of the local social setting where migration, including human trafficking of migrants, is one of the limited options available for work. It explores how these social configurations contribute to exploitation both domestically and internationally. This book also draws on first-person accounts from those who have experienced trafficking or exploitation, offering lived experiences which reveal deep and complex cultural, social, and personal expressions of meaning, resilience, and hope within constrained, unequal, and even violent circumstances.

This book will appeal to students and scholars researching and studying in the fields of social and cultural anthropology, and Southeast Asian studies.

Amie L. Lennox is a New Zealand-based social anthropologist. Her research interests include migration, human trafficking, and the relationships between individual experiences of exploitation and wider social structures in the Philippines.

Routledge Studies in Anthropology

Surfaces
Transformations of Body, Materials and Earth
Edited by Mike Anusas and Cristián Simonetti

Mambila Divination
Framing Questions, Constructing Answers
David Zeitlyn

Suckling
Kinship More Fluid
Fadwa El Guindi

Amerindian Socio-Cosmologies between the Andes, Amazonia and Mesoamerica
Toward an Anthropological Understanding of the
Isthmo–Colombian Area
Edited by Ernst Halbmayer

Africa and Urban Anthropology
Theoretical And Methodological Contributions from
Contemporary Fieldwork
Edited by Deborah Pellow and Suzanne Scheld

Human Trafficking, Structural Violence, and Resilience
Ethnographic Life Narratives from the Philippines
Amie L. Lennox

https://www.routledge.com/Routledge-Studies-in-Anthropology/book-series/SE0724

Human Trafficking, Structural Violence, and Resilience

Ethnographic Life Narratives from the Philippines

Amie L. Lennox

LONDON AND NEW YORK

First published 2023
by Routledge
4 Park Square, Milton Park, Abingdon, Oxon OX14 4RN

and by Routledge
605 Third Avenue, New York, NY 10158

Routledge is an imprint of the Taylor & Francis Group, an informa business

© 2023 Amie L. Lennox

The right of Amie L. Lennox to be identified as author of this work
has been asserted in accordance with sections 77 and 78 of the
Copyright, Designs and Patents Act 1988.

All rights reserved. No part of this book may be reprinted or
reproduced or utilised in any form or by any electronic, mechanical,
or other means, now known or hereafter invented, including
photocopying and recording, or in any information storage or
retrieval system, without permission in writing from the publishers.

Trademark notice: Product or corporate names may be trademarks
or registered trademarks, and are used only for identification and
explanation without intent to infringe.

British Library Cataloguing-in-Publication Data
A catalogue record for this book is available from the British Library

Library of Congress Cataloging-in-Publication Data
Names: Lennox, Amie L., author.
Title: Human trafficking, structural violence, and resilience :
ethnographic life narratives from the Philippines / Amie L. Lennox.
Description: 1 Edition. | New York, NY : Routledge, 2023. |
Series: Routledge studies in anthropology | Includes bibliographical
references and index.
Identifiers: LCCN 2022017276 (print) | LCCN 2022017277 (ebook) | ISBN
9781032198279 (hardback) | ISBN 9781032198286 (paperback) | ISBN
9781003261049 (ebook)
Subjects: LCSH: Human trafficking—Philippines. | Philippines—Social
conditions—21st century. | Human trafficking victims—Philippines—
Social conditions.
Classification: LCC HQ281 .L466 2023 (print) | LCC HQ281 (ebook) | DDC
306.36209599—dc23/eng/20220627
LC record available at https://lccn.loc.gov/2022017276
LC ebook record available at https://lccn.loc.gov/2022017277

ISBN: 978-1-032-19827-9 (hbk)
ISBN: 978-1-032-19828-6 (pbk)
ISBN: 978-1-003-26104-9 (ebk)

DOI: 10.4324/9781003261049

Typeset in Times New Roman
by codeMantra

Contents

List of figures	xi
List of tables	xiii
Acknowledgements	xv
List of abbreviations	xvii
Glossary of terms	xix

1 Researching human trafficking in a local context: research design, challenges, and aims   1

  1.1 Introduction 1
  1.2 Defining and measuring human trafficking 2
  1.3 Human trafficking and the Philippines 4
  1.4 Research design and research aim 5
  1.5 Ethnography and fieldwork in Mindanao 8
  1.6 Suroy-suroy: to roam around; to wander; to run errands 13
  1.7 Gatekeepers 15
  1.8 Matarong pamatasan [ethics], pain, and writing 17
  1.9 Interviews 19
  1.10 Analysis and personal narratives 21
  1.11 Conceptual framework 23
  1.12 Overview of the book 26
  1.13 Conclusions 27

2 Rural Mindanao: history, conflict, and underage soldiers   36

  2.1 Introduction 36
  2.2 Rural history and poverty 38
  2.3 Definitions of poverty 39
  2.4 History of conflict in Mindanao 41
  2.5 Definitions of children and child 42
  2.6 Marcus' story 44

viii *Contents*

2.7 *Jun's story 49*
2.8 *Trauma, force, and agency in global comparison 52*
2.9 *Coercion and agency 54*
2.10 *Soldiers, rural poverty and structural violence 56*
2.11 *Conclusions 60*

3 Labour and exploitation: employment and work
in Mindanao   68

3.1 *Introduction 68*
3.2 *Part 1: employment, economics, law, and structural violence 70*
3.3 *DonDon's story 77*
3.4 *Gabriel's story 79*
3.5 *Melissa's story 81*
3.6 *Structural violence, labour, and human trafficking 83*
3.7 *Part 2: sexual labour and sexual traffic: women in
Mindanao seeking work 87*
3.8 *Erica's story 93*
3.9 *Crystal's story 98*
3.10 *Joramae's story 101*
3.11 *Choice, coercion, agency 102*
3.12 *Structural violence, labour, and gender 106*
3.13 *Conclusions 108*

4 Migration and globalisation: migrant experience and
multiple violences   116

4.1 *Introduction 116*
4.2 *Migration in the Philippines: state control and
social norms 119*
4.3 *Bianca's story 124*
4.4 *Jasmine's story 129*
4.5 *Coercion, consent, control, and agency: trafficking of
migrants in context 132*
4.6 *Social pressures and the culture of migration 134*
4.7 *Global pressures and local lives: history,
stories, and migration 137*
4.8 *History and colonial legacy: structural and symbolic violences 140*
4.9 *Conclusions 142*

Contents ix

5 Risk and violence: producing and reproducing
vulnerability   150
  5.1 Introduction 150
  5.2 Susan's story 151
  5.3 Risk and compounding violence 157
  5.4 Mariel's story 161
  5.5 Navigating violence: choices and structure 165
  5.6 Conclusions 168

6 Agency, sacrifice, and human trafficking in Mindanao:
conclusions   172
  6.1 Agency and meaning 172
  6.2 Agency, sacrifice, and suffering 174
  6.3 Sacrifice and symbolic violence 176
  6.4 Summary 178
  6.5 Implications 181

Index   187

Figures

1.1	Research design	3
1.2	Representations of home?	8
1.3	My children at the market; my son enjoying some pakwan [watermelon]	9
1.4	My daughter aboard a crowded jeepney	10
1.5	Shoppers queueing at the packed supermarket after payday	10
1.6	An urban scene: a goat tied up beside a main road in an industrial area	11
2.1	Rural health services in Mindanao's rural municipalities. Areas in grey have some form of birthing facilities and emergency transport; unshaded areas do not. Map is indicative only	59
3.1	Wandering anthropologist, street-side as a row of jeepneys pass by	69
3.2	"Wanted 10 girls 18–25 yrs old apply inside"	73
3.3	Job advertisements in Davao City. Note requirements that include gender, height, "plessing" [sic] personality, and tertiary education for cashier/waiter roles	74
3.4	Job advertisement in Davao City, specifying gender, age, appearance, and "pleasing personality"	75
3.5	Job advertisements. Child attendant must be single, age 18–23; the other ad offers a pay range starting below minimum wage	76
3.6	"Baby Face Night Bar" gentleman's club in Davao City	93
4.1	Migration agents' advertisements around Davao City – "Good life awaits you"	117
4.2	"Work as a Factory worker in South Korea." Note the requirements of minimum high school graduate and age 18–36 years	122
4.3	Supporter of Duterte displaying a sign on a car during the 2016 campaign period	142

Tables

1.1 List of life narratives presented in this book   26

Acknowledgements

I would first like to thank my participants including the organisations who contributed to this study. The participants who so generously shared their stories and their lives with me each inspired and taught me, and also motivated me to complete this research and fulfil my promises to share their accounts. Many thanks as well to the multiple organisations and workers who helped me in ways too numerous to count, from granting me interviews and information, introductions, accessing participants, and building friendships. Thank you also to my mga maestra, Ate Mercy and Ate Bebe, who taught me so much more than language, and to Mercy for her work in translating and transcribing the interview recordings.

Salamat kaayo, akong mga higala ug mga magtutudlo, ako anaa sa kamong utang.

Many grateful thanks go to my supervisors at Massey University while I was conducting this research, Dr. Sita Venkateswar, Professor Kathryn Rountree, and Dr. Maria Borovnik. The intellectual, practical, and moral support that they have provided throughout my candidature has been invaluable. In this time, I have grown as an academic and a person because of their contributions to my research and my life. Thank you, daghang salamat, I am so grateful for all you have done.

The anthropology department at Massey University, Albany, has become almost a second family to me over my years of study, and I would like to express my appreciation to Professor Kathryn Rountree, Dr. Graeme Macrae, Dr. Eleanor Rimoldi, Dr. Barbara Anderson, and all of the postgraduate anthropology students I have had the pleasure of knowing. You have taught me what it is to be an anthropologist.

I am grateful to have received several scholarships which allowed me to carry out this research. Thanks to MFAT for the NZ Aid Programme Award for Postgraduate Field Research, and to Massey University for financial support from the Graduate Research Fund and the Alumni Doctoral Completion Bursary. Thanks also to the publishing team at Routledge for their efforts in bringing this book to publication.

Part of Chapter 4 was previously published in a revised version as: Precarity and improvisation: challenges and strategies in Filipino labour

xvi *Acknowledgements*

migration. *SITES: A Journal of Social Anthropology and Cultural Studies, 16*(2019 Special Issue). It is reprinted with permission from *SITES*.

Finally, I would like to thank my parents, family, and friends who have supported and encouraged me through many years of study. Above all, thanks to my husband, Jono, and our children, Africa, Jordan, and Rio, who have been unintentional research assistants in the Philippines, and have patiently adapted family life around the demands of my work. You have given me the strength I needed to finish this adventure. Thank you; let's go find another.

Abbreviations

ALS	Alternative Learning System (High School Equivalency)
AMOSUP	Associated Marine Officers and Seamen's Union of the Philippines
BLES	Bureau of Labor and Employment Statistics (Philippines)
CPP	Communist Party of the Philippines
CSEC	Commercial Sexual Exploitation of Children
GO/NGO	Government Organisation/Non-Government Organisation
GRO	Guest relations officer; euphemism for club-based sexual labourers
HIV/AIDS	Human Immunodeficiency Virus/Acquired Immunodeficiency Syndrome
IACAT	Inter-Agency Council Against Trafficking
ILO	International Labour Office
IMF	International Monetary Fund
MILF	Moro Independence Liberation Front
NPA	New People's Army
OFW	Overseas Filipino Worker
OWWA	Overseas Workers Welfare Association
PHP (₱)	Philippine Peso
POEA	Philippines Overseas Employment Administration
PSA	Philippines Statistics Authority
STI	Sexually transmitted infection
TIP Report	Trafficking in Persons Report (US State Department)
UN	United Nations
UNESCO	United Nations Educational, Scientific and Cultural Organization
UNICEF	United Nations International Children's Emergency Fund
UNODC	United Nations Office on Drugs and Crime

Glossary of terms

Ako, ko   Me or I, short form "ko"
Amerikano   American
Apo   Grandchild
Ate   Older sister
Bago   New
Bagong bayani   Modern-day hero (Bago - new + bayani - hero)
Balay   House
Barangay   Municipal division
Bayad/walay bayad   Payment/no payment
Bayani   Hero
Bukado   Avocado
Cebuano   Language of the Southern Philippines
Copra   Dried coconut meat
CR (Comfort room)   Toilet (Lavatory)
Daghan   Many
Daghang salamat/Salamat kayo   Many thanks/thank you very much
Daog-daog   (To) oppress/Oppressed
Davao   Capital city of Mindanao
Dili   No or not
Dili maayo   Bad (literally, not good; there is no word for "bad" alone)
Diri/diha/didto   Here/there (near)/"over there" (far)
Estudyante   student
Filipino/Filipina   Person or man from the Philippines/woman from the Philippines
Gago(ng)   Stupid, silly, idiot
Ikaw, ka   You, short form "ka"
Ispatay pangpang   Killer (pangpang) cliff (ispatay)
Jeepney   Specific local transport, small bus
Kaayo   Very
Kamote   Kumara/sweet potato
Karenderiya   Small restaurant
Katabang   Helper; generally a domestic helper

xx   *Glossary of terms*

Katsila   Spanish
Kaya/Dili kaya   Can or able/cannot or unable
Keso   Cheese
Kulata   (To) beat with great violence
Kuya   Older brother
Lang   Only
Lola   Grandmother
Lisod/lisod gyud   Difficult/very difficult
Lumad   Indigenous rural people
Maayo   Good or well
Maayong Buntag   Good morning
Maayong Gabii   Good evening
Maayong Hapon   Good afternoon
Maayong Udto   Good noon or lunchtime
Maestro/a   Teacher (male / female)
Mama-san   Female manager of sexual labourers
Matarong pamatasan   Ethics, correct or moral behaviour
Mindanao   Southern region of the Philippines
Mga   Plural (added before the word)
(Mga) Numero   Numbers:
  usa, duha, tulo, upat, lima…: 1, 2, 3, 4, 5
  uno, dos, tres, kuwatro, singko…: For some situations the Spanish-derived numbers are used
Pancit   Noodles
Salamat   Thank you
"Sa kadtong mga tao nga akong nautang ang kinabuhi nila"   "Those people whose lives are my debt"
Sakripisyo   Sacrifice; Suffering
Sundanon   Prolific
Suroy-suroy   (To) roam or wander
Tindahan   Small shop
Trisikad, sikad   Tricycle, short form; pedicab / rickshaw, motorised or pedal powered
(mga) Tsinelas, slippers   Jandals (inexpensive, plastic thong-style sandals)
Utang Debt
Visayas   Central region of the Philippines, north of Mindanao
"Wala ka kahibalo unsay mahitabo"   "You don't know what will happen"
Zamboanga   City in south-west Mindanao, common transit point to Malaysia

1 Researching human trafficking in a local context

Research design, challenges, and aims

1.1 Introduction

"I will tell you everything"
- Crystal (formerly trafficked into the sex industry at age 15)

Crystal, like many of the people I met, wanted to tell her story as often as she could, in the hope that it would help raise awareness, and be part of exposing and reducing the frequency of human trafficking in the Philippines.[i] Now, Crystal is out of the sex industry, working as an advocate for other sexual labourers, and pursuing her education:

> I love reaching out to people. For them to be educated. For them not to be victims in human trafficking. As well as the STI-HIV (prevention) because it is not easy for them when they get sick. So, this is why I volunteer (with an NGO supporting sexual labourers).

When I was in Mindanao I was privileged to hear Crystal's story, and many others, that expressed hope and pain, triumph and loss, and survival through difficulties. These words, experiences, and stories are the centre of this book. I will tell you everything.

It was a meandering journey which brought me to Mindanao for research, and even once there I could not have guessed the number and diversity of people who eventually contributed to this study. It was the second time I had been to Davao City when I arrived, on what then seemed to be an unbearably hot day, with my husband and three children in tow. Waiting helplessly with our luggage on a shaded, grassy spot, while the apartment building's staff struggled to locate our booking, I hoped that I was prepared for whatever lay ahead.

The first time I travelled to Davao had been eighteen months prior. A friend in New Zealand was planning to go to the Philippines to visit some mutual friends, and I thought it would be a good opportunity to travel to a new place, visit friends, and learn about the work that their NGO (Non-Government Organisation) was doing. I ended up travelling alone,

DOI: 10.4324/9781003261049-1

2 Researching human trafficking

and spent two weeks in Davao, joining the NGO and learning about the anti-trafficking, school breakfast, child and youth support, and community development programs that they were undertaking.

I had learned from local community organisations that in Davao human trafficking was a significant problem, but measures to counter it were still in their infancy. The NGO I was with, for example, was the only group doing any form of human trafficking prevention with young people at the time, and the program they used had been developed overseas rather than locally.[ii] I had wanted to learn more about the Philippines for my own education about the world, but I eventually decided to pursue a PhD study that would meet my own goals as well as support the local organisations I had met by providing locally based research.

The Philippines is widely understood to be a "source" country for international human trafficking, but there are also problems with domestic trafficking.[1–4] At a community summit I attended in Davao City, Mindanao in 2014, local organisations estimated that 150 people per month were disappearing from the local area. Programs to counter human trafficking were in their early stages, and all aspects from prevention strategies to prosecutions were still minimal. Filipinos face a unique set of circumstances which, at times, result in exploitation, and understanding this connection requires research-based information which is currently underdeveloped. In this book, I approach the concept of human trafficking from an anthropological perspective which suggests that the practice and experience of trafficking are not universal, but specific to the geographic, social, cultural, and personal settings from which events and individuals emerge.

Despite the robust anti-trafficking laws and migrant support systems, human trafficking in and from the Philippines remains a significant problem. In 2015, 1465 Filipino trafficking victims received government assistance[iii]; related research, such as with migrants and sex workers, has indicated that trafficking is significantly underrepresented by official victim counts.[6–8] Research in other contexts, such as Thailand, Nepal, and Mexico, suggests significant connections between human trafficking and social conditions including unemployment, poverty, and discrimination.[9–11] These relationships have not been extensively explored either theoretically, or locally in the Philippines context.

1.2 Defining and measuring human trafficking

Despite the rapid increase of both academic and popular attention to trafficking over the last two decades, the ongoing problems of how to measure and define human trafficking accurately and appropriately have not yet been fully resolved. Trafficking is a clandestine activity, intentionally hidden from official systems, and as such the people affected are impossible to count directly. The impossibility of measuring the size of the problem or gathering accurate numbers, as well as differing methodologies and criteria for inclusion in global estimates, mean that "statistics on trafficking worldwide are notoriously unreliable."[12(p. 117),13,14] In this book, I have intentionally omitted broad attempts to measure human trafficking in the Philippines or globally, considering both the tenuous data in this area and the overarching aim which is to show how patterns that maintain exploitation are embedded in social processes that have wide ranging impacts beyond those whose experiences fit within certain definitions.

Human trafficking was initially defined as "forced movement" into exploitative labour, to address transnational crime. However, current definitions in practice usually include the subsequent exploitation, and there is a great deal of overlap and confusion between the terms human trafficking, modern slavery, and forced labour.[iv16–18(p. 15)] The UN describes modern slavery as "situations of exploitation that a person cannot refuse or leave because of threats, violence, coercion, deception, and/or abuse of power."[19] Apart from the movement of people, their human trafficking definition is essentially the same: "The recruitment, transportation, transfer, harbouring, or receipt of persons, by means of the threat or use of force or other forms of coercion... for the purpose of exploitation[v]."[20(p. 51)] The term "human trafficking" is important, however, not only because it is used to include other descriptors, but because it has been so widely ratified internationally through the UN Palermo Protocol, with a universal set of legal obligations under a single, shared definition on which, in theory, most laws, policies, and approaches are based.[18(p. 16),21].

In this book I use the UN's definition as the international legal standard, on which the Philippines' legislation has also been based. However, in doing so, I also explore its limitations and ambiguities in the context of actual experiences which do not necessarily fit neatly into the categories

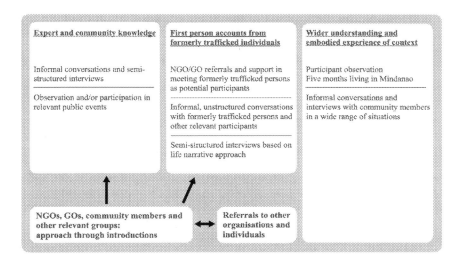

Figure 1.1 Research design.

4   *Researching human trafficking*

defined above. In particular, the central defining notion of force, coercion, and control is contextualised beyond individual-level relationships to the social, cultural, economic, and political settings that shape and constrain lives, choices, and individual relationships. All the participants meet the general criteria of the UN definition to varying degrees[vi] and reveal that within it, there are broad continuums of abuse and exploitation, and a wide range of experiences.

1.3 Human trafficking and the Philippines

The Philippines is primarily but not exclusively considered a "source" country for international human trafficking.[20] Malaysia, Singapore, and the Middle East are common destinations. Females are most often trafficked in domestic service or forced sex work, while trafficking and forced labour on fishing boats or construction sites are most common for males. Men and women (and boys and girls) have also been forced labourers in factories, on plantations or construction sites.[4,22] Filipinos also experience labour or sexual exploitation in the Western world. These locations are often associated with legal and documented migration, whereas other locations in Asia are more likely to also find irregular migrants being exploited. Trafficking also occurs domestically in the Philippines, including sexual exploitation of mainly women and children, exploitative and indentured labour including forms of debt bondage, child soldiers, exploitation of domestic workers including children, and often involves domestic migration from rural to urban areas.[23–25] All the pathways identified in trafficking situations are also the primary routes for legitimate labour migration and travel.[26(p. 29)]

Although it is widely recognised that debt bondage and labour trafficking of both men and women are occurring in the Philippines and abroad, the literature is heavily weighted towards sex trafficking, women's experiences, and the exploitation of land-based migrants. Labour migration is a common strategy for both men and women, and Filipinos face significant challenges in navigating economic opportunities and constraints at home and in the global labour market.

The Philippines' unique history, geography, and social context has seldom been considered in human trafficking analyses. On a macro level, the role of poverty in shaping migration and the risks of human trafficking is taken for granted. Most close studies focus on Filipino migrants overseas and do not have the scope to explore the local context for migration in depth. While the category of human trafficking has been criticised for conflating multiple diverse situations and types of exploitation, the fact that multiple forms of trafficking are emerging from Mindanao and the Philippines, raises significant questions about the social context and specific localised risks, that people here are facing. As such, this "bottom-up" study presents a local-level perspective on global processes in society and as lived realities.

1.4 Research design and research aim

This research has been designed as a "micro-level" study to extend an understanding of human trafficking in a local setting. From the initial planning stages, it was clear to me that any study of human trafficking had to be centred on those who had experienced it and their own accounts of their lives. However, this emphasis included several ethical and practical limitations. For one, it would have been practically difficult and ethically problematic to conduct research among people who were still under exploitative control.[27–29] Ethical concerns for both the participants and researcher meant that I also decided to exclude people who were still going through legal proceedings or initial rehabilitation. Therefore, the target participants were identified as people who had experienced human trafficking in the past and were now moving on with their lives, as guided by the organisations that were supporting me, which I discuss below.

Like many other human trafficking researchers, I designed this study knowing that the most appropriate way to access participants is usually through other support agencies.[30–33] Working through other institutions has its own limitations and challenges, discussed further in Chapter 3. However, the significant issues of safety, access, and even identification are mitigated through this collaboration, as well as the trust, ongoing relationship, and trained support that agencies offer to participants. The role of support agencies is further explained below and in Figure 1.1.

To extend an understanding of people's life paths overall, I decided that my research would be based on life narrative interviews where the participants would have the opportunity to describe and reflect on the circumstances of their lives. I felt this was most appropriate as this approach would allow me to consider people's experiences as part of a whole life and part of a social setting, rather than a single unconnected event.[34(p. 3),35] Brennan[27(p. 36)] has pointed out the lack of attention given to formerly trafficked persons' lives and experiences outside of their dramatic trafficking account. Research with formerly trafficked persons has included life narrative interviews to emphasise both the context for trafficking and individual agency over a life course.[32(p. 107),36(p. 77)] The use of life narrative is an ethical as well as methodological choice to consider exploitation as part of a wider life course that is shaped by personal and social factors. It was important to me that any approach would give primacy to the participants' own accounts and voices,[37] and present a much wider view of participants as whole people rather than "victims."

As an anthropologist, I am also deeply aware that individual narratives are also never only personal, but reflect the society, culture, relationships, and point in geography and history that a person inhabits.[34] As such, the perspective of individual lived experience gives a concrete and ground level basis for inquiry into the wider society, culture, and social processes, through a focus on how they play out in day-to-day life.[34(p. 32),38(p. 78),39(p. 46)]

6 *Researching human trafficking*

Through a personal and subjective point of view, and grounded in the Philippines' context, narratives offer a unique lens on social realities. The focus on day-to-day, lived realities in a specific local context, suggested narrative based interviews set in an ethnographic methodology. This approach has been successfully used to consider both exploitation and lived experience without ignoring individual people and situations. My research has thus been inspired by a number of diverse studies which have taken this approach in order to consider exploitation and vulnerability from a ground level view, studying groups such as undocumented migrants, sex workers, low paid factory workers, international surrogate mothers, leprosy sufferers, and social welfare beneficiaries.[38,40–44] Ethnographies contribute to the literature by exploring people's lives without assuming they are one group with the same experiences, and have the potential to illuminate the complexities of trafficking and migration in society beyond definitions and statistics.

The aim of this study was to explore how human trafficking in Mindanao relates to wider social processes. Based on an anthropological approach to human trafficking which gave primacy to individuals' accounts of their own experiences, the following research objectives emerged:

- To tell returned trafficked persons' stories which include but are not limited to trafficking experiences
- To explore the relationships between social factors and human trafficking from a local perspective

The methods used have been based on this ethnographic approach which involved spending five months in Mindanao, the Philippines. During this time, I talked with and interviewed people who had experienced exploitative labour, human trafficking, or trafficking-like practices.[vii] I also interviewed a wide variety of government and NGO workers from anti-trafficking and related agencies, and attended many organisational meetings and public awareness events. I extended these approaches with additional interviews with community members who had other relevant experiences, particularly former migrants and sexual labourers. Spending five months living in Davao also allowed me to participate in the practice of everyday life such as through navigating the practicalities of food, accommodation, and transport for my family and in sharing in my friends' lives. The strategies for accessing these three sources of knowledge – expert and community perspectives, first-person accounts, and wider experience of everyday life – are illustrated in Figure 1.1. Note that the first step for locating both community knowledge and participants who had experienced human trafficking was approaching a wide range of local organisations through introductions. From these, I sought further introductions, interviews with their staff on issues facing Mindanao, and support in accessing people who had previously experienced trafficking.

Fulfilling the aim of this study demanded attention to both individual accounts of trafficking and the complex cultural setting where human trafficking was occurring. Anthropological methods are particularly suited to developing a deep understanding of a local setting, in part because of the flexibility that they allow in adapting fieldwork to the discoveries and opportunities in the field, and also because of the "holistic" emphasis of ethnographic research which does not limit who or what may be a source of knowledge and understanding. On reaching the field, I found that the category of "trafficking" could apply in multiple situations, and that many people's experiences were difficult to categorise concretely. In attempting to engage with this complexity, I sought to understand local life in Mindanao from multiple perspectives and through conversations and insight from a wide variety of people, beyond those directly affected by trafficking, over the course of my fieldwork.

The focus of this research is participants' experiences, narratives, and perspectives. Reliable quantitative data regarding the numbers of people trafficked or using support services is not fully available, nor is it within the limits of this project to try to obtain better data. I depended heavily on networked introductions, and as such did not have access to minority groups such as Muslims or Chinese immigrants. My work did also not cover all demographics, and particularly certain types of trafficking were only represented by either heterosexual men or heterosexual women, nor did I meet participants who were Muslim. The emphasis is also primarily on the experiences of the poor, who are at greatest risk from trafficking, and those who have experienced trafficking, rather than the middle and upper classes. While I interviewed workers from human trafficking related agencies such as the police and women's organisations, fully analysing the measures against human trafficking or effectiveness of the anti-trafficking efforts is outside the scope of this study.

One characteristic of ethnographic research is the flexibility and "messiness" of navigating relationships, multiple sources of knowledge, competing pressures, and the researcher's own position and well-being, particularly in emotionally sensitive topics such as human trafficking.[32(p. 84)] The variety of experiences, from shopping for groceries to meeting and interviewing such a diverse range of participants and organisations, was indeed messy and I often found myself questioning whether I was pursuing the right directions, or learning anything useful to my research. However, it is the messy and ordinary living of everyday life where the "entrenched processes of ordering the social world" exist, and where social processes are worked out and ultimately felt.[45(pp. 238–239)] The multiple experiences, relationships, and encounters that shaped my research include everything from the "official" events and interviews, to the mundane tasks of life that together built a fuller and more holistic picture of life in Mindanao.

The basis of ethnographic research has traditionally been participant observation. While the research topic presented challenges for this

8 *Researching human trafficking*

Figure 1.2 Representations of home?

approach, the design of the study has been based on the need for close-level accounts and understanding based on immersive experiences. Research on human trafficking demands significant sensitivity towards ethical issues, and I designed and carried out this project based on a primary and ongoing consideration for my participants who had experienced trafficking and exploitation.

1.5 Ethnography and fieldwork in Mindanao

To fulfil the objectives of this research, I started from an ethnographic research design to explore social structures from an in-depth, personal and lived perspective. The ethnographic approach gives the individual experience primacy in understanding and interpreting the wider social realities, through sharing the experiences of day-to-day life. The locus of inquiry is individual lived experience and the participants' own perspectives, from which insights can be drawn about society, culture, and social processes. While ethnography is thus highly personal and subjective, ethnographic inquiry has been successfully contextualised and situated within historic,

Figure 1.3 My children at the market; my son enjoying some pakwan [watermelon].

geographic, and social settings.[10,38,46] As such, ethnographic research has produced alternative accounts and challenges to quantitative and global-level studies, as are prevalent in the human trafficking literature, which frequently ignore the local and individual realities and perspectives.

The combination of ethnographic research and life-narrative interviews was designed to provide anthropologically sound insights into human trafficking in a specific location. The challenge of this approach was that people who have experienced human trafficking share a general social context, but do not necessarily have any personal connection to each other, and I found that this was true in Mindanao as in other locations[27,28,47] This eliminated traditional participant observation as a potential research methodology. I addressed the problem of accessing participants who are hidden as individuals in society, rather than a socially or geographically distinct group, by working with multiple organisations and slowly increasing my social network through introductions. The life narrative interviews that participants shared with me are understood in part through the understanding of the local society that I gained through five months of living day-to-day in the same local environment.

Although ethnographic research traditionally depends on participant observation which was impossible with the specific participants I was seeking, the five months that I spent participating in life and community in Mindanao gave a grounded and experienced understanding of the wider context to my participants' lives. Gerassi's[28] research team recommended using a variety of sources and strategies when attempting to access "hidden populations" as a technique to find a wider variety of participants and experiences. This

10   *Researching human trafficking*

Figure 1.4 My daughter aboard a crowded jeepney.

Figure 1.5 Shoppers queueing at the packed supermarket after payday.

Researching human trafficking 11

Figure 1.6 An urban scene: a goat tied up beside a main road in an industrial area.

approach demanded modifying the ideal strategy of participant observation to obtain deep data based on immersive experiences, while accepting that participant observation was not feasible with the majority of my key participants to the degree I would have liked. The methodology of ethnographic research was thus adapted to the specific context, limitations, and research objectives. In-depth interviews with key participants gave their own accounts primacy in understanding human trafficking, and during the five months of fieldwork I also sought local community knowledge and insights into the local context so that I could effectively situate these accounts in the wider social setting. While interviews and narrative accounts have been criticised as subjective and therefore of limited analytic relevance, here the methodological triangulation of multiple perspectives on human trafficking, in-depth community participation, and attention to the wider social realities supports the validity of narrative and ethnographic approaches in this context.[32(p. 84)]

One concern was the central anthropological topic of researching the "other" as a blonde Western woman in the Philippines, a place I knew little about prior to this research. This raised questions such as issues of power relationships, the limits of "outsider" research, and how I would be

12   *Researching human trafficking*

received. Indeed, I found that the initial assumptions people had on meeting me were that I was (1) American, (2) a missionary, (3) rich. Although I would attempt to amend these perceptions, the general assumption that I was a missionary – religious workers have a high social status in Davao in general, and foreign ones in particular – was something I always struggled with, and I would do my best to gently clarify that I was a student from New Zealand[viii] doing research about life in Davao.[ix] Although being an "outsider" means that there are undoubtedly many things that I do not understand, I found that in people's reactions and conversations with me this position did contribute unique insights through experiencing local perceptions of America and the outside world.

Through the preparation, fieldwork, and writing up stages, I continued to grapple with the question of whether I was the right person to be carrying out this research. Adamson and Donovan[48(p. 823)] reported that this is a common concern and emotional response among researchers who do not share ethnicity with the research participants, particularly when white researchers are aware of the racial and cultural power imbalances in society that also imbue their position and people's perceptions. I recognise that I will never fully be an insider to Philippine society, and I continue to view research as my education on the Philippines, which will always be incomplete.

My family came with me for the first three months of fieldwork, and I often found that having my children along, as well as conducting practical family life such as grocery shopping and exploring, enabled me to interact with a wide variety of people on a more personal relational level. Indeed, I found that getting to know some of my neighbours' ordinary life practices often illuminated aspects of the wider culture. In the mornings, for example, there was always an early bustle of activity, and we would greet each other, *Maayong buntag!* [Good morning!], as I passed people in pyjamas out sweeping their drives and curbs or washing their cars. In the library at a local university, I had read about an official edict that households should be responsible for keeping their road frontage tidy. In my neighbourhood, it seemed to be just what was done, go out early to sweep, sweep, sweep, creating the music of the early day. I would guiltily wonder, momentarily, if my curbsides were letting the neighbourhood down, and what it would take to compel me to arise before seven to wield a broom on the public roadway for temporary relocation of dust and leaves. It seemed to me, however, to illustrate how Filipinos often accepted and adapted to conditions that were set from above. Queueing for groceries, asking for directions, eating in restaurants, using public transportation, and living daily life with my family, all contributed to a better understanding of the ways that people saw the world and made their lives in Davao.

Beyond the attention that my children's blond heads attracted (see Figure 1.3), I began to see glimpses of the position I occupied in the social imagination. Local primary school students, well-groomed and in perfectly laundered brightly coloured uniforms, would walk past me saying, "money,

Researching human trafficking 13

give me money?" People stared as my family walked past, and the brave approached to ask if they could take a picture with us. Others took pictures anyway. After we had posed with one man prior to an event at the town square, I asked him why he wanted a photo. "For a souvenir" was his somewhat cryptic reply. I was not sure if he just wanted a souvenir of having seen a white family, or of the event that was so exciting even foreigners turned up.

I had been assured it would not be a problem to conduct research and interview in English, but I had decided to learn Cebuano to communicate both in and out of interviews and to, ideally, get a better sense of the culture and worldview. Although Tagalog (Filipino) is the official national language, Cebuano (or Visayan) is the vernacular for Mindanao and the Visayas. I took regular lessons via Skype for the year leading up to fieldwork, and my teacher in Manila also began to introduce me to Filipino ways of thinking about the world. It ended up that only a few of my interviews with key participants were in English,[x] and my Cebuano, even as limited as it was, was incredibly useful in both "practical" and fieldwork scenarios, such as navigating *jeepneys* and other public transport (Figure 1.4).

Davao city is an odd mix of religions and the secular, although in the city the overall impression is that the various groups seem to coexist peacefully and openly. At the local universities, both Catholic and non-religious, for example, I did not see any segregation between students who were or were not wearing Muslim headscarves. Catholicism, as the dominant religion, is the most officially entrenched in daily public life. I often found myself in the supermarket, (see Figure 1.5) following the lead of other shoppers, standing solemnly in silence as the garbled recording of a deep male voice led us in a "Hail Mary." Subsequently, the staff would sometimes perform a simple dance in their colourful uniforms (often rather unenthusiastically) to the company's theme song. Once I had finished shopping, I would wait in the queue alongside the "impulse buy" section stacked with chocolate, toothbrushes, and condoms. It was in the practice of daily life that the intricacies and contradictions of urban social life and practice – such as the normal juxtaposition of agriculture and industry (see Figure 1.6) – began to come into focus as I attempted to both inhabit and comprehend the world around me.

1.6 Suroy-suroy: to roam around; to wander; to run errands

The word *suroy-suroy* is used to mean running errands, and is often the answer to the question, what have you been doing today? It also has the connotation of being "out and about," not anywhere in particular. This was the best way I could describe the fieldwork experience, that of wandering from one place to the next without a fixed route or final destination.

The first thing that I did in the field was to begin approaching organisations that work in anti-trafficking, both government and NGO, to ask for interviews with their workers and for support in accessing formerly trafficked people. Introductions and personal connections were indispensable

14 *Researching human trafficking*

in this effort, as they are in Mindanao social life. In contrast to this personal approach, I had sent out over 50 emails introducing myself and my research to various organisations prior to and during fieldwork; I did not get a single reply.

My husband and I knew several people who have been involved with a local NGO in Davao including its American founder; at the time of my research she and her husband, and friends I had known for over ten years, including a Kiwi woman and two Filipino women, were working there. Their connections, insights and friendship were all invaluable to the practical and emotional sides of the time I spent in the Philippines. My primary source of introductions and support was one of the NGO employees known as *Mamu* [Mama], who took me, my research, and my family under her wing. As she had worked in and with a wide variety of GO/NGOs in development and human rights areas, she generously introduced me to many contacts. Some of my fondest memories of my time in the Philippines are from the steps of Mamu's house, watching my children run around and play with some of her many *mga apo* [grandchildren[xi]], relatives and neighbours' children in the hard-packed dirt yard amid the coconut palms.

Through these introductions came further introductions, and I was able to spend time with people who included: police officers experienced in human trafficking; researchers from local universities who kindly spent time discussing my work and making introductions; social workers from several government departments; GO/NGO migrant support workers; workers and residents at halfway houses for sex workers and former rebel soldiers; and workers from other NGOs with focuses including migration, women, children, sex workers, and legal support. Research with multiple stakeholders in various locations was a central technique to explore the relationships between various facets of social life including the rural-urban flows and disparities. I travelled as much as my contacts could arrange to take me to meetings in other parts of Eastern Mindanao. This was always interesting, and I became acquainted with a wide variety of public transport options from the local pedal powered *trisikad* [tricycle, also known as a pedicab] to the fancy, movie playing, over-air-conditioned large buses. The latter was the only experience I had in the Philippines of ever being too cold, and I returned to Davao with the flu.

To visit street-based sex workers, I would go along with women from an NGO at night, but early in the evening before the workers were busy. We would join in the gathering around the *karenderiya*[xii] where the women were laughing and eating, texting and chatting. When I interviewed Susan, we spoke soon after I had arrived so that she would not be losing potential earnings for the night. I felt a responsibility that, at least, I would not cost anything to Susan and the other women, as well as my other participants. I found that getting to know these women provided a fruitful perspective on local life and work, and was personally very enjoyable. They found it humourous on one of my first nights when a customer asked the women,

Researching human trafficking   15

"Can we buy the American girls?," when I and another white woman were visiting.[xiii] The women were a lot of fun, and spending time "hanging out" with them contrasted sharply to the experience of sitting through official meetings.

I attended many Inter-Agency Council Against Trafficking (IACAT)[xiv] meetings and events to better understand the local situation and to make connections for research. These were often conducted in Cebuano, and I struggled at times to catch the details of what was being said. The process was rather painful and mainly involved eight-hour stints of sitting through government bureaucracy. The worst part, though, was that no one would translate or explain "adult" themed jokes to me because as a student I was assumed to be much younger than I actually was.[xv] Although I learned a lot from some of these meetings, in this way I continued to feel like an outsider, more so than in one-to-one conversations. However, attendance did pay off as it led to meetings with many of the organisations that were represented, and introductions to further groups, and towards the end of my fieldwork I stopped attending and would contact the people I had met there directly. Several organisations working in the rehabilitation stages of human trafficking were also able to help me to interview people who had experienced human trafficking themselves.

Most of the formerly trafficked or exploited people I spoke to had been through government or NGO assistance of some kind, and this is how I met them. These interviews were recorded, while during most interviews with GO/NGO workers I only took notes. I did not compensate these workers, but I would pay for the transportation costs and snacks to share with the participants, and I was grateful for the generous support I received. Due to the relationships based on the GO/NGO facilitators, I was not able to spend additional time with most participants beyond the interviews, with a few exceptions.

1.7 Gatekeepers

Much has been written about the role of "gatekeepers" in accessing formerly trafficked persons for research purposes.[29,31,33(p. 175),49–52] Indeed, some researchers have encountered challenges or even hostility, to the point that research proved impossible with some or all of the institutions contacted.[31,49,51,52] In Davao, I found that there was only one organisation, the government-run women's shelter, which provided me information but would not have allowed me any access to participants, as they were short-term residents who had very recently exited abuse of various kinds. My research, however, would also have excluded these women as I was intentionally seeking people who had already completed legal and rehabilitative processes, and I found this to be an entirely appropriate policy in the case of the shelter. The significant issues of safety, access, and even identification are mitigated through this collaboration, as well as the trust, ongoing relationship, and

16 Researching human trafficking

trained support that agencies offer to participants. This corresponded well with the other aims of my study in understanding the human trafficking situation and local context, and many organisations beyond those working directly with formerly trafficked persons generously shared information and expertise regarding the social situation in general and problems that their work was addressing. However, I found that the process of building relationships, trust, and "goodwill" with relevant organisations did take time as well as personal introductions.[52]

Locating participants was heavily dependent on networking widely with a variety of groups; I accessed two participants at most through each organisation or individual who served as the gatekeeper, and none through other participants. The organisations were extremely helpful in finding appropriate participants, but the limitations of this method correspond to what has been observed about trafficked persons in general. As a "hidden population," and "non-associative hard to reach population" – meaning, that whether formerly or currently trafficked, people with these experiences are not frequently a socially or geographically connected group.[28,31,53(p. 101),54] Formerly and currently trafficked persons have also been identified as not only hidden but often marginalised, stigmatised, and vulnerable, contributing to both social and intentional invisibility.[50,53] Gatekeepers played a central role in locating and ethically accessing such disconnected participants, but this also depended on my patience and perseverance in building relationships within the government agency and NGO communities, meeting with a wide variety of organisations, and demonstrating my credibility over time.

It was through perseverance, and flexibility in my willingness to *suroy-suroy* that I also came to meet a few participants with trafficking or related experiences who had not been formally identified or assisted by the official organisations.[xvi] This of course raises a question about ethical research with people who may have experienced trauma which had not been addressed or resolved.[51] However, I did meet these participants through NGO or community workers who knew them personally, and facilitated introductions as a mutual friend rather than a caseworker. In each case, the mutual friend also either remained nearby or acted as a translator, fulfilling the support role for participants which I considered necessary for interviewing people who might have experienced trauma. I make no distinction between "official" (as in, categorised and counted by support services) and "unofficial" formerly trafficked persons. Surtees[51(p. 119)] has pointed out that there may be differences between people who have been identified or sought support and those who have not. However, the purpose of this research is to present the narratives from people who have experienced a range of trafficking, trafficking-like, and related experiences such as migration within a generally shared social context, rather than analysing the role of support services. The potential limitation may be where, a few of the interviews were done with the government caseworkers present and so I may have heard a slightly

Researching human trafficking   17

more "official" version of events, which can be a limitation of this method of accessing people to interview.

My approach, then, most closely corresponds to the recommendation that participants, gatekeepers, and researchers work collaboratively.[27,29,33,55] The aim is not only facilitating interviews and access, but also "positioning each as experts for the purposes of creating a more complete and applicable knowledge," and extending this with multiple forms and sources of "community knowledge."[29(p. 39)] Many times, I invited my participants to reflect on their lives as well as general social issues in an effort to engage their contribution to knowledge and analysis within and beyond their own life story. Although the centre of this research is individual narratives rather than, say, their caseworkers' commentaries, the methodology of including multiple types of participants as well as a significant period of cultural immersion supports a better understanding of the social setting and factors at play in my key participants' lives.

1.8 Matarong pamatasan [ethics],[xvii] pain, and writing

"Just wait, I'm crying"
  – Erica

"It's very difficult to talk about my experiences of the abuse"
  – Gabriel

"I would like to have some counselling"
  – Mariel

There are significant ethical considerations in working with people who have experienced abuse and exploitation. These quotes from some of the interviews that I conducted demonstrate just one of the considerations, that of the research participant's well-being. Indeed, researchers have established that people who have experienced human trafficking are likely to have experienced trauma, and this was a continual caution in ethically designing the research.[56] Ethical considerations have been part of every stage of this research, from planning, to gaining access to participants and the field site, considering my position within the wider community, carrying out interviews and interacting with participants, and in representing and analysing the interviews and field data.

Primary ethical issues included the safety and confidentiality of participants, the safety of myself as researcher, and the potential for my being confused with an employee of anti-trafficking organisations. In addressing these, my main strategies were to arrange interviews through organisations already working with potential participants, and to go through the

18 *Researching human trafficking*

information sheet I had prepared in English and Cebuano to ensure that participants were aware of their rights and my role as a researcher. The participants who needed legal or rehabilitative support had also already completed those processes, apart from ongoing case management in a few instances, and a trained support worker would be available in each interview. I also offered to arrange counselling if any participants desired, although only Mariel requested it and her social worker offered to arrange it.

In each interview, there was a trained support person present, generally a social worker, and usually someone the participant knew. The support workers at times filled several roles, such as supporting me with language interpretation and being a cultural medium, for example, asking me to clarify questions that they thought would not be easily understood with the same implications. I was also careful to make sure that people knew they did not have to participate, answer any question, or could end the interview at any time, and that the support person understood this as well. There were times when people did become emotional in recalling traumatic or difficult events, such as Erica while talking about childhood sexual abuse. I would have felt uncomfortable in bringing up these emotions without a support person present; this would have created another ethical problem if I had stopped a participant from telling their story and determining their own comfort related to any emotional response.[50(p. 12)]

As part of designing the research plan, I completed and submitted a full application to the Massey University Human Ethics Committee which was approved prior to fieldwork (Application MUHECN 15/039). However, the application of safeguards does not eliminate the fact that all anthropology work is relational, and the ethics of fieldwork with people is further complicated by the fact that most of my participants had experienced some form of trauma, abuse, or exploitation. Despite careful preparations and research designs, most of the ethical dilemmas and decisions can only be "negotiated in real time with real people."[29(p. 33)]

In terms of writing this book, the primary ethical decision was to present the life narratives as whole accounts. This aligns to my objective of telling the stories from those who had experienced human trafficking, but also consciously places participants' voices at the centre of this work. It allows a degree of separation between the narratives and my analyses, so that my voice does not diminish the participants' own perspectives on their lives, but instead interprets the stories alongside the participants' accounts and interpretations.

Writing the stories has also raised ethical questions on a very personal level that can often never be fully resolved. The interview process is relational, intimate, and emotional; exposing this process and the resulting narratives in writing demanded a second level of sensitivity towards the interview process. Questions over the ethics of this research continued to haunt me. Although I have criticised others for work that turns people who have experienced trafficking into "just" trafficking victims, in selecting

Researching human trafficking 19

participants for this reason, am I doing the same? As a white Westerner coming in, collecting stories, and then leaving, am I re-enacting a form of colonial exploitation? My only justifications have come from my participants themselves: how eagerly, willingly, and hopefully these stories were shared; how key participants, gatekeepers, Mamu, and GO/NGO workers told me that my work was important; and how I was taught by each person that I met. Most importantly, though I received these stories with gratitude, my participants relayed them with the intention that they would be shared more broadly. The stories have been translated and narrated as directly and respectfully as possible under this ethical sense of both sensitivity and duty.

1.9 Interviews

Ethnographically based individual life accounts "offer unique lenses through which the interplay of social categories might be observed and better understood," and interviews with key participants were based on this life narrative format.[38(p. 78)] Individual narratives are also never only personal, but reflect the society, culture, relationships, and point in geography and history that a person inhabits.[34(p. 3)] This approach emphasises how beliefs, values, and ideals are often embedded in stories as well as the way that people interpret the world around them and their own lives and experiences.

Formerly trafficked individuals' narratives reflect not only the shared values in making decisions prior to and within a trafficking event, but also culturally situated understandings of the situations.[9,57,58] Near the end of the life story interviews, I would specifically ask participants to reflect on their lives and consider what was important, and I found that these analyses added depth to the reflections they had already conveyed throughout their narrative accounts. Through a personal and subjective point of view, and grounded in an understanding of the wider context, individual and groups of narratives offer a unique lens on social realities.[34(p. 32),39(p. 46)] Moreover, narratives are unique in reflecting something of both inner and shared social worlds in that the narrative structure is also a primary way that people understand the world and their place in it, and construct meaning from their experiences.[59]

Most of the key participants' interviews were conducted in Cebuano, either by their choice or by necessity when they did not speak English. I appreciated the value of stories told in participants' vernacular, given the close relationships between language and views of the world, in attempting to understand their own perspectives. My language skills allowed me to understand generally what was being said which helped the interview process, and support workers also supported me with some interpretation. I enjoyed it when participants would laugh at me for my language skills, feign disbelief when they asked my age ("you look so young!"), or laugh with me when I described how many children I had ("*daghan* [many], too many"). Being in the position of *estudyante* [student] in terms of language learning as

20   *Researching human trafficking*

well as research also set me in a less powerful position, particularly in contrast with the social workers, where I hoped people would feel comfortable to make their own decision as to whether and how they spoke to me.

During interviews, I did not usually ask many questions. After orally discussing the information sheet participants had been given, I would then explain that I wanted to hear their life story – from where they grew up to where they are now. Sometimes participants would immediately start telling their story, without any questions or prompting, and sometimes I would ask, "what was it like where you grew up?" I usually did not need or have opportunity to ask many more questions until close to the end of the interview. Brennan[27] reported a similar approach to interviews with the formerly trafficked migrants in her research, placing the emphasis on the participant's narrative and what they want to tell, rather than on the exploitation or trauma they might have experienced.

The compensation of participants for their time is always a question in research.[33(p. 182)] A social rather than financial contribution correlated to my position as a guest and student, although the presumption that as a foreigner I was wealthy also created a certain expectation. I would usually bring snacks and drinks to people's homes, as guided by the person introducing me, or pay for the food and drinks if we were at a cafe. I also tried to avoid inconveniencing anyone, and made sure that interviews were set around the participants' schedules, such as meeting employed people in the evenings. I was constantly aware of my perceived status, and beyond asserting that I was not a religious authority, I made additional efforts to address potential power imbalances that came from my position as a foreigner and a researcher.

However, an interview is a reciprocal human connection. It demands emotional labour of both the researcher and the participant in connection, empathy, moderating responses, as well as speaking and telling the story. I became aware of the personal and ethical implications where asking for an interview was also requesting participants' emotional labour in connecting with me, and accepting my attempts to connect and bridge the language and culture gaps between us. One of my participants, for example, was a migrant who had returned due to health problems and was now struggling to provide for her family. She spoke about her Christian faith which gave her a sense of unity and equality with other people in the world – "God made all of us" – and added that she was a woman and a mother, and, placing her arm against mine, remarked, "We are different because of our past, but we have two hands, one heart, one life, right? *Ako* [I am] Filipina, *ikaw* [you are] from New Zealand, but we are the same." I was incredibly touched by the gesture, particularly as I was very aware of how visibly foreign I was in Davao. This interaction contrasted sharply with many other experiences, such as when we took our children to the local zoo, and we took pictures of the crocodiles while local visitors took pictures of us, seemingly in the same way.

Researching human trafficking 21

This experience as well as many of the other friendships and moments of connection that developed in my fieldwork challenge the binary dichotomy of "native and non-native" in considering relationships between the self and other.[60,61(p. 12)] Narayan[60(p. 680)] argued that "given the multiplex nature of identity, there will inevitably be certain facets of self that join us up with the people we study, other facets that emphasize our difference." Indeed, as a woman, a mother, an English-speaker, a Cebuano learner, having a Christian background,[xviii] inhabiting and doing life in Davao and the neighbouring area, I found that there were many ways that people accepted my identification with them and built relationships that did not erase, but crossed the "self and other" divide. I found this participant's actions particularly touching as her experiences of poverty, working overseas away from her children, and serious health problems were things that I could empathise with but had no experience of myself; despite this gulf between her story and my (comparatively, very privileged) life, the fact that she saw us as similar and equals was deeply joyful and humanising for me in a very lonely time.

Listening to, reading, and writing up the stories[xix] also meant reliving the interviews, which I sometimes found quite emotional. I found myself again reconciling the memory of the person I had spent time with to the often very difficult story that they recounted of their experiences, at times making the process very draining.[xx] A theme of this research is that of violence, both personal and structural, immediate and cumulative. For me it also became a metaphor for writing, in the carving of stories and experiences down into words on paper, the impact of painful accounts on the reader, and the bleeding of emotion[xxi] and pain in the narratives into ink as a writer. At the same time, I have tried to craft the writing to avoid directing violence back towards the participants, through protecting identities, and recounting faithfully, carefully, and respectfully the narratives that my participants shared.

1.10 Analysis and personal narratives

The methods for accessing participants affect not only the outcomes but the analysis. For me, the wide variety of experiences that my participants recounted was not an intentional but incidental outcome of these open-ended methods. This approach corresponds to the anthropological tradition of grounded theory where the analyses and foci emerge from fieldwork and participants' perspectives.

In attempting to write and analyse my participants' stories, my starting point is the knowledge that the narrative itself is a person's analysis of their own life and experiences in the world. This analysis is personally and culturally shaped, but is also the most valid one. Brennan[27(p. 35)] presented a challenge to researchers working with formerly trafficked persons to consider the possibilities that arise from moving past a "victim status"

22 *Researching human trafficking*

including commenting on the anti-trafficking movement and contributing to its future. For my research at this stage, this means taking people's narratives and analyses seriously in attempting to make sense of the social factors which have shaped their lives. As such, the ethical considerations of representation, including the agency of the participant, continued through the writing stages of research.

The main strength of this approach, particularly when working with people who have experienced exploitation, is that narrative accounts of biography and experiences give primacy to a person's own words, agency in selecting and making accounts, and self-positioning within the events and narratives.[39(pp. 39–40)] Further, for people who had generally already shared their experiences of trafficking "officially," an unstructured interview with focus on their wider life stories including plans for the future, and on their own reflections and analysis, offered a venue for my research participants to reconstruct their narratives beyond that of a "victim." As such, narratives can also be useful in challenging dominant perspectives, approaches, and voices in attending to the intersubjective, partial, and constructed knowledge and narratives by which marginalised populations negotiate and re-narrate their own identities, positions, and experiences.[34(p. 34),39(p. 40),63] I am aware that each interview was a unique interaction and a story told at a particular moment, in a particular context and relationship; it was, however, how people chose, in that moment, to represent themselves and their experiences.

Ethnographic methods are flexible, but often messy, and a multiplicity of voices can strengthen the validity of observations about a society.[32(p. 84)] The pressure to find participants, combined with my willingness to pursue any opportunity to meet relevant people, resulted in a wide variety of interactions and interviews, from successful and unsuccessful migrants, to sexual labourers, taxi drivers, former underage soldiers, affluent high school leavers planning their futures, as well as GO/NGO/community workers, and people who had experienced a wide range of exploitative labour situations. Although their lives were mostly unconnected and often vastly different, these stories together helped to build a more complete picture of local society from multiple angles. However, the diversity of the participants may also be considered a limitation of this research method in terms of gaining a deep understanding of the phenomena in question. While I spoke to multitudes of community workers as well as "ordinary" people who contributed to my understanding of local society, the central participants whose life narratives are presented in this book are listed in Table 1.1.

Although interviews are highly subjective, narratives provide glimpses of the fundamental logic which governs people's actions and choices, and the ways that they understand and represent themselves and their lives.[64] I recognise that an interview and the narrative produced is not a mere account of events, but a creation emerging from the relational interview space and the temporal meaning-making which accompanies the telling.[65(p. 40),66,67(p. 279)]

Researching human trafficking   23

The locus of my inquiry is these personal and socially shaped narratives and the *meanings* given to exploitation as part of the wider social context. As such, narratives can be significant representations of the social worlds in which people live their lives. Moreover, a focus on stories which reveal points of exploitation give the social factors concrete expression and basis for analysis, as Arnold and Blackburn[68(pp. 5–6)] have argued:

> Life histories enable us to render more intelligible precisely the complex of forces at work in modern societies and to reflect further, and from more solid foundations, on many of the major themes… gender, modernity, colonialism and nationalism, religion, social changes, family and kinship, and interrelationship between self and society.

My analysis, then, is interpretive in nature and has focused on the links between individual stories and wider social processes. The themes and primary points of analysis have emerged from participants' stories, with a focus on how the participants interpreted and made choices within the circumstances and contexts of their lives. I have first focused on the events my participants described, the choices that they have reported making, and the ways that they articulated and analysed their narrative. Further, I have considered how participants' stories relate to the wider society, with a focus on opportunities and constraints, and the role of social structures and relationships in shaping their lives. These topics have then been analysed through the concepts of structural violence that have been described. Through presenting the narratives as whole accounts, I have attempted to retain participants' voices within my analysis as well as offering transparency for the methods of interpretation.

1.11 Conceptual framework

The question at the heart of this book is how human trafficking relates to wider social processes. Central to this question are the relationships between individuals and society, the role and limits of agency, and the place of vulnerability and violence within society. My view is that widespread violence within a society, particularly pertaining to human trafficking in the Philippines, implies a connection to wider social processes including normal, everyday life. I argue that anthropological analysis can contribute to an understanding of human trafficking within wider discussions of suffering, vulnerability, and social inequality through a framework based on structural violence.

The focus on this research is individual narratives as a window on social configurations. Other approaches, such as intersectionality, that focus on individual experiences of oppression thus were insufficient to make sense of society-level patterns and processes. Further, as Farmer[69(p. 279)] pointed out, identity politics can obscure structural violence. As such, although Filipinos

24 *Researching human trafficking*

abroad face inequalities that align to intersectional concerns of race, ethnicity, language, gender, migration status, and other distinctions that come to the forefront in multicultural settings, within the Philippines, structural violence is highly gendered, but also manifest in distinctions in geography and socioeconomic conditions. Considering, then, social factors that shape unequal access is more pertinent than looking at the individual as the locus of inequality and violence. Filipinos experiencing structural violence as a result of living in or coming from a rural area, for example, experience constraints primarily due to inequality in accessing social resources and opportunities rather than in how other Filipinos might respond to them. Accordingly, this research considers the interplay between the social and structural and individual life stories in order to query "by what mechanisms do social forces ranging from poverty to racism become embodied as individual experience?"[69(pp. 261–262)]

Approaches to explaining vulnerability are insufficient unless they encompass not only individuals in marginal, risky situations, but the wider social, political, and historical structures which create and maintain conditions of inequality as they relate to risk.[70(p. 89),71(p. 179)] The legal system, social norms, business procedures, and government support structures are all part of the context where some groups experience higher levels of exploitation, abuse, and hazards, while others are more sheltered from these events.[70(p. 89)] Anthropologists researching human trafficking have emphasised the role of ethnography in identifying and critiquing the structural and social dimensions of risk and of violence.[10,12,72]

Social structural factors have been implicated in many studies of human trafficking. In Europe, the social marginalisation and exclusion of Serbian Romas maintain conditions of vulnerability which contribute to their disproportionate experience of human trafficking.[73] Trafficking from Nepal to India follows a unique pattern and is highly gendered, and Crawford[74] argued that it is tolerated as part of the widespread and ingrained patterns of violence towards women. Accounts from Central America have highlighted the role of extreme and often violent border politics in shaping the risks and experiences of human trafficking for irregular migrants.[75,76] In the Philippines as in other parts of Southeast Asia, the massive disparity between rural and urban areas has maintained the increased vulnerability of rural people for multiple negative outcomes which include human trafficking.[1,77,78] As in other locations, trafficking in the Philippines is experienced most frequently by those already at risk, suggesting a need to explore the relationship between trafficking and wider social conditions which maintain inequality and vulnerability.

It is in recognising the structural, "unchosen" determinants of risk that the question emerges of what is considered "violence" – is it in the event of human trafficking alone, or is there violence implicated in the process by which people are made vulnerable and "at-risk"? Galtung[79] introduced the concept of "structural violence" as a way to consider the relationship between direct, physical violence and indirect, socially-shaped forms of violence and suffering.[46,80(p. 295),81,82] Structural violence refers to how social processes such as inequality, exclusion, poverty, and lack of access to resources, rather than direct physical violence alone, contribute to suffering, thus termed *social* suffering.[45,46,79,80,83-85]

Human trafficking, which is exploitation for financial gain, is a criminal matter of perpetrators and victims; it is also an economic matter which implies political and social structures. At the same time, gender, poverty, and geographic location are all strongly implicated in the risk of experiencing human trafficking, which reveals that it is a "social indicator and indeed a social process."[86(p. ix)] Suffering is interpersonal and social, not a solely individual experience; suffering reveals "clustering" of multiple forms among individuals in some groups; suffering reveals "a causal web in the global political economy" where violence, economic insecurity, ill-health, social instability, and disorder are overlapping within the processes that create and maintain inequalities and exclusion.[86(p. x)]

The backdrop for this discussion, however, is the knowledge that cultural representations of suffering, imbued with moral, political, and essentialised agendas, and misidentifying structural violence as cultural difference, have been central to the deployment of human trafficking as a category and the creation of "moral panic."[86(p. 2),87,88(p. 23)] As such, while recognising suffering in my participants' lives, in this book I do not conflate trafficking with suffering, nor suffering with victimhood or lack of agency. Instead, I focus on both suffering and experiences of trafficking as social realities, social *events*, which are illuminated by moments where they appear in participants' stories. To put it another way, the individual experiences of exploitation, trafficking, and violence where the ever-present possibility becomes reality are used as windows into the normal, the way-things-are, and how social reality already contains the violence that erupts at certain points in time, space, and biography.

For the purposes of this study, structural and social violences become the lens with which to view society from the perspective of individual life narratives, and to consider the temporal aspects of inequality, risk, and violence over a life course. Structural violence extends an understanding of risk through acknowledging the processes by which some populations or demographic categories are exposed to greater harm through social structures and social inequality, where "violence is built into the structure and shows up as unequal power and consequently as unequal life chances."[79(p. 171)] Giving primacy to participants' accounts highlights the agency they have deployed in facing and navigating unequal life chances and experiences of violence. It also highlights their biography, choices, and sense of meaning;[89(p. 254)] the focus on structural violences as a lens on *society* does not imply a focus or dramatisation of *individual* suffering. Through

26 *Researching human trafficking*

this book, I consider aspects of life in Mindanao and how they relate to aspects of structural violence, from official policy and legal systems to the social and symbolic processes that are embedded in language and culture. I contend that violence in all its forms, but particularly structural and other social violences, can be compounding over a life path to produce further violences, both direct and indirect, by shaping a person's available options, social position, and internalised identity within the world.

1.12 Overview of the book

This book has been structured to reflect the research aims and my participants' experiences. The chapters are based on outward movement, from rural to urban to international, which mirrors many of my participants' accounts of movement which became a place of trafficking or exploitation. This pattern also reflects wider accounts of labour flows, migration, and human trafficking. The chapters each contain stories from participants which have been grouped according to this movement, location, and experience. As discussed, the stories are told separately from the analysis and discussion in order to emphasise and maintain participants' voices and lives.

Following this discussion of the design and methodology of this research, Chapter 2 focuses on former underage soldiers as a window into the realities of rural Mindanao. Narrative accounts are contextualised in the history and unequal (under-)development that have shaped experiences of rural life. Underage soldiers demonstrate rural-rural movement of people. This chapter also introduces several key concepts that run throughout the book, such as childhood and age in exploitation, definitions of poverty, consent, control, coercion, and agency.

Table 1.1 List of life narratives presented in this book

Participant (pseudonym)	Chapter	Past experience:
Marcus	2	Underage soldier
Jun	2	Underage soldier
DonDon	3.1	Labour exploitation
Gabriel	3.1	Labour trafficking
Melissa	3.1	Labour exploitation/abuse
Erica	3.2	Trafficking for sexual labour
Crystal	3.2	Trafficking for sexual labour
Joramae	3.2	Underage sexual labour
Bianca	4	Migrant trafficking
Jasmine	4	Migrant trafficking
Susan	5	Underage labour exploitation
Mariel	5	Migrant trafficking

Researching human trafficking 27

Chapter 3 explores experiences of labour exploitation including trafficking for sexual labour within the Philippines, which is frequently (and predominantly among my participants) rural-urban movement. This chapter explores the often-precarious labour conditions that workers face, in the light of people who had experienced a variety of exploitative labour situations. It goes on to consider the specific gender-based constraints that affect labour through the experiences of women who had experienced trafficking for sexual labour. The distinction between parts 1 and 2 is not to separate trafficking for sexual labour from other forms of labour exploitation, but to reflect my participants' experiences and allow space for a discussion of gender that came to the fore in the lives of the sexual labourers and those formerly trafficked for sexual labour.

In Chapter 4, I begin by exploring the widespread practice of international labour migration, its role in Philippine society, and accounts of trafficking from several former migrants. I then further explore migration as part of the social imagination, in the context of globalisation as it is experienced in Philippine life. Trafficking of migrants is part of the range of migrants' experiences, and as such wider migration patterns, constraints, and realities are implicated in discussions of human trafficking as part of migration issues. The structure of the book has thus been designed to reflect the general movement of migration and my participants' experiences – rural, rural to urban, and urban to international.

In Chapter 5, I build on the discussion of structural violence to consider the relationships between human trafficking and risk in local society. I explore the ideas of risk and vulnerability as they relate to my participants' experiences and as windows into the social realities and cultural narratives which shape people's life paths. I argue that multiple, overlapping and entrenched social processes maintain violences – both direct and indirect – which shape the prevalence and experience of human trafficking as part of wider social realities.

I conclude in Chapter 6 with a discussion of agency amid constraint through the topic of sacrifice as a central part of participants' narratives and wider cultural idioms. Although the focus of this book has been on structural violence as the social setting of exploitation, agency is a major theme in my participants' lives and accounts as they have strategically and creatively navigated their worlds and experiences. Hope, resilience, and agency are central to my participants' accounts and lives, and active forces even in the midst of violences.

1.13 Conclusions

The narratives and analyses that follow are the result of these methodological strategies and the research that I have carried out. I have presented the narratives as wholes, as closely as possible to how they were told to me.[xxii] The analyses of the stories and central themes are grounded in the

28 *Researching human trafficking*

understanding of Mindanao society that I gained from my own fieldwork experiences, as well as the multiple forms of community knowledge that was shared with me. Close attention to individual accounts and the local context through ethnographic methodologies give a grounded basis for analysis of the wider society, and the processes which contribute to the exploitation that my participants experienced as part of their life paths.

I have explored Mindanao society through individual experience and embedded in stories, in the texture of people's ordinary lives, not limited to experiences of human trafficking/exploitation. The next part of the book begins by considering the phenomenon of underage soldiers, defined officially as a form of human trafficking, through personal accounts situated in the context of rural Mindanao.

Notes

i Crystal's full story is presented in Chapter 3, in the context of sexual labour and sex trafficking. To refer to participants' stories, see the Table of Contents or list in Section 1.12.

ii They have since created their own curriculum based on local needs and culture; it is based on a narrative story which warns about dangers and is usually presented in Cebuano.

iii The Recovery and Reintegration Program for Trafficked Persons (RRPTP) is administered under the DSWD (Department of Social Welfare and Development).[5] There are ten components available:

> "livelihood assistance; skills training; support for victims/witnesses; Balik-Probinsya (financial and food assistance); temporary shelter; educational assistance; finding assistance (for medical assistance, purchase of assistive devices, etc.); psycho-social counselling; referral; and airport assistance for offloaded and/or intercepted and repatriated (potential) victims of trafficking."[5]

Several of the formerly trafficked persons I met had been assisted under this program.

iv The ILO's[15] document, for example, used the terms "modern slavery" and "forced labour" almost synonymously; their global overview, however, included only forced labour including sexual labour, and forced marriage. Their exclusion of underage/"child" soldiers, which fall under the definition of human trafficking, is relevant to this study and another reason I have referred to "human trafficking" rather than modern slavery or forced labour.

v According to this definition, there are three criteria that must be met:

> − The recruitment, transportation, transfer, harbouring or receipt of persons,
> − by means of the threat or use of force or other forms of coercion, of abduction, of fraud, of deception, of the abuse of power or of a position of vulnerability or of the giving or receiving of payments or benefits to achieve the consent of a person having control over another person,
> − for the purpose of exploitation. Exploitation shall include, at a minimum, the exploitation of the prostitution of others or other forms of sexual exploitation, forced labour or services, slavery or practices similar to slavery, servitude or the removal of organs *[spacing added]*.[20(p. 51)]

Researching human trafficking   29

vi   Degrees include: the type and severity of force, coercion, and control; the range of control over movement; the age of the person as a defining factor; the single or plural, direct and indirect sources of force, coercion and control; the type, severity and/or beneficiaries of exploitation.

vii   The UN definition of human trafficking is the standard analytical base for trafficking research, and I consider the ways that the participants' stories do and do not fit within its parameters. However, I also acknowledge the problems inherent in defining people as "trafficked" when this is not the way they would refer to their own experiences; this tension is discussed with regard to individual cases (see Susan's story and Jasmine's story, for examples). The only narrative about exploitation which would likely not fit clearly within the definition of human trafficking is DonDon's account of labour exploitation, as will be discussed. However, the elements of deception, coercion and control, and financial exploitation are all present, and this narrative is included to highlight the fact that continuums of exploitation and control go beyond strict definitions of trafficking, and that labour trafficking is best understood within the wider range of employment practices.

viii   Although I grew up in Canada, I had lived in New Zealand for fifteen years; although people in NZ still notice my accent, my Filipino friends laughed with disbelief when I mentioned this: "But you sound the same as [another friend from New Zealand]!" In general, therefore, I found it simplest to usually only mention that I was from New Zealand, and the assumption that I was American was based primarily on my skin colour.

ix   Many people I met did not know where or what New Zealand was; those who admitted it would ask me questions such as, 'Is that an American state?' or 'Is that in Europe?' A New Zealand friend showed me a rare reference, advertising dairy products from "where the cows are happier," much to our amusement (Figure 1.2).

x   Interviews with government/NGO workers were usually in English, although they were given the option of Cebuano.

xi   *Mga* is a pluraliser.

xii   Small restaurant or food stand; this one was a trestle table with food and drink set up on top.

xiii   I and the street workers found it rather funny, but the other European woman had often been pestered by the Mama-san that her curvier figure would fetch a high market return. I did get a once-over look from Mama-san, who appraised that I had a "good nose," but I gathered that she thought I should keep my day job.

xiv   This was the regional chapter of a nation-wide initiative.

xv   I was 34, I had been married for twelve years, and had three children, but people guessed my age as 25.

xvi   Susan is an exception, but an example of how an open approach to fieldwork can result in unexpected connections for seeking "hidden" populations. I met Susan through an NGO working with street sex workers who facilitated an interview, as I thought that Susan's experiences and insights as a long-time sex worker would be relevant and valuable; I did not know that she had worked as a child labourer, in a situation that could be easily classified as human trafficking under the UN and local legal definitions, until partway through the interview.

xvii   *Matarong pamatasan* also refers to "correct behaviour" or "moral conduct," both also important as part of the ethics of fieldwork.

xviii   Being familiar with a wide range of Christian practices, although in various Western settings, I also felt it was a part of Filipino life that I could begin to partially understand. In this case, the differences in attitude that we might

30 *Researching human trafficking*

have had on doctrinal, political, and social issues was never a major discussion, although I did not particularly hide my views which I suspected were often more critical/liberal than many of the people I met.

xix I employed one of my language teachers, based in Manila, to initially transcribe and translate the interviews; I also listened to the interviews and checked the transcription and translation myself and with support of other native speakers in places where there seemed to be ambiguity.

xx Warden[32(p. 119)] openly discussed her experiences of PTSD following research with sex workers and trafficked persons; I did not have this level of effect from my research, but can identify similar emotions in the fieldwork and post-fieldwork stages of research. For example, I felt unable to write this chapter and re-explore my own position, emotions, and experiences of fieldwork until many months after I had returned home. In this and other chapters, I found that I experienced strong emotional responses and I felt that this writing was often a form of emotional labour.

xxi Despite criticisms of research into social suffering as sentimentally/morally-inspired (or worse), I make no apology for the emotional and moral investment of myself into this work and into the relationships I formed in the Philippines. As discussed, these stories deserve to be told, at the risk of this work being misused or misinterpreted for purposes contrary to my intent, such as sensationalising or "other"-ing the people whose lives I have explored, for which I take full responsibility and risk.[62(pp. 150–152)]

xxii The stories, as mentioned, have been carefully translated (where necessary) from the Cebuano, or local English phrases at times. They have been slightly rearranged, as necessary, to follow a chronological format. I have been particularly attentive to including comments where participants expressed their own opinions and analyses on their lives and experiences.

References

1 Guth, A. (2010). Human trafficking in the Philippines: The need for an effective anti-corruption program. *Trends in Organized Crime, 13*(2–3), 147–166. https://doi.org/10.1007/s12117-009-9082-0

2 Jani, N., & Anstadt, S. (2013). Contributing factors in trafficking from South Asia. *Journal of Human Behavior in the Social Environment, 23*(3), 298–311. https://doi.org/10.1080/10911359.2013.739010

3 Saat, G. (2009). Human trafficking from the Philippines to Malaysia: The impact of urbanism. *South Asian Survey, 16*(1), 137–148. https://doi.org/10.1177/097152310801600109

4 van Schendel, W., Lyons, L., & Ford, M. (Eds.). (2012). *Labour migration and human trafficking in Southeast Asia: Critical perspectives.* Routledge.

5 Pajarito, D. (2016). *IACAT secretariat year end accomplishment report* 2015 [Annual Report]. Inter-Agency Council against Trafficking. http://www.iacat.net/index.php/annual-report

6 Huang, S., & Yeoh, B. (2007). Emotional labour and transnational domestic work: The moving geographies of 'maid abuse' in Singapore. *Mobilities, 2*(2), 195–217. https://doi.org/10.1080/17450100701381557

7 Urada, L., Silverman, J., Tsai, L., & Morisky, D. (2014). Underage youth trading sex in the Philippines: Trafficking and HIV risk. *AIDS Care, 26*(12), 1586–1591. https://doi.org/10.1080/09540121.2014.936818

8 Visayan Forum. (2016). *Facts & figures.* Visayan Forum Foundation. http://visayanforum.org/facts-figures/

Researching human trafficking 31

9 Dahal, P., Joshi, S., & Swahnberg, K. (2015). 'We are looked down upon and rejected socially': A qualitative study on the experiences of trafficking survivors in Nepal. *Global Health Action, 8*(1), 1–9. https://doi.org/10.3402/gha.v8.29267

10 Feingold, D. (2014). Virgin territory re-explored: Ethnographic insight, public policy and the trade in minority women in Southeast Asia. In S. Yea (Ed.), *Human trafficking in Asia: Forcing issues* (pp. 81–100). Routledge/Taylor & Francis Group.

11 Holmes, S. (2013). "Is it worth risking your life?": Ethnography, risk and death on the U.S.–Mexico border. *Social Science & Medicine, 2013*(99), 153–161. https://doi.org/10.1016/j.socscimed.2013.05.029

12 Brennan, D. (2014). Trafficking, scandal, and abuse of migrant workers in Argentina and the United States. *The ANNALS of the American Academy of Political and Social Science, 653*(1), 107–123. https://doi.org/10.1177/0002716213519239

13 Saner, R., Yiu, L., & Rush, L. (2018). The measuring and monitoring of human trafficking. *Public Administration and Policy, 21*(2), 94–106. https://doi.org/10.1108/PAP-10-2018-011

14 Youle, J., & Long, A. (2020). The same ruler for everyone: Improving trafficking estimates. *Forced Migration Review, 2020*(64), 39–42.

15 ILO, & Walk Free. (2017). *Global estimates of modern slavery: Forced labour and forced marriage.* International Labour Organization. http://www.ilo.org/global/publications/books/WCMS_575479/lang--en/index.htm

16 Allain, J., & Bales, K. (2012). *Slavery and its definition* (Research Paper No. 12–06; School of Law). Queen's University.

17 Choi-Fitzpatrick, A. (2015). From rescue to representation: A human rights approach to the contemporary antislavery movement. *Journal of Human Rights, 14*(4), 486–503. https://doi.org/10.1080/14754835.2015.1032222

18 UNODC. (2016). *2016 global report on trafficking in persons.* http://www.unodc.org/documents/data-and-analysis/glotip/2016_Global_Report_on_Trafficking_in_Persons.pdf

19 UN. (n.d.). *International Day for the Abolition of Slavery.* United Nations; United Nations. Retrieved November 11, 2021, from https://www.un.org/en/observances/slavery-abolition-day

20 UNODC. (2006). *Trafficking in persons: Global patterns* [United Nations Office on Drugs and Crime]. Anti-Human Trafficking Unit Global Programme against Trafficking in Human Beings. http://www.unodc.org/pdf/traffickinginpersons_report_2006ver2.pdf

21 UNODC. (2000). *United Nations convention against transnational organized crime and the protocols thereto.* United Nations Office on Drugs and Crime. https://www.unodc.org/documents/treaties/UNTOC/Publications/TOC%20Convention/TOCebook-e.pdf

22 Aronowitz, A. (2009). *Human trafficking, human misery: The global trade in human* beings. Praeger.

23 Ferolin, M., & Dunaway, W. (2013). Globalized fisheries, depeasantization and debt bondage in Philippine seafood exporting. *International Journal of Humanities and Social Science, 3*(13), 45–54.

24 Nonnenmacher, S. (2014). Trafficking at sea: The situation of enslaved fishermen in Southeast Asia. In S. Yea (Ed.), *Human trafficking in Asia: Forcing issues* (pp. 141–164). Routledge/Taylor & Francis Group.

25 Williams, T., Alpert, E., Ahn, R., Cafferty, E., Konstantopoulos, W., Wolferstan, N., Castor, J., McGahan, A., & Burke, T. (2010). Sex trafficking and health care

32 *Researching human trafficking*

in metro Manila: Identifying social determinants to inform an effective health system response. *Health and Human Rights in Practice, 12*(2), 135–147.

26 Oishi, N. (2017). Gender and migration policies in Asia. In D. Tittensor & F. Mansouri (Eds.), *The politics of women and migration in the global south* (pp. 27–48). Palgrave Macmillan UK.

27 Brennan, D. (2005). Methodological challenges in research with trafficked persons: Tales from the field. *International Migration, 43*(1–2), 35–54. https://doi.org/10.1111/j.0020-7985.2005.00311.x

28 Gerassi, L., Edmond, T., & Nichols, A. (2017). Design strategies from sexual exploitation and sex work studies among women and girls: Methodological considerations in a hidden and vulnerable population. *Action Research, 15*(2), 161–176. https://doi.org/10.1177/1476750316630387

29 Kelly, L., & Coy, M. (2016). Ethics as process, ethics in practice: Researching the sex industry and trafficking. In D. Siegel & R. de Wildt (Eds.), *Ethical concerns in research on human trafficking* (Vol. 13, pp. 33–50). Springer International Publishing.

30 West, C. (2014). *The migration-trafficking nexus: An investigation into the survival strategies of the Philippines' poorest migrants* [MA Thesis, Massey University]. http://mro.massey.ac.nz/handle/10179/7263

31 Brunovskis, A., & Surtees, R. (2010). Untold stories: Biases and selection effects in research with victims of trafficking for sexual exploitation. *International Migration, 48*(4), 1–37. https://doi.org/10.1111/j.1468-2435.2010.00628.x

32 Warden, T. (2013). *The cost of dreaming: Identifying the underlying social and cultural structures which push/pull victims into human traffic and commercial sexual exploitation in Central America* [PhD Thesis, University of Stirling]. https://dspace.stir.ac.uk/bitstream/1893/18521/1/Tara_Warden_PhD.pdf

33 Boyd, Z., & Bales, K. (2016). Getting what we want: Experience and impact in research with survivors of slavery. In D. Siegel & R. de Wildt (Eds.), *Ethical concerns in research on human trafficking* (Vol. 13, pp. 173–190). Springer International Publishing.

34 Maynes, M., Pierce, J., & Laslett, B. (2008). *Telling stories: The use of personal narratives in the social sciences and history.* Cornell University Press.

35 Moen, T. (2006). Reflections on the narrative research approach. *International Journal of Qualitative Methods, 5*(4), 56–69. https://doi.org/10.1177/160940690600500405

36 de Angelis, M. (2012). *Human trafficking: Women's stories of agency* [PhD Thesis, University of Hull]. https://hydra.hull.ac.uk/assets/hull:5823a/content

37 Visser, A., du Preez, P., & Simmonds, S. (2019). Reflections on life design narrative inquiry as a methodology for research with child sex trafficking survivors. *International Journal of Qualitative Methods, 18*. https://doi.org/10.1177/1609406919857553

38 Staples, J. (2015). An "up and down life": Understanding leprosy through biography. In K. Smith, J. Staples, & N. Rapport (Eds.), *Authenticity and the interview* (pp. 60–82). Berghahn Books.

39 Willemse, K. (2014). "Everything I told you was true": The biographic narrative as a method of critical feminist knowledge production. *Women's Studies International Forum, 43*, 38–49. https://doi.org/10.1016/j.wsif.2014.02.005

Researching human trafficking 33

40 Goldade, K. (2011). Babies and belonging: Reproduction, citizenship, and undocumented Nicaraguan labor migrant women in Costa Rica. *Medical Anthropology, 30*(5), 545–568. https://doi.org/10.1080/01459740.2011.577043

41 Panitch, V. (2013). Global surrogacy: Exploitation to empowerment. *Journal of Global Ethics, 9*(3), 329–343. https://doi.org/10.1080/17449626.2013.818390

42 Pun, N. (2005). *Made in China: Women factory workers in a global workplace.* Duke University Press/Hong Kong University Press.

43 de León-Torres, M. (2014). Niños, niñas, y mujeres: Una amalgama vulnerable. *Revista Latinoamericana de Ciencias Sociales, Niñez y Juventud, 12*(1), 105–119.

44 Zheng, T. (2014). Migrant sex workers and trafficking in China. In K. Hoang & R. Parreñas (Eds.), *Human trafficking reconsidered: Rethinking the problem, envisioning new solutions* (pp. 139–148). International Debate Education Association.

45 Kleinman, A. (2000). The violences of everyday life: The multiple forms and dynamics of social violence. In V. Das, A. Kleinman, M. Ramphele, & P. Reynolds (Eds.), *Violence and subjectivity* (pp. 226–241). University of California Press.

46 Farmer, P. (2004). An anthropology of structural violence. *Current Anthropology, 45*(3), 305–325. https://doi.org/10.1086/382250

47 Ellard-Gray, A., Jeffrey, N., Choubak, M., & Crann, S. (2015). Finding the hidden participant: Solutions for recruiting hidden, hard-to-reach, and vulnerable populations. *International Journal of Qualitative Methods, 14*(5), 1–10. https://doi.org/10.1177/1609406915621420

48 Adamson, J., & Donovan, J. (2002). Research in black and white. *Qualitative Health Research, 12*(6), 816–825. https://doi.org/10.1177/10432302012006008

49 Bosworth, M., Hoyle, C., & Dempsey, M. (2011). Researching trafficked women: On institutional resistance and the limits to feminist reflexivity. *Qualitative Inquiry, 17*(9), 769–779. https://doi.org/10.1177/1077800411423192

50 Easton, H., & Matthews, R. (2016). Getting the balance right: The ethics of researching women trafficked for commercial sexual exploitation. In D. Siegel & R. de Wildt (Eds.), *Ethical concerns in research on human trafficking* (Vol. 13, pp. 11–32). Springer International Publishing.

51 Surtees, R. (2014). Another side of the story: Challenges in research with unidentified and unassisted trafficking victims. In S. Yea (Ed.), *Human trafficking in Asia: Forcing issues* (pp. 118–137). Routledge/Taylor & Francis Group.

52 van Dyke, R. (2013). Investigating human trafficking from the Andean community to Europe: The role of goodwill in the researcher–gatekeeper relationship and in negotiating access to data. *International Journal of Social Research Methodology, 16*(6), 515–523. https://doi.org/10.1080/13645579.2013.823280

53 Lewis, H. (2016). Negotiating anonymity, informed consent and 'illegality': Researching forced labour experiences among refugees and asylum seekers in the UK. In D. Siegel & R. de Wildt (Eds.), *Ethical concerns in research on human trafficking* (Vol. 13, pp. 99–116). Springer International Publishing.

54 Tyldum, G., & Brunovskis, A. (2005). Describing the unobserved: Methodological challenges in empirical studies on human trafficking. *International Migration, 43*(1–2), 17–34. https://doi.org/10.1111/j.0020-7985.2005.00310.x

55 UNIAP. (2008). *Guide to ethics and human rights in counter-trafficking: Ethical standards for counter-trafficking research and programming* [United Nations

34 Researching human trafficking

Inter-Agency Project on Human Trafficking]. United Nations. http://un-act.org/publication/guide-ethics-human-rights-counter-trafficking/

56 Ottisova, L., Hemmings, S., Howard, L. M., Zimmerman, C., & Oram, S. (2016). Prevalence and risk of violence and the mental, physical and sexual health problems associated with human trafficking: An updated systematic review. *Epidemiology and Psychiatric Sciences, 25*(4), 317–341. https://doi.org/10.1017/S2045796016000135

57 Gurung, S. (2014). Sex trafficking and sex trade industry: The processes and experiences of Nepali women. *Journal of Intercultural Studies, 35*(2), 163–181. https://doi.org/10.1080/07256868.2014.885415

58 Jose, D., & Erpelo, M. (Eds.). (1998). *Halfway through the circle: The lives of eight Filipino women survivors of prostitution and trafficking.* Women's Education, Development, Productivity and Research Organization.

59 Czarniawska, B. (2005). *Narratives in social science research* (Reprinted). SAGE.

60 Narayan, K. (1993). How native is a "native" anthropologist? *American Anthropologist, 95*(3), 671–686.

61 Seligmann, L. (2014). Between storytelling and critical analysis: Going native and crossing borders. *Anthropology and Humanism, 39*(1), 10–17.

62 Wilkinson, I., & Kleinman, A. (2016). *A passion for society: How we think about human suffering.* University of California Press.

63 Ryen, A. (2011). Exploring or exporting? Qualitative methods in times of globalisation. *International Journal of Social Research Methodology, 14*(6), 439–453. https://doi.org/10.1080/13645579.2011.611380

64 Byrne, G. (2017). Narrative inquiry and the problem of representation: 'Giving voice', making meaning. *International Journal of Research & Method in Education, 40*(1), 36–52. https://doi.org/10.1080/1743727X.2015.1034097

65 Atkinson, R. (1998). *The life story interview.* SAGE Publications, Inc.

66 Bräuchler, B. (2018). Contextualizing ethnographic peace research. In G. Millar (Ed.), *Ethnographic peace research* (pp. 21–42). Springer International.

67 Stanley, L., & Temple, B. (2008). Narrative methodologies: Subjects, silences, re-readings and analyses. *Qualitative Research, 8*(3), 275–281. https://doi.org/10.1177/1468794106093622

68 Arnold, D., & Blackburn, S. (Eds.). (2004). *Telling lives in India: Biography, autobiography, and life history.* Indiana University Press.

69 Farmer, P. (1997). On suffering and social violence: A view from below. In A. Kleinman, V. Das, & M. Lock (Eds.), *Social suffering* (pp. 261–284). University of California Press.

70 Spencer, D. (2014). Exposing the conditions of precarity: Compounding victimization and marginalized young people. *Contemporary Justice Review, 17*(1), 87–103. https://doi.org/10.1080/10282580.2014.883846

71 Tombs, S., & Whyte, D. (2006). Work and risk. In G. Mythen & S. Walklate (Eds.), *Beyond the risk society: Critical reflections on risk and human security* (pp. 169–193). Open University Press.

72 Weitzer, R. (2014). New directions in research on human trafficking. *The ANNALS of the American Academy of Political and Social Science, 653*(1), 6–24. https://doi.org/10.1177/0002716214521562

73 Poucki, S., & Bryan, N. (2014). Vulnerability to human trafficking among the Roma population in Serbia: The role of social exclusion and marginalization. *Journal of Intercultural Studies, 35*(2), 145–162. https://doi.org/10.1080/07256868.2014.885417

Researching human trafficking 35

74 Crawford, M. (2016). International sex trafficking. *Women & Therapy, 40*(1–2), 101–122.

75 Schmidt, L., & Buechler, S. (2017). "I risk everything because I have already lost everything": Central American female migrants speak out on the migrant trail in Oaxaca, Mexico. *Journal of Latin American Geography, 16*(1), 139–164. https://doi.org/10.1353/lag.2017.0012

76. Vogt, W. (2013). Crossing Mexico: Structural violence and the commodification of undocumented Central American migrants. *American Ethnologist, 40*(4), 764–780. https://doi.org/10.1111/amet.12053

77 Bulloch, H. (2017). Ambivalent moralities of cooperation and corruption: Local explanations for (under)development on a Philippine island. *The Australian Journal of Anthropology, 28*(1), 56–71.

78 Mialhe, F., Walpole, P., Bruno, E., Dendoncker, N., Richelle, L., & Henry, S. (2014). Spatio-temporal migration patterns to and from an upland village of Mindanao, Philippines. *Population and Environment, 36*(2), 155–179.

79 Galtung, J. (1969). Violence, peace, and peace research. *Journal of Peace Research, 6*(3), 167–191. https://doi.org/10.1177/002234336900600301

80 Galtung, J. (1990). Cultural violence. *Journal of Peace Research, 27*(3), 291–305. https://doi.org/10.1177/0022343390027003005

81 Kaufman, A. (2014). Thinking beyond direct violence. *International Journal of Middle East Studies, 46*(02), 441–444. https://doi.org/10.1017/S0020743814000427

82 Scheper-Hughes, N., & Bourgois, P. (Eds.). (2007). *Violence in war and peace: An anthology.* Blackwell.

83 Das, V., & Das, R. (2007). How the body speaks: Illness and the lifeworld among the urban poor. In J. Biehl, B. Good, & A. Kleinman (Eds.), *Subjectivity: Ethnographic investigations* (pp. 66–97). University of California Press.

84 Kleinman, A., & Kleinman, J. (1997). The appeal of experience; the dismay of images: Cultural appropriations of suffering in our times. In A. Kleinman, V. Das, & M. Lock (Eds.), *Social suffering* (pp. 1–24). University of California Press.

85 Scheper-Hughes, N. (2006). Dangerous and endangered youth: Social structures and determinants of violence. *Annals of the New York Academy of Sciences, 1036*(1), 13–46. https://doi.org/10.1196/annals.1330.002

86 Kleinman, A., Das, V., & Lock, M. (1997). Introduction. In A. Kleinman, V. Das, & M. Lock (Eds.), *Social suffering* (pp. ix–xxvii). University of California Press.

87 Brennan, D. (2017). Fighting human trafficking today: Moral panics, zombie data, and the seduction of rescue. *Wake Forest Law Review, 52*(2017), 477–496.

88 Das, V., & Kleinman, A. (2001). Introduction. In V. Das, A. Kleinman, M. Lock, M. Ramphele, & P. Reynolds (Eds.), *Remaking a world: Violence, social suffering, and recovery* (pp. 1–30). University of California Press.

89 Fassin, D. (2012). *Humanitarian reason: A moral history of the present times.* University of California Press.

2 Rural Mindanao

History, conflict, and underage soldiers

2.1 Introduction

> My fear when I was in the mountains was that I might die there. If a comrade of yours dies, they will just bury you knee-deep and leave you in the forest. That's my fear if I died, (no one would know where I was). If you have an encounter here, and a comrade of yours dies, you would carry him and upon getting (to safety), you will bury him. So, I would be afraid that I would die.
>
> - (Marcus, reflecting on his time as a rebel soldier from age 15–18)

Rebel soldiers like Marcus routinely faced the risk of death for themselves and their comrades. During the time I was in Mindanao for fieldwork, a military skirmish in a rural area had left four rebels dead, the youngest aged only fifteen. Reportedly, New People's Army (NPA) forces had attacked a military delivery of civilian relief supplies to an impoverished area. In rural Mindanao, NGOs and police told me about their human trafficking concerns which included the issue of underage soldiers. One of the former soldiers I met through police and NGO workers was just sixteen years old, and I watched female police officers hug him and fuss over him maternally.[i] The officers had initially facilitated his surrender to the military, and later visited him in their off-hours to teach him to read. He had been told by the rebels that if he was captured, the government forces would torture him and "skin him alive." This same day, one of my NGO friends had confided that there were NPA soldiers hiding out at her house, wanting to surrender to the military, but wary of a reported corrupt official who had not been facilitating the social support packages offered to former soldiers but pocketing the processing payments.[ii]

The prevalence of underage soldiers in Mindanao is closely related to other rural problems including violent conflict, poverty, and unemployment. Globally, underage soldiers are often presumed to represent one of the "worst" forms of human trafficking; accounts from other parts of the world, however, are often significantly removed from both the experiences of young soldiers in the Philippines and their social context. In the Philippines, the

DOI: 10.4324/9781003261049-2

History and conflict in Rural Mindanao 37

multiple ongoing conflicts in rural Mindanao are implicated in human trafficking in the form of underage soldiers; further, multiple risks, including that of human trafficking, emerge in combat zones as a result of the conflict due to disrupted livelihoods, the threat of violence, and displacement from their homes.[1] Researchers have increasingly emphasised the role of local studies that acknowledge (former) underage soldiers' own experiences of the complex and distinct settings that shape their lives.[2(p. 224),3(p. 321),4] In the Philippines, both the rural-urban disparities and the ideologically based operations of the NPA create a unique situation for underage soldiers compared to other locations.[5]

I use the term "underage soldiers" rather than "child soldiers" to include older teenage combatants without infantilising them, and to recognise that my participants, like most Filipino underage soldiers, were teenagers, and in many ways already economically independent from their parents prior to becoming soldiers. The multiple rebel uprisings in Mindanao represent a specifically rural discontentment, and the issues affecting rural populations have been implicated heavily in both individual and group decisions to take up arms. Underage soldiers' stories reveal their own experiences, choices, and constraints, as well as aspects of the specific rural context in which much of their lives have been lived.

The aim of this chapter is to explore the conditions facing rural populations in Mindanao through the experiences of former underage soldiers, who under international definitions would also be considered victims of human trafficking. Although there are several non-state military groups known to have used underage soldiers, the primary focus will be on the CPP-NPA (Communist Party of the Philippines – New People's Army) as this is the group where my participants had been enlisted. This chapter contributes to the discussion of human trafficking and structural violence in Mindanao by describing the realities of rural life including the massive disparities between rural and urban communities. The experiences of underage soldiers are points where the relationships between structural and physical violence become clearly manifest. This relationship is also significant in then understanding the ways that rural poverty can be a risk factor for most other types of human trafficking in Mindanao.

Structural violence has been used by multiple disciplines as a way to analyse the links between the past and the present in terms of suffering. Economic deprivation, institutionalised racism, and colonial violence have been demonstrated to have transgenerational impacts on multiple aspects of life including physical health, economic and educational success, and cultural belief systems.[6-8] Colonial legacies have included both structural violence, such as racialised hierarchies or unproductive economic systems which maintain impoverished conditions, and symbolic violence.[6,7] The suppression of native languages and cultures in many former colonies, for example, has been identified as symbolic violence with far-reaching effects.[9-11]

38 *History and conflict in Rural Mindanao*

The Philippines' history which includes colonisation, displays multiple violences which continue to impact local society. The legacies of colonial rule and their relationships to current social configurations and cultural systems are themes that particularly emerge in this chapter which explores the legacy of rural underdevelopment. Dwyer[12(p. 21)] suggested that when the connections between "the cultural, the social, and the political, between representation and social experience" are analysed in terms of violence, violence then can "illuminate the past" – and, I would argue, violences of the past can also illuminate the present.

2.2 Rural history and poverty

The current social configuration of rural/urban relationships and inequalities has emerged from a long colonial history. Spanish rule (1565–1898) was based on Roman Catholicism underpinning political power. The social landscape began to transition from agrarian regions to townships around a small centre with a church, a resident priest, and schools (one for boys and one for girls); the majority of contemporary towns were established in this period.[13(p. 48)] This physical and political restructuring of traditional social organisation enabled colonial control through religion, education, economic systems as part of "the deliberate cultivation of local mentalities towards subservience,"[14(p. 34)] relevant to the discussions of domestic and migrant labour in later chapters. Spanish control also began the exploitation of natural resources, deforestation, and loss of traditional land use, which would characterise the next centuries of Philippine history.

Spanish laws on land ownership meant that some private owners began to acquire and commercially develop what had been traditionally shared land and resources, a legacy of inequality and exploitation which has only been partially addressed today.[7,15] Further, violence, oppression, and forced labour were common elements of the Spanish rule. An account from Filipino oral history illustrates the way that political and religious rule were entwined, as well as the conditions for locals:

> The first thing that had to be done was the construction of the town, or pueblo, and the next was the church. This was why a great number of the natives (indios) were captured and forced to destroy the mountains, to cut the trees, and gather adobe from faraway places. This was punishing work for the natives and what was most hateful about it was that they were not paid for their labor.
>
> The natives had no choice but to obey orders; they were forced to obey these cruel masters so as to erect the church, which was the town's foundation.
>
> The natives endured many months of this, but some ran away to faraway places and to mountains just so they could escape the Spaniards' cruelty. The family members who were left behind had to take on the

History and conflict in Rural Mindanao 39

work of those who escaped, and they bore unbearable suffering and poverty.

Shall we tell you about the misery and suffering the natives endured at the hands of the Spaniards? Shall we tell you how many native lives were lost at the hands of the oppressors?[16(p. 42)]

As the account above illustrates, forced labour was part of the Spanish dominance, and central to the beginning of the contrast between urban areas and the mountains where "disobedient" Filipinos ran to escape. The social geography of the Philippines is still based on the Catholic distinction between lowlanders, and uplanders who had fled and been pushed to the mountains and outside of religious jurisdiction.[17] Lowlands and cities were converted, and considered civilised, real Filipinos, while the mountainous areas were those of heathen spirituality, backwards and primitive peoples. Even now, the category of *lumad* [indigenous] is based on this arbitrary distinction between "us and them" based on these old Catholic forms of dominance.[17,18] The end of Spanish rule, after local uprisings began to challenge colonial dominance, came when Spain sold the Philippines to the USA in 1898. American rule continued the land and resource degradation, concentration of wealth and power in certain land-owning families, and underdevelopment of impoverished rural areas which characterise the Philippines today and are the results of the colonial period and ongoing uneven relationships.

Rural areas of the Philippines have the lowest levels of infrastructure, health services, and commercial activities. They also have the worst rates of poverty,[iii] malnutrition, education attainment, and infant mortality.[21(p. 168),22,23,24(p. 365)] Crime statistics are often unknown, not because there are not cases of, say, domestic violence or theft, but because remote or indigenous areas often operate under customary law which does not have higher outside or government accountability.[25(p. 128)] The lack of infrastructure has multiple effects, where inadequate roads and transport options limit access to social services as well as commercial opportunities such as markets; the lack of educational opportunities further reinforces cycles of poverty.[21,24] Displacement due to conflict and natural disasters, ongoing in Mindanao, is extended and the negative consequences multiplied when there is no resolution, or infrastructure to rebuild and recover.

2.3 Definitions of poverty

For this research, the primary concern is the subjective meanings of poverty – the ordinary day-to-day experience, the social meanings and identities, the way people engage with lack in their decision making. The objective measurements – and the limits and ambiguities within the objective measurements – of poverty in the Philippines are discussed in Chapter 3. The uneven distribution across genders and geography suggests attention

40 *History and conflict in Rural Mindanao*

to the social configurations embedded in structure and daily life that shape the risk and experience of poverty. Subjective meanings include not only the effort to meet basic needs but also whether people have the resources to participate in family and community life, and meet social obligations.[26(p. 12),27] Many participants emphasised times when they were able to support others in their family, an important aspect of relationship and marker of economic success in the Philippines. Poverty is comparative, both to others locally and by global standards in terms of resources and meeting basic needs. In the Philippines, the migration-focused economy, widespread English use, and specific colonial history mean that poverty is interpreted in both local and global context.

My experiences confirmed what other scholars in various disciplines have noted where Filipinos would readily describe themselves as operating from a "colonial mentality."[6(p. 1),28] Researchers have described how this manifests as a sense of inherent personal and cultural inferiority, and a type of "auto-racism" in an ongoing comparison to the powerful colonial ther,[6,28,29(p. 53)] when Filipino culture is set against images of America and automatically judged inferior. White people are assumed to be rich, and American. Of course, by Philippine standards my family was very wealthy, as most New Zealanders would be. But even well-fed private school students would ask for money, as I mentioned in Chapter 1, as we passed by groups in their tidy uniforms. Further, when overseas, Filipinos are often treated as impoverished – whether they are or not. The Philippines' position in relation to the rest of the world is keenly felt, and the experiences of poverty and precarity colour Filipinos' self-perceptions.

Poverty is not a fixed state; however, being "poor" is not only a descriptor but a social identity. Most of my participants whose stories are included would likely fall into the category of "poor" (and, most identified themselves as such). In their stories, I see related factors that contribute to this framing: low income, or insufficient income to meet the family's needs; lack of a permanent home, or having a home in a "squatter" settlement which implies uncertainty due to its irregular status; dependency on family for present or future survival; dependency on subsistence agriculture. Living paycheque-to-paycheque seemed to be the norm, regardless of income level, including for those in stable, well-paid employment; one notable exception was an industrious sexual labourer who saved money and supplies, buying rice in bulk and offering micro-loans to other sexual labourers. Thus, the experience of being poor exists on continuums and in the context of social norms.

One of the topics that these stories illuminate is what it means to be poor. Being poor is a family experience, and economic decisions are made from a corporate sense of responsibility – including decisions about work, labour, and migration. For many participants across a range of experiences, being poor meant experiencing lack – identified as a form of violence – that pushed them to seek better options and opportunities. For labourers, it meant increased dependence on their employers and less power to object to

History and conflict in Rural Mindanao   41

being treated badly. For (potential) migrants, it meant significant hurdles to accessing regular migration paths before even leaving the country. For rural Filipinos, it often meant experiencing ongoing conditions of hardship combined with a lack of both resources and infrastructure; for those who became NPA insurgents, it meant being positioned to see the injustice of the government system from the perspective of those among the most marginalised of Filipino society.

2.4 History of conflict in Mindanao

Various communist and Muslim separatist groups had existed from the 1930s, but the MNLF (Moro National Liberation Front) and NPA (CPP-NPA) were both mobilised to violent rebellion under the Marcos (1965–1986) dictatorship with accompanying oppressive policies and violent martial law state.[18(p. 170),30] The Marcos family are believed to have embezzled up to $US 5 billion, and further assets were assigned to their relatives and supporters, while poverty levels increased dramatically.[31(p. 90)] The dictatorial Marcos regime is known for imposing martial law with consequent human rights abuses including torture and other military atrocities, censorship of the media and individuals, and seizing corporate assets.[32,33(p. 199),34(p. 147)] Marcos' political opponents, public critics, and the CPP-NPA and Moro Independence Liberation Front (MILF)[iv] organisations were particularly targeted, although the NPA in particular, grew in numbers as a vessel for Marcos' detractors to unify in opposition.[32(p. 176)] Despite this negative legacy, the Marcos family continues to be politically active and maintains some level of public support. However, the violent Martial Law years remain in popular memory.[v]

Since that time, the MILF and BIFF (Bangsamoro Islamic Freedom Fighters) have broken away from the MNLF and continued the violent uprisings in Western Mindanao. After the establishment of the ARMM (Autonomous Region in Muslim Mindanao), conflict has continued, as the future of the ARMM has been negotiated; the consequences to indigenous and Christian communities in this area have been particularly devastating and meant significant population displacement.[18(p. 171),35(p. 21)] The Abu-Sayyaf is a recent militant Islamic group which, although smaller, has received attention for the terrorist attacks on civilians as well as government forces.[vi]

The NPA exists across the Philippines, with significant activity in Eastern Mindanao.[30] From its height in 1987 with over 25,000 troops who had been mobilised against the Marcos dictatorship, the AFP's 2009 estimates suggested that there were only 4,700 active NPA insurgents.[37] In 2016, military activity against the NPA was ongoing, but the government was also offering significant livelihood packages and holistic support for surrendering soldiers.

Analysts have argued that from about 2,000, governments have been increasingly authoritarian.[38] President Duterte (2016–) has extended this

42 *History and conflict in Rural Mindanao*

tendency of heavy-handed government, raising concerns that history may be repeating itself; one year following my fieldwork, martial law had been declared in Mindanao in response to security concerns.[39,40] Until recently, the NPA-CPP and MILF were acknowledged as political dissenting organisations, and the focus was on disarmament and rehabilitation; Duterte instead labelled them terrorist organisations and increased AFP hostility.[41(p. 108)]

The longstanding conflicts in Mindanao are on the surface conflicts of ideologies – Muslims against Christians, communists against the government regime. However, researchers agree that rural underdevelopment, and particularly feudal economic systems and lack of land access, are the underlying catalysts,[22,42,43] supporting Paredes'[18(p. 170)] claim that "land is usually at the root of any serious armed conflict within Mindanao." Resistance to eviction from traditionally held land for government economic development has sparked conflict between various rural groups and the government, and increased support for dissenting organisation like the NPA.[44(p. 349)] Ongoing conflict, however, has perpetuated land access problems, contributing to the 152,380 displaced persons in Mindanao in 2016 – a known correlate to increases in underage combatants.[45,46]

2.5 Definitions of children and child

In the Philippines, underage soldiers are found in many different conflict zones in Mindanao as well as other areas. On 10 March 2017, for example, hundreds of underage soldiers were released by the MILF (Moro Islamic Liberation Front) in Western Mindanao, as part of an arrangement with the UN to eventually disengage over 1,800 children.[47] The most common characteristics of underage soldiers in the Philippines include being uneducated, teenagers rather than young children, coming from rural, impoverished, large or separated families, and recruited without physical force.[48,49(pp. 60–63)] These characteristics have been similar for most armed struggles over the past decades.

Youth have been central to the development of the NPA since its humble origins in communist-oriented University student groups.[36] In the NPA, minors have historically had a variety of roles from semi-civilian scouts and messengers to direct support roles and active combat.[36] From 1999 to 2007, the AFP (Armed Forces of the Philippines) reported processing 265 NPA "child-combatants."[vii, 37] Further numbers of NPA will have joined as youth, although evidence from participants and other stakeholders suggests that the NPA often and increasingly avoids directly recruiting underage participants.

Questions over the age of consent or majority have often, particularly in the context of human trafficking, been primarily about identifying culpability versus victimhood. A particular aspect of the UN definition is the universal identification of a child as anyone under eighteen and whose consent is considered irrelevant in a trafficking case.[50(p. 15)] This discussion is relevant to all forms of human trafficking, but particularly underage soldiers and sex work where voluntary participants are often labelled trafficked by their age alone. Criminal prosecution, support and benefits, and community reintegration are often shaped around the question of whether someone is a victim or a perpetrator; for former soldiers, age can be the single defining factor in answering that question.[51,52(p. 92),53(p. 63)] Although minor status has meant that perpetrators of crimes, for example, are considered less culpable, it has also meant that those under eighteen have been presumed "victims" or lacking agency and prevented from making decisions about their own lives.[52]

Most scholars would agree that in general, minors have greater vulnerability to coercion and less ability to make informed long-term commitments such as enlisting as a rebel soldier.[25(p. 126),51] Where this agreement usually ends, however, is on the question of agency.[54(p. 3)] Some have argued that as those under eighteen years are ineligible to enter into contractual arrangements legally, they are always victims when participating in conflict.[53(pp. 62–63),55(p. 7)] Others have maintained that constraints including the limitations that come with age and maturity do not override the legitimate agency and decision-making processes that even underage soldiers display in navigating the world around them, including the decision to enlist.[52,56] This issue is important, however, as defining child or underage soldiers as distinct from adult soldiers has real-life consequences.[52(p. 92)]

The primary difficulty in terms of defining underage soldiers as exploited or trafficked hinges on the definition of a "child" and the degree to which a minor is ascribed the ability to make informed and socially accountable decisions.[51,52] The definition and legal age are different in various cultural and legal settings, making universal proclamations or comparisons difficult.[5,52,56–59] Although some have suggested that the UN's recommendations have increasingly led to eighteen being considered the universal benchmark, this still varies across locations in policy and practice.[53,55] Others have suggested that the age should be set according to local cultural traditions, or a variable context-based scale which can acknowledge both agency and vulnerabilities.[52,56]

At the same time, where such choices are made by (or for) minors amid highly constrained circumstances, there is a legitimate mandate to question whether and what type of intervention is appropriate. Swart and Hassen[56] suggested that a sensitive understanding of local traditions, maturity, voluntariness, cultural context, and local laws is necessary, particularly for older (fifteen to eighteen year old) youths, in evaluating whether a young person can choose military participation. Derluyn[51] recommended integrated approaches which accommodate legal rights, psychological and social needs, through culturally appropriate forms of restorative justice which can transcend binary distinctions between victim and perpetrator. However, these recommendations also highlight the difficulty in reconciling concrete legal policy to actual experience in the case of underage soldiers.

44 *History and conflict in Rural Mindanao*

Marcus and Jun's stories both reveal elements of coercion and exploitation as minors, as well as agency and choice in their experiences of rebel military life. Both men have received education, financial, and well-being support offered to surrendering soldiers. Sacrifice, suffering, death, endurance, and strength are among the central themes of Marcus and Jun's narratives. These are themes that also link their stories to others of my participants who had experienced various types of human trafficking and related events.

2.6 Marcus' story

> "Those people that I have killed,[viii] I hope they can forgive me and God will forgive me too."

Marcus was eighteen years old, but gentle and soft-spoken, he seemed younger when I met with him in a café along with his guardian.[ix] He had come to stay with an NGO worker I knew after recently surrendering to the AFP. The NGO worker was a forthright, petite, motherly woman, and she had told me how Marcus seemed to be reclaiming his lost childhood, planting in her garden and playing happily with her young grandchildren when they often visited. She obviously cared for Marcus, and during the interview any time Marcus mentioned something in his past that she did not approve of, she would start swatting and threatening him teasingly. I knew her well, though, and would swat her arm playfully in turn and remind her with similar feigned annoyance, "this is *my* interview! You can't punish him for this!"

Marcus came from a rural area. When he was young, he attended primary school and helped at home. The family was poor but survived. His father was sick and could not work due to ongoing bad health, so Marcus' mother worked as an agricultural labourer harvesting rice. "When I was little, I went to elementary school there. After that, when I was turning eight, my mother died. There are nine of us siblings, I am the sixth." At that point, his siblings separated. One sister was "adopted" by a family in another town,[x] while the oldest brother migrated to Manila for work. Another moved to a mining area and found work as a labourer. Two older brothers and one older sister joined the NPA. Marcus was left with his disabled father and two younger siblings. "I was turning ten then, but my father couldn't get a job because he was sickly. So that's why I was helping him in looking for food. I had already stopped school at that time." Marcus took on the responsibility of earning a living to feed the family. He was employed as a casual agricultural labourer, primarily harvesting bananas, before he was yet ten years old.

By the time Marcus was thirteen, he had had enough of the struggle for survival in his home village. He had started getting into trouble, joining his friends in experimenting with marijuana. Finally, he left home, leaving his father and younger siblings. He was thirteen when he joined an older sister to work as agricultural labourer working on a banana plantation. However, "my sister and I didn't understand each other," he described, "because

History and conflict in Rural Mindanao 45

whenever I made a small error, just a little mistake, she would always hit me, straight away." Eventually Marcus left his sister to get away from her treatment, and travelled again to another town. He stayed with an uncle, and found a job as a labourer in construction. He worked in this job until he was fifteen.

At this point, Marcus met up with one of his older brothers, Ian, who was visiting. With Marcus leaving home and Ian having been in the mountains with the NPA, they had not seen each other in five years. Marcus was happy to see one of his siblings after spending several years living with other relatives, and realised how much he had missed his family. He decided to accompany Ian back to the mountains. When they arrived, Ian announced Marcus as a new recruit, and Marcus realised he had been enlisted without his knowledge. The next morning, he began training. Training lasted for 20 days, during which time the trainees learned how to shoot, how to avoid crossfire, and what to do in battle. They practiced target shooting with a tarpaulin shaped to look like a person and placed at a distance. Marcus was given a gun, bandolier [bullet holder], bag, and dressed as a soldier. He was very proud of completing the training and wore his new gear with bravado, showing off his new status. "I graduated from the training, I already had a gun and I looked like a typical soldier." Ian, by this time, had moved on with his separate battalion.

After this, however, "I really went through *sakripisyo* [suffering] that I had never experienced outside. Like when there was no food for a week, none, only water. When there were many (government) soldiers around, we could not get through to get rice. We would just keep on hiding. We knew we couldn't fight back because we hadn't been eating. So, we would just have to watch and wait." There was little Marcus and the other soldiers could do at these times. "My comrades, when the hunger got to be too much, would just eat sugar, grass, rattan, whatever we could find in the jungle."

Marcus also described enduring long and dangerous treks on top of the hunger that he felt. "We would leave at night, carrying heavy loads. We would walk along *ispatay pangpang* [killer cliffs] in the dark, without any flashlight. In our bags we had bombs, bullets, medicines, and emergency supplies for the wounded. For the first two months when I got there, I bore all of this, I just suffered all the hardships, but I hadn't encountered a real battle yet."

Two months after Marcus arrived in the mountains, he experienced his first battle. His camp was raided and attacked by the AFP. "There were only fourteen of us there and thirty of them. We fought back for an hour, exchanging gunshots. They were able to take fifteen of our packs as well as a magazine full of bullets. They stole those from us. After an hour the (government) reinforcements arrived, including a military helicopter, and we had to withdraw. I was only fifteen years old at that time."

After this, Marcus' battalion joined another group to form a large squadron, and for a time, he was reunited with Ian. Marcus was assigned the duty

46 *History and conflict in Rural Mindanao*

of setting landmines, while other NPA were placed as snipers. They aimed to take out military forces while they were operating checkpoints along the highway. But before the attack, the AFP soldiers were tipped off and advanced towards the camp.

Marcus and his comrades had to flee, walking out at midnight during Typhoon Yolanda. It was raining hard, cold and tempestuous, and rivers were swollen with rainwater. "The current was very strong. When we crossed the river, one of my comrades was carried away by the current. When he crossed, he got hit by a piece of driftwood. It was dark, and there was no flashlight. We looked for him anyway, even though the current was strong. We swam and dived under the water, but we couldn't find him. His body was found the next morning."

After three hours of searching, they had to carry on through the miserable conditions and darkness. "We got tired looking for him, and we continued walking. We were tired and weak because we had empty stomachs and no food. Then it was uphill, really steep. It was very slippery, and our loads were heavy. It took a long time climbing uphill. When we reached (a place we could stop), we made a barracks. We didn't want to go anymore because emotions were running very high. We were very angry at the soldiers. We were very mad at them, thinking 'we will stay here, even if we die. We will not withdraw anymore.' We set up our camp, and planted bombs around it. We dug foxholes, so we could hide. We waited in silence, only talking to each other very slowly using bird calls[xi] so that we would not be heard. Day and night, we stood guard, and we did not sleep."

In the typhoon, however, the AFP did not continue pursuing Marcus' unit. They returned soon after though and encountered another paramilitary group. These indigenous local "blackfighters" were also active in rural areas. A battle broke out. "The soldiers thought that the blackfighters were NPAs. The blackfighters thought that the soldiers were NPA, because they wear the same uniforms. So, they shot at each other. After a week, the soldiers left, and everything was quiet." At this point, the battalions split off again and dispersed.

By this point, Marcus was well entrenched into the rebel movement. "I had already internalised the communist way of thinking. We were angry at the government. We were angry at the soldiers. Besides the (combat) encounters, (the NPA) would also educate us, and tell us what the government was like."

Between skirmishes, Marcus would participate in combat training, communist education, and medical skills. He was trained in emergency medicine, surgery, and basic skills for common ailments. Once trained, Marcus provided basic medical services to the other NPA troops as well as local rural populations. He and the other medics would perform circumcisions, tooth extractions, surgical cyst removal, and make dentures.

In rural civilian towns, as well as providing medical services, Marcus and his comrades would gather the people around an NPA speaker with a

History and conflict in Rural Mindanao   47

blackboard. "We would gather them, just like going to school. Then we would teach them the traits of a soldier, and how the government has exploited us. We would teach them why we are still poor until now. Then after we had organised them, we would choose who would become their leader. Then we would recruit to become members of the New People's Army. Anyone who wanted to could join, but underage (youths) were not allowed. I was accepted because my brother was responsible there and he recommended me." Ian, however, was part of a different battalion and seldom saw Marcus.

"When I turned sixteen, (my comrades) celebrated my birthday. They threw a party for me. They bought me a pig, and chicken. I also got promoted, and I got a higher rank. They changed my gun, my gun was new. I became a medic in the squadron. Then I was the one giving my comrades medical aid when they were sick. So, I stayed *nagkadugay-nagkadugay* [longer and longer]. While I stayed longer and longer in the NPA, I also began to think, 'will my life be like this always? Feeling like I'm always in the dark?' I started to think that it was really not good[xii] for me to continue in this kind of life."

However, Marcus' comrades discouraged him from trying to leave, saying that he could not go back to civilian life. "(They) would advise me, that if I left, it would be just the same. If I was a civilian, the government would exploit me, and nothing would change. And that the army was already looking for me, and because the soldiers are fascists, I might be caught and then they would kill me. So, my commitment to serve was revived and I continued on."

Marcus recounted one of the memorable events for him. "There was a time that we had a medical mission in one community. We held it in the *barangay* hall. When I came in, a man saluted me. He greeted me, '*maayong udto* [good noon/midday],' and saluted, but in the NPA, saluting is not done. It is only done by (government) soldiers. I told our office (what had happened). So, we captured him, and we did not continue our medical mission. We captured him and took him back to our camp." Initially, the soldier would not admit that he was an intelligence agent, but after a week of being kept in handcuffs, he finally confessed.

"It was decided among the officials that he should be killed. When the officials decided to kill him, I was the one who was ordered to kill. It was nighttime, and the commander said to me, 'you're going to kill him at night. You will take him up to the road, and you will shoot him there. When he dies, remove the handcuffs.'"

"So that was it." Marcus and another rebel soldier took the prisoner up to the road. Marcus told his comrade to hold onto him in the dark, and Marcus followed, carrying a gun. "When we got to the road, the soldier thought we would set him free. But, unfortunately not. He would be killed instead. So I shot him."

Marcus remained with the movement for about three years. Long treks and hunger became a way of life. He described the ongoing movement, such

48   *History and conflict in Rural Mindanao*

as an event where "we had to flee. We walked away. We walked for nine days straight." He also described the constant fear that had accompanied him through his years of service. "My fear when I was in the mountains was that I might die there. If a comrade of yours dies, they will just bury you knee-deep and leave you in the forest. That's my fear if I died, (no one would know where I was). If you have an encounter here, and a comrade of yours dies, you would carry him and upon getting (to safety), you will bury him. So, I would be afraid that I would die. But if you heard the sound of a gunshot your fears would vanish." With a gun in his hand and in the fury of battle, Marcus described feeling invincible in those moments. "All the more if you can smell gunpowder. All the more if you can fire your gun. You are immortal."

Marcus continued his work as a medic. He was also promoted to team leader, and given new responsibilities as an assassin for targeted government troops. Eventually, however, Marcus received word that his father was in hospital. He was given permission to go and stay with his father. A female friend and former NPA member had been supporting Marcus, and when he needed medicine for his father, she offered to drive him to the city for it. However, she took him to a mall and introduced him to a female AFP soldier. "I was shocked. I was really surprised at that because I did not expect that I would come face to face with a soldier. Because I had no plans to surrender. So that was it. Two soldiers sat beside me. I thought whether I could flee, but I had no money. I could not go home." He was angry at his friend, but she continued to text him, reassuring him that he would not be harmed.

Marcus was taken to be interviewed. "We talked. We understood each other. I understood after that, and I thought 'there are still soldiers who are kind.' I had thought all soldiers were cruel. So, my fear vanished. Then my anger also vanished. Then (my friend) and I also became close again."

"When I surrendered, that's when I realised all the things that I had done." After Marcus' guardian had translated, she also commented on Marcus' experiences since he had come to live with her. "He really realised everything, the wrongdoing he has done, the sacrifices he went through, the hard life; it's been a big realisation for him."

Marcus expressed his gratitude for having come to her house and finding people who cared about him, and getting to attend church and participate in religious community life. "I am thankful that I met (my guardian), and here I discovered God. When I got here outside (of the conflict), when I would lie down I would think about the differences between the movement and here outside. I would think that life here is great because here is where you find the real democracy. Here, whatever you want to do, no one will tell you not to do that. There (in the mountains) you cannot just do anything that you want to do if you don't go through your commander. You even have to ask permission to go to the CR ("comfort room," the toilet)."

When I spoke to Marcus, he was considering going back to school. He had been working in the garden at his new home, to the delight of his guardian.

History and conflict in Rural Mindanao   49

He enjoyed looking after plants and wanted to go into farming and agriculture; his guardian teased that she was finding him a wife. Marcus reflected on his experiences and how glad he was to be out of NPA life.

"Those people that I have killed, I hope they can forgive me and God will forgive me too. I also don't want those things that I have experienced to walk at night with no flashlight." The long, arduous treks were something Marcus had emphasised as a struggle of rebel life. As a medic, Marcus also had to endure seeing the effects of violence very close-up. "Those hardships in life that I encountered, like holding your comrade and his life ending in your hands. During an encounter, he got hit. I held him in my arms, I just let him lie here, like that. I just held him and told him, 'I will not leave you.' Then, after a few minutes, his breathing stopped. So that's why – those kind of sacrifices, I don't want to bring that back in my life."

2.7 Jun's story

Being remembered as a martyr –
because you're a martyr during the revolution –
there is that honour.
But the question is, will we end there?
Those that became martyrs during the movement,
didn't they have their own dreams?
Of course they did.
You arrive at that point because you have dreams.
Your dream was to change yourself and change the system.
The question is, until when?
Until when will we dream of that?
Until we are gone?

Even with visible scars, Jun was handsome and athletic, the picture of glowing health now that he was out of the jungle. His social worker had done a thorough job asking if he would mind doing an interview with me, stressing that he did not have to by any means. He had shared his story on other occasions, and wanted to make his experiences known. He sat facing away at a 90-degree angle to Adrian and me, his eyes averted to the wall, his face neutral but hard, appearing wary and alert. I was slightly concerned that he was uncomfortable with the interview, but Jun had chosen to be here, and we continued through the informed consent process. I first asked him to describe his life where he had grown up, and my apprehensions began to lift as he spoke at length, thoughtfully but not hesitantly, and gave the impression that he was in control of himself and what he wanted to say.

I met Jun early in my fieldwork and I was not used to working with a translator, and Adrian, the social worker who was accompanying me, was not used to being one, but we managed to communicate. Slowly Jun's body language relaxed and became more open and towards us, and he began

50 *History and conflict in Rural Mindanao*

to make eye contact with Adrian, although I only received the occasional glance. He had been a soldier from the age of 13–33, when he surrendered a few months prior to my meeting him, making him almost exactly my age. I watched and listened as he spoke, trying to picture him as the thirteen-year-old he once was when he began rebel life.

Jun described how he was never really able to have a childhood. For some time, he had a happy but poor life in the remote rural village with his agricultural family. He would work hard on the farm as well as going to school. He remembered how his parents cared for him and that the children would have enough to eat, even snacks during the day as well as their meals. Things changed drastically, though, when Jun's mother died when he was seven, and his father less than three years later. "In my youth, I did not really experience childhood life because first my mother died, then my father also died." Jun and his siblings were left to support each other, and Jun found himself in the role of breadwinner from an early age. He and his siblings suddenly found themselves in dire poverty with little hope for a better life, and the demands meant that Jun did not continue his schooling past grade one. When he was thirteen, recruiters came through the area, and he joined the NPA.

Jun had had an ambition to finish school, and the offer of free school and training towards any chosen career was too good to pass up – there was no such opportunity in the rural area otherwise, and Jun was not in school at all. They offered "free school and whatever course you want. That propaganda, I was really convinced, because I really wanted to finish school." The lessons, though, were solely based on the NPA's specific communist ideology and would not be any use outside of the forest. Eventually he realised that he would not gain any qualification this way, and in particular, that the anti-government teachings would not help him to get a legitimate job.

The NPA promised him an education that would lead him to a career in the city. He would be able to provide for his siblings and make something of himself. Reality was far removed from the promises, though. Food was scarce, and during combat there was no chance to prepare what little food there was. "Sometimes breakfast would become dinner, dinner would become lunch. It wasn't regular; really, the situation was *dili mayo* [not good]." Arduous treks without regular meals were part of the way of life. "On our monthly walks, sometimes we wouldn't have enough sleep, not enough food, because we were on the run. If there was any food to be eaten, we couldn't cook it."

Jun described that as a soldier, the trees were like his parents, and his comrades became his siblings as they travelled and lived together. Jun reflected that he was in combat in the forest for "(so) many years that I had forgotten the responsibilities of being me. What my responsibilities were to myself and to my family. The one thing that I considered to be my parents... was the forest. It's what I recognised as my parents and what raised me."

"I really was not able to enjoy childhood life because it was so early that I was pushed into (combat). I carried a big responsibility as a guerrilla even

History and conflict in Rural Mindanao 51

then. I really didn't feel (like a child) because at thirteen years old I had already joined and was in the mountains. Thirteen years old until 33."

There were two things that Jun identified as characterising his long period of service in the NPA. The first was the discipline. As a soldier, the demands were not only to obey the group's orders but to discipline himself – he described the ongoing self-discipline as central to his experience. "Those experiences – not enough sleep, not enough food, long walks, even if you are asleep, you wake up, and you will walk just to defend, and to avoid (the government troops) – they gave me strength. Those experiences gave me resolve. It gave me strength and I learned to be careful and alert, so that I can also see what is going on around me. So those experiences really gave me fortitude and discipline."

The second characteristic of life in the rebel militia that Jun identified was the constant danger, being used to seeing death, losing comrades, and fearing for one's own life. "It is normal to experience risking life, risking death in the crossfire of an encounter between the military troops and the revolutionaries. Both sides have to defend something, that's just the standard operating procedure. Whether it would happen now or later, it's expected to happen, you expected eventually there would come a time when you would lose, and death would come." Jun had watched several of his friends die during encounters. He lamented that even though there was honour in dying for a cause, all of their dreams and hopes for the future would never be realised.

Jun described that most of the other former soldiers had a similar background. Rural, poor, and most had not only never reached high school, but had only been in school to grade one or two. He attributed this as a cause of vulnerability to propaganda as well as age. "In the documents of the former rebels, they really lack education. Nearly all the surrenderees, their profiles say, Grade One, Grade Two. We rarely see a high school level. If anyone did reach high school, they did not finish."

It was Jun's ambition for an education and a career that finally made him realise that staying in the rebel movement would not help him in his life. However, he had not been aware of the level of support he would receive, and he was grateful for the opportunities offered. "When I surrendered, we did not expect that this (organisation) existed."

Jun came across as thoughtful and intelligent, and he had proven his abilities by completing high school. Not only had he quickly graduated, but he also won a nation-wide writing competition. The title quote came from some of Jun's reflections on being a rebel soldier. I found his poetic prose deeply moving, and he conveyed a deep sense of meaning within his experiences and perspective.

Jun reflected on his life as he moved forward. "For me it's *sayon* [easy]. First, before we make decisions or act, we should first consider what the benefits will be. We are not perfect, we have wronged people. But what is important is that the mistakes can really teach us lessons. For me, what happened to me, gave me a big challenge. How will I support myself, and

52 *History and conflict in Rural Mindanao*

fulfil my dreams. The dream I had to continue my education never faded, never faded even up until the time I surrendered. It was always on my mind that while there is life, there is also hope. Poverty is not a hindrance to my dream. It's not a hindrance that I am an orphan. My having been a rebel is not a hindrance. All of these things, poverty, being an orphan, being an older (student), these became my bridge to become stronger than I am. So, for others, I can only suggest that we should not make poverty, seniority, or other things a basis, because if you could see past them, there are many possibilities to reach your dreams."

Adrian thanked Jun and shook his hand as we got up to go. Adrian later confided how much Jun's words had touched his heart; I was also rather in awe at the depth of Jun's reflection and the strength of character in his narrative. I reached out to shake Jun's hand as well, looking him in the eyes. "*Daghang salamat, Kuya*[xiii]" [Thank you very much, (older) brother], and he finally returned my gaze, as well as my smile, which warmed my heart although I left feeling somewhat shaken.

2.8 Trauma, force, and agency in global comparison

Although "child soldier" is presented by the UN and other international humanitarian organisations as a universal category, and a form of human trafficking, there are significant differences in the experiences of underage soldiers worldwide.[5,60–63] Underage soldiers, in a local context, have often been found to have more similarities to other local rebel soldiers or local young non-combatants than they would with international underage soldiers; in particular, the experiences and treatment of underage soldiers in Africa and even other parts of Asia have been vastly different from those in the Philippines.[5,64] The primary use of ideological propaganda rather than force for recruitment, for example, as well as the rehabilitation and livelihood support now offered to all surrendering soldiers make the Philippines a unique context and the continued conflict particularly revealing.[25,48,65]

The NPA's recruitment is a combination of ideology, a chance to fight against the government that has oppressed the rural people, and a chance for an alternative and opportunity to succeed and be educated outside of the limitations of rural villages. Both draw on the poverty of rural areas – a chance to escape and overcome it. This is significantly different from places that force children and youths into service. The NPA continues to operate under strong ideological principles such as equality and respect, where in other locations, rape and abuse have been used to force compliance. The NPA also provides basic services for remote areas, in contrast to other places where dissident non-state military groups rob, harass, or abuse local populations. While some concerns over child soldiers are universal, such as questions over the ability to agree to participate and exposing young people to harm, the experiences of underage soldiers in the NPA cannot be so easily defined as forced service or abuse.

Researchers have consistently found that trauma is a common outcome of military service, and particularly so for minors, but there are many variations which have included positive experiences and outcomes.[25,67] Most accounts of underage soldiers have come from Africa, where children have at times been kidnapped, raped, forced to watch or commit violence, and forced into labour, "marriage," or armed service among the rebel forces.[5,61,68] Accounts from the Philippines have been used to illustrate the incidence of underage soldiers, but most experiences do not align to the severe cases elsewhere. In combat, the most severe war atrocities, such as murder of civilians or rape, are rare.[xiv25,36,48] Being a soldier, even when underage, cannot be defined as an exclusively traumatic experience.

Former Filipino underage soldiers, in fact, have reported that although they left the movement because of the violence, they otherwise found the experience empowering and gained valuable life skills.[48(p. 13)] Jun and Marcus both identified positive skills, attributes, and sense of self because of their experiences. Young women in the Philippines reported that they received greater respect and equality within the rebel military than in wider society, and some reported joining to escape being forced by their family to marry or work as a domestic helper.[xv48(pp. 7,14),49(p. 69),69(p. 71)] Marcus and Jun both sought opportunities and social support that were otherwise not available to them. Researchers working with former underage soldiers in the Philippines have found that the young people often exhibited a great deal of agency, strategy, and ideological commitment, as opposed to the forced service prevalent in other locations.[48,65]

In the case of the Philippines' NPA, it can in fact be leaving the so-called trafficking situation of underage soldiers that is a greater source of trauma. The sudden severing of the close relationships which developed through difficult times can itself be a source of trauma.[70(p. 140)] For Marcus, both his relationships with his family and with his comrades have significantly shaped his life path; Jun's transition out of the NPA meant severing virtually every relationship in his life. The significant work of forging new plans, relationships, identity, and worldview – particularly for soldiers who have grown to adults through conflict – suggests holistic support is needed beyond a focus on trauma, victimhood, and age.[3(p. 3)]

The NPA has been reported to operate from strong principles which include respect for women and mutual consent, and duty to the group from an egalitarian basis.[48] They have also been known to offer practical support to rural villages particularly in times of difficulty, besides working to spread their particular communist ideology.[30,48(p. 9),69(p. 51)] At the same time, members were exposed to violence and the risk of violence as well as expected to commit violence. As such, there is the high possibility of soldiers experiencing a "moral injury" which is trauma sustained through acting against their own beliefs and values.[71] For Marcus and Jun, both acknowledged wrong that they had done as well as the positive aspects of NPA life, identifying an inner tension and conflict over their own role and the complicated

54 *History and conflict in Rural Mindanao*

embodiment of constraint, control, and agency in micro- and macro-level participation in armed conflict. However, the possibility of "moral injury" further suggests the need to consider even forced and/or coerced soldiers alongside other soldiers, rather than grouping them according to a binary definition of force/choice or victim/perpetrator.

Reintegration includes working through the trauma of violence, and particularly for long-serving soldiers such as Jun, creating new plans for the future. Social workers in this area stressed the importance of effective livelihood support including training and grants as part of the transition out of militia and into a new life, as other researchers have noted.[3(p. 8)] They expressed feeling discouraged over the cases they had seen where the livelihood grants had been given to surrendered soldiers without other support. At times, the young people had subsequently returned to their rural homes where the money was spent supporting their families, and when it was gone there were still no opportunities, so they had re-joined the rebel forces. Comparison between the trauma of conflict's violence and the trauma of poverty's violence is central to questions of how young people make choices within their environment.

2.9 Coercion and agency

One important outcome of qualitative research has been examining more closely the issues of coercion, consent, and control, which are central to the UN's definition of human trafficking. This and other universal models of human trafficking have been frequently based on Western assumptions about the freedom of individual choice.[72(p. 188)] Although the UN definition acknowledges both coercion and abuses of power, its role as a primarily legal device has shaped its applications towards concrete legal definitions which hinge on victim-perpetrator distinctions.[51,73,74(p. 51)] Emphasising this distinction has led to false dichotomies between freedom or force, and victimisation or agency, which reduce complex situations to questions of individual choice.[75(p. 620),76(p. 369)] Coercion, consent, and control can each have continuums within a relationship, but can also be shaped by personal, social, and structural factors.[73]

As a response to the legal and moral emphases on this "free versus forced" dichotomy, the idea of agency has emerged as one of the central theoretical concepts in the human trafficking literature. Research, which has focused on the actual people who have experienced trafficking, including their accounts and active roles in choosing courses of strategic action in response to experiences of trafficking, has provided a much-needed critique of the "victim or perpetrator" and "innocent or guilty" dichotomies which have shaped the human trafficking discourse.[77,78] However, recognising that victims can have a degree of agency and choice does not negate the necessity of exploring the social contexts which shape their choices, the constraints which frame them, and people's diverse experiences.

History and conflict in Rural Mindanao   55

Here, Marcus' and Jun's stories demonstrate both coercion and agency. Marcus' brother enlisted him without his consent, but Marcus wanted to be near his brother and remained rather than trying to leave. He embraced the soldier identity, but maintained a critical view of the practices and experiences in his first period in the rebel army. When he later considered leaving, however, his comrades pushed him to stay and distorted the truth to prevent him from going. His young age was undoubtedly a factor; he had to respect and obey his older brother, and he did not have the wider knowledge that might have allowed him to question the reports his comrades gave him. Jun also chose from a limited number of options, and although the recruiters lied to him, the promise of potential education was compared to remaining in the village where he knew with certainty that he would not get an education and was already not in school. Keairns[48] reported similar stories from other Filipino former underage soldiers; although they, like Marcus and Jun, eventually left the rebel group, the coercive pressure including stories about potential violence were significant factors in remaining longer than they would have liked.

The young men's embracing of the communist ideology and voluntary participation suggests agency in adapting their personal identities in becoming soldiers. Researchers in the Middle East found that when former underage soldiers' experiences of violence occurred in the context of a genuine belief in the rightness of their liberation struggle, there were fewer ongoing negative impacts from trauma.[70(p. 139)] For Marcus and Jun, selectively adapting their mindsets was a way to endure and make sense of the experiences. However, both men maintained a critical stance on some of their experiences, and Jun continually retained his goal of education beyond the NPA. Agency is central to developing internal resources and explanations, which reveal the process by which self-identity and self-efficacy can be expressed.

It is significant that Jun articulated, not an outright rejection of the teachings and worldview he was taught by the rebels, but a process of making sense, reintegrating, and reinterpreting the world around him. This implies agency not only in reintegrating to civilian life but in the adopting of communist ideology; he took ownership of the beliefs he came to hold and gave weight to his own experiences and choices from the time he was young. At the same time, Jun identified his age and lack of education as contributing to his vulnerability to propaganda; Marcus, too, mentioned his youth as significant in the effects of the violence he experienced – "I was only fifteen." However, Marcus related his regrets specifically to the violence and hardship he experienced; he did not cast himself as a victim, despite the coercion he had experienced.

Leaving the NPA demanded the work of developing new mindsets after years of indoctrination. Jun particularly demonstrated significant agency and autonomy in retaining many of the values that inspired him to fight as a rebel soldier, specifically, believing that change was needed for rural people living in poverty, while undergoing a dramatic shift in adapting to civilian

56 *History and conflict in Rural Mindanao*

life. The ideas of endurance, sacrifice, and suffering as creating strength for the future were among those that the men described as central to the transition they were undergoing. Both Jun and Marcus had to work through the new knowledge that much of what they had been told about life outside the movement was untrue. Marcus too gained a new perspective on his time in the forest, and noted how much freedom he experienced in a home environment that was not regimented like military camp.

Both men acknowledged having made mistakes, hurt, and wronged people, and Marcus directly articulated his hope for forgiveness. They experienced a contradiction between believing in the movement and the actual violence and killing. Jun alluded to the impersonal nature of violence between the sides – "standard operating procedure" – and also recognised that in ordinary life, it was not normal to be surrounded by danger and death. Research with female underage rebel soldiers in the Philippines has shown that violence was one of the main reasons many had left the movements.[48,49] Marcus, as a medic, viewed physical suffering up close but also had a responsibility for the consequences of violence his comrades endured – his young age, as well as limited medical resources, contributed to this being a significant emotional weight. Another underage soldier had been cited reflecting on the violence, "I think my comrades felt bad when they killed a soldier in an encounter. No matter how you looked at it, they were all Filipinos" ("Brian," sixteen year old former NPA soldier).[25(p. 132)] Violence against others, for this soldier as well as for Marcus and Jun, was also experienced as some level of violence against themselves.

2.10 Soldiers, rural poverty and structural violence

Historically, even beyond the Marcos years, military troops have given rural Filipinos legitimate reasons to question their legitimacy as protector.[79] The contemporary focus on disarmament and victim-status of underage soldiers stands in stark contrast to the treatment of CPP-NPA participants historically. From 1976 until 1995, there were 415[xvi] documented cases of torture by the military and paramilitary groups when interrogating suspected CPP-NPA members or sympathisers.[36] Of these, 326 (79%) were young people between the ages of fifteen to eighteen; almost all were rural agricultural workers, poor and likely uneducated.[25(p. 129),36] For this period, "the NPA has a better human rights record than the AFP."[80(p. 108)] Even since 2001, the military is assumed to be behind several activist assassinations.[81(p. 208)] This history of violence is reinforced through the government's contemporary neglect of rural areas and unequal development.

It is significant that the false propaganda that was used to control recruits was often based on conditions that may have been true at one time. The Marcos era Martial Law years saw multiple, widespread human rights abuses including extrajudicial killings, imprisonment, and torture, the kind of treatment that NPA members expected to receive if they did encounter government troops. At that time, properties and businesses were seized arbitrarily and dispersed among political cronies. There is a clear link between these conditions and the rise of opposition based on alternate political and financial configurations. From the perspective of rural Mindanao, little has changed in terms of the distribution of infrastructure, opportunity, and poverty levels. Indeed, economists have observed that even in periods of economic growth, wealth remained concentrated in a small segment of the population without proportionate increases in jobs; in fact, the number of domestic jobs in relation to the population has often decreased year to year.[82(p. 389)] In rural areas, particularly those furthest from major centres, economic growth has been virtually non-existent for decades.

The NPA frequently provided basic social services, replacing the government in this role for remote rural villages. The government left a void to be filled. The NPA also dealt with some of the conflict and damage from other warring groups; this validated their role, perpetuated their existence, and built support and sympathy from the public. Studies have shown that non-state militant groups, although often presented as a national security threat, actually pose the biggest threat to local civilian populations.[18,83] That the NPA took an immediate, active role in ameliorating the effects of conflict reinforced belief in the idea that the government oppressed, exploited, and neglected the rural farmers. However, their proximity as well as active recruitment continued to expose rural populations to violence. The positive role that the NPA often took in society also demonstrates how different rebel groups can operate in quite different ways, and thus the rationales for underage soldiers enlisting or being sent to the front can also vary quite dramatically.

The NPA's militant communist worldview offered Marcus and Jun a way to make sense of the conditions that they experienced. It was a framework that allowed acknowledging the violence and injustice of poverty, that did not assign blame to the individual poor rural agriculturalists, but that offered a language to describe the problem and limitations, and even to state concretely that they existed. They had a sense that farmers who toiled away for little reward were oppressed somehow. When the choices available were to stay in this poverty and hard labour, or to join a rebel group fighting against this oppression, the decision to enlist made sense in this context.

> The absence of reasonable structural conditions...has resulted in widespread oppression and neglect that continues to fuel the armed struggle of CPP-NPA. The other factors...are all derived from the inability of the GRP[xvii] to extend effective governance around the country.[22]

Through this language that brought the violence of poverty and marginalisation into concrete expression, and the available opportunity to contest these conditions and to join in violent rebellion, structural violence was transformed into physical violence.

58   History and conflict in Rural Mindanao

Indeed, even agrarian reform projects which have redistributed commercial land to individual agriculturalists have had limited success in disrupting control by the "landed elites" who have historically wielded significant social, political, and economic power.[15(p. 233),22,84] Researchers have frequently commented on the dependency-based, feudal style relationships in the Philippines, particularly in agricultural areas.[15,81(p. 208),84(p. 44),85(p. 558)] Adam[15(pp. 233–235)] found in an area of Mindanao that resistance from commercial elites – intertwined with political authority – through practices from direct violence to debt bondage meant that few beneficiaries of the program were able to escape dependency relationships and either keep or benefit from the land packages. The farmers who did access land were barely able to survive from the land's produce, and spiralled into debt which eventually left them landless agricultural labourers once more.[15]

The risks of violence and victimisation are also "amplified...due to poverty and limited access to health care services."[86] Unequal access to essential services has been identified as a form of structural violence.[87] In the Philippines, the effects of rural poverty are compounded through the lack of social services (for example, see Figure 2.1). The combination of suspicious government military forces known to harass rural civilians including apolitical church organisations, and the neglect in providing basic services or economic development, mean that rural Filipinos have frequently experienced the normal operations of the state as violent, unjust, and oppressive.[81,88(p. 5)]

The forms of structural violence that disproportionately affect the rural areas of the Philippines include poverty and lack of services (Figure 2.1), inequality, punitive and neglectful treatment from the government, lack of land access, and an unchallenged economic structure based on feudal-style dependent relationships.[22] Each of these situations demonstrates inequality between urban and rural areas, and structural, pervasive challenges to survival for rural people. Recruiting underage soldiers draws on the lack of services, particularly lack of education, as well as poverty in offering young people a chance to pursue a better life (as is claimed) as well as to oppose the government's role in the inequality and difficult conditions inherent to rural life. Recruiting can be coercive in deceiving young people into service, and often involves false propaganda as well as ideology, and is considered human trafficking because of this coercion and minor status. Coercion in this way is an indirect violence in drawing young people into difficult conditions including direct violence and mortal risk. However, despite deceit and coercion, young people also play an active role that in navigating the options available to them and making choices within and from local realities and systems of meaning. The complex choices whereby young people enlist in rebel forces are points where structural violence erupts into the potential for physical violence.

In accounts from underage soldiers in the Philippines, researchers have found that combinations of structural and personal factors influenced their participation in conflict. Reasons for enlisting have often included leaving difficult circumstances including poverty and family

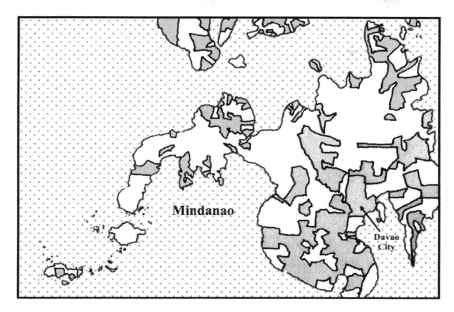

Figure 2.1 Rural health services in Mindanao's rural municipalities.[66] Areas in grey have some form of birthing facilities and emergency transport; unshaded areas do not. Map is indicative only.

separation.[25,36,48,49(pp. 60–62)] Marcus' and Jun's stories confirmed these aspects of other former underage soldiers' reports. Jun joined the rebel forces for personal rather than ideological reasons which were closely related to the lack of opportunities and severe poverty that he experienced in his rural home. Marcus went from underage labour into underage soldiering; although the work he did was paid and he was free to leave, agricultural labour is physically demanding and among the lowest paid sector of work in the Philippines. When his mother died, the family went from just surviving to absolute desperation. Jun similarly lost his parents and along with his siblings was suddenly in dire poverty. The context of these men's lives, like others in rural Mindanao, was poverty, lack of opportunity, and exploitative and underpaid work options. These structural conditions were exacerbated by Marcus and Jun's status as minors amid disrupted family support networks.

For rural areas of Mindanao and the Philippines, the expansion of government and commercial land use to traditionally held land continues a colonial legacy of seizure and exclusion.[89(p. 124)] The government has frequently considered rural populations a problem to be civilised and brought into commercial systems and under neo-liberal systems of personhood. Despite the lack of services, extending governance and civilisation to rural areas has primarily been through land acquisition and displacement of

60 *History and conflict in Rural Mindanao*

rural persons. "Civilisation" and political programs have not included these populations, but further excluded them and demanded assimilation. Rural people attempting to escape the margins have faced multiple risks including exploitation and becoming part of the working poor, rather than the rural poor. Like in colonial times, people are pushed further from the centre unless they accept not only governance but participation in the economic system. The structural violence against rural populations suggests a "critical geography of vulnerability that maps the spatial linkages between the hurt and the hurter—between the vulnerable and the powerful."[90(p. 10)] The NPA and other rebel groups (primarily) exist in this space between, demonstrating how resistance against the state's actions is criminalised to the point of violence.[90]

2.11 Conclusions

The Philippines has high rates of poverty in general, but the rural areas are significantly poorer than urban as well as often lacking even basic infrastructure. Both the poverty and the sense of injustice have contributed to the prevalence of underage soldiers who seek an alternative to the poverty in village life. Structural violence is compounding against a person's life directly, but violence is also compounding in how it incites violence in response. In this case, injustice and very real inequality have pushed people out of their villages as well as inspiring a response to take up arms in demanding change. Pushing back against this violence through rebel participation created more violence; it became a point where structural violence was transformed into physical, military violence.

The violence of armed conflict is implicated in human trafficking beyond the use of underage soldiers. The ARMM and other conflict zones are also notorious for "employment" recruiters who would offer young people a chance to find work in cities such as Iligan or Manila. This presented an opportunity to remit earnings back to their rural families, who would often be under added strain due to displacement or conflict. Local community workers told me how they had seen this happen where young people would never be heard from again. NGO workers visiting from Western Mindanao, as well as those around where I was in Eastern Mindanao, described what they had seen and heard, but lamented that there was no way to know how many people had been trafficked from rural areas, without infrastructure, telephones, legal systems, or often even birth certificates. Conflict as well as rural poverty are thus implicated in sex and labour trafficking.

As many of my participants originated in rural areas, the issues facing rural Filipino communities seemed an appropriate place to begin considering the context for human trafficking. Trafficking most often occurs at a point of movement, and for underage (and other) soldiers, this movement could be described as rural-to-rural. Other forms of trafficking occur most frequently alongside movement that is rural-to-urban and urban-to-international. As such, the rural conditions that shape multiple pathways for

History and conflict in Rural Mindanao 61

movement are implicated for understanding the background of many forms of exploitation. Rural areas are thought to have the fewest and worst opportunities for people hoping to improve their and their families' lives, whereas urban areas are considered more promising, and overseas destinations most ideal. Movement of people for economic opportunity, thus, flows from rural areas in an outward direction.

Both conflict and poverty push people away from their homes. Enlisting as a rebel soldier entails rural to rural movement, while labour trafficking is often associated with rural to urban movement in looking for better work opportunities. In the chapter that follows, I present the stories from people who have experienced trafficking or exploitation for labour, including sexual labour, domestically in Mindanao. Many of these participants moved from rural areas with similar circumstances as Jun and Marcus. Several stories involve those trafficked or exploited as young people, continuing the discussions of age, agency, consent, and coercion in relation to human trafficking.

Notes

i He was not one of the former soldiers whose narratives will be presented; I did not have the option to request an interview as the social workers and police officers I was with did not speak his local dialect, and he did not sufficiently speak Cebuano, Tagalog, or English.

ii From what I heard from various organisations, this report turned out to be correct, and was dealt with by higher authorities. Corruption is a known and ongoing issue in the Philippine government.

iii Of the Filipinos considered "poor," approximately 2/3 are rural despite about ½ the population being rural/urban.[19,20(p. 295)] See Chapter 3 for further discussion of poverty in the Philippines.

iv NPA (New People's Army) is the militant wing of the CPP (Communist Party of the Philippines). The Moro Independence Liberation Front (MILF) is a militant, primarily Muslim, separatist group in Eastern Mindanao which eventually achieved recognition as a limited autonomous region.

v While in the Philippines, I met a woman who had been imprisoned and tortured under the Marcos regime, and a former leader within the NPA at the time, both of whom are now NGO workers and activists.

vi While the government (prior to Duterte) has recognised groups such as the MNLF, MILF, and CPP-NPA as political rebels, the Abu-Sayyaf has been considered a criminal terrorist organisation based on its violent attacks on civilians.[36] The Maute and Abu-Kalifar also have recently emerged as small, militant Islamic terrorist groups.

vii This included both captured (96) and voluntarily surrendered (169) soldiers, but did not include others who may have left the movement without military processing or were killed in battle.[37(p.4)]

viii "*Sa kadtong mga tao nga akong nautang ang kinabuhi nila*": literally, those people whose lives are my debt.

ix He may indeed have been younger, his guardian surmised, but surrenderees were apparently often taught to say they were eighteen to protect their comrades.

x This is a common practice, particularly for rural families, to send a child usually to work as a domestic helper in exchange for room, board, and schooling costs; rural communities may not have schools past elementary. However, this can also

62 History and conflict in Rural Mindanao

be a site of abuse or exploitation. Refer to Susan's story, for an example of this practice.

xi "*Pati mag-istorya mag-kanang mura na lang ug pato*," literally, "we were only talking like ducks."

xii There is no direct word for "bad" in Cebuano: *dili mayo* [not good] could also be translated as bad, but I have retained the literal translation here. However, as elsewhere, this phrase can be read as an understatement of the sentiment implied.

xiii *Kuya* is an honorific title meaning older brother. Its use is not restricted to natal siblings, and denotes respect.

xiv The recent exception, where civilians were targeted in 2014, was by the recently formed Abu-Sayyaf group, an extremist Islamic breakaway group from the other Muslim separatists. NPA violence has included political targets, particularly in its early days, and there was an attack on civilians in 1989, but most contemporary violence has been directed towards the military.[37]

xv The NPA include female and male soldiers, but for this project, I was only able to meet male former underage soldiers.

xvi 85% were male; 15% were female. I was privileged to meet a woman who was a former torture victim under the government's forces during the Marcos era. She was working as an activist at an NGO supporting minors in the justice system. Note that these figures include documented cases alone.

xvii Government of the Republic of the Philippines.

References

1 Martin, S., & Callaway, A. (2011). Internal displacement and internal trafficking: Developing a new framework for protection. In K. Koser & S. Martin (Eds.), *The migration-displacement nexus: Patterns, processes, and policies* (pp. 216–238). Berghahn Books.

2 Kerig, P., & Wainryb, C. (2014). *Trauma and resilience among child soldiers around the world*. Routledge.

3 Özerdem, A., & Podder, S. (Eds.). (2011). *Child soldiers: From recruitment to reintegration*. Palgrave Macmillan.

4 Pedersen, J., & Sommerfelt, T. (2007). Studying children in armed conflict: Data production, social indicators and analysis. *Social Indicators Research, 84*(3), 251–269. https://doi.org/10.1007/s11205-007-9117-3

5 Keairns, Y. (2003). *The voices of girl child soldiers: Summary*. Quaker United Nations Office. https://quno.org/resource/2003/1/voices-girl-child-soldiers

6 David, E., & Okazaki, S. (2006). Colonial mentality: A review and recommendation for Filipino American psychology. *Cultural Diversity and Ethnic Minority Psychology, 12*(1), 1–16. https://doi.org/10.1037/1099-9809.12.1.1

7 Hedman, E., & Sidel, J. (2000). *Philippine politics and society in the twentieth century: Colonial legacies, post-colonial trajectories*. Routledge.

8 Rutten, R. (2007). Losing face in Philippine labor confrontations: How shame may inhibit worker activism. In L. Joseph, M. Mahler, & J. Auyero (Eds.), *New perspectives in political ethnography* (pp. 37–59). Springer.

9 Bourdieu, P. (1997). *Language and symbolic power* (J. Thompson, Ed.; G. Raymond & M. Adamson, Trans.; Reprint). Polity Press.

10 Ha, M. (2003). From "nos ancetres, les Gaulois" to "leur culture ancestrale": Symbolic violence and the politics of colonial schooling in Indochina. *French Colonial History, 3*(1), 101–117. https://doi.org/10.1353/fch.2003.0006

History and conflict in Rural Mindanao 63

11 Khanal, P. (2017). Falling prey to the dominant culture? Demystifying symbolic violence against ethnic minority students in Nepal. *Pedagogy, Culture & Society, 25*(3), 457–467. https://doi.org/10.1080/14681366.2017.1280841

12 Dwyer, P. (2017). Violence and its histories: Meanings, methods, problems. *History and Theory, 56*(4), 7–22. https://doi.org/10.1111/hith.12035

13 Arcilla, J. (1998). *An introduction to Philippine history* (4th ed.). Ateneo de Manila University Press.

14 Chong, A. (2020). José Rizal attacks imperialism softly: Comprehending the depths of psychological conversion and the temptations of violent solutions. In F. A. Cruz & N. M. Adiong (Eds.), *International studies in the Philippines: Mapping new frontiers in theory and practice* (pp. 34–49). Routledge.

15 Adam, J. (2013). Land reform, dispossession and new elites: A case study on coconut plantations in Davao Oriental, Philippines. *Asia Pacific Viewpoint, 54*(2), 232–245. https://doi.org/10.1111/apv.12011

16 Cruz-Lucero, R. (2006). Judas and his phallus: The carnivalesque narratives of holy week in Catholic Philippines. *History and Anthropology, 17*(1), 39–56. https://doi.org/10.1080/02757200500395568

17 Paredes, O. (2017). Projecting order in the pericolonial Philippines: An anthropology of Catholicism beyond Catholics. *The Australian Journal of Anthropology, 28*(2), 225–241. https://doi.org/10.1111/taja.12234

18 Paredes, O. (2015). Indigenous vs. native: Negotiating the place of Lumads in the Bangsamoro homeland. *Asian Ethnicity, 16*(2), 166–185. https://doi.org/10.1080/1 4631369.2015.1003690

19 PSA. (2019). *Urban population in the Philippines.* Philippine Statistics Authority. https://psa.gov.ph/content/urban-population-philippines-results-2015-census-population

20 Timberman, D. G. (2018). Persistent poverty and elite-dominated policymaking. In M. R. Thompson, E. C. Batalla, & P. N. Abinales (Eds.), *Routledge handbook of the contemporary Philippines* (pp. 293–306). Routledge Taylor & Francis Group.

21 Delgado, M., & Canters, F. (2011). Measuring the accessibility of different household income groups to basic community services in upland Misamis Oriental, Northern Mindanao, Philippines. *Singapore Journal of Tropical Geography, 32*(2), 168–184. https://doi.org/10.1111/j.1467-9493.2011.00427.x

22 Domingo, F. (2013). Explaining the sustainability of the communist party of the Philippines-New People's Army. *Small Wars Journal, 2013.* http://smallwarsjournal.com/jrnl/art/explaining-the-sustainability-of-the-communist-party-of-the-philippines-new-people%E2%80%99s-army

23 Fukuta, E., Sudo, N., & Kato, N. (2008). Barriers to compliance with the daily food guide for children among first-grade pupils in a rural area in the Philippine island of Mindanao. *European Journal of Clinical Nutrition, 62*(4), 502–510. https://doi.org/10.1038/sj.ejcn.1602734

24 Pe Symaco, L. (2013). Geographies of social exclusion: Education access in the Philippines. *Comparative Education, 49*(3), 361–373. https://doi.org/10.1080/0305 0068.2013.803784

25 Protacio de Castro, E. (2001). Children in armed conflict situations: Focus on child soldiers in the Philippines. *Kasarinlan, 16*(2), 123–142.

26 Daly, M. R., Kelly, G., & Policy Press. (2015). *Families and poverty: Everyday life on a low income.* Policy Press. University of Bristol.

64 History and conflict in Rural Mindanao

27 MacPherson, S., & Silburn, R. (2002). The meaning and measurement of poverty. In P. J. Dixon, J. Dixon, & D. Macarov (Eds.), *Poverty: A persistent global reality* (0 ed., pp. 1–3). Routledge. https://doi.org/10.4324/978020 3029183

28 Bulloch, H. (2013). Concerning constructions of self and other: Auto-racism and imagining *Amerika* in the Christian Philippines. *Anthropological Forum, 23*(3), 221–241. https://doi.org/10.1080/00664677.2013.804400

29 Gonzaga, E. (2009). *Globalization and becoming-nation: Subjectivity, nationhood, and narrative in the period of global capitalism.* University of the Philippines Press.

30 Stanford University. (2015). *Communist party of the Philippines—new people's army* (Mapping Militant Organizations). Stanford University. http://web.stanford.edu/group/mappingmilitants/cgi-bin/groups/view/149

31 Niu, G. (1999). Wives, widows, and workers: Corazon Aquino, Imelda Marcos, and the Filipina "other." *NWSA Journal, 11*(2), 88–102.

32 Abinales, P. (2008). Fragments of history, silhouettes of resurgence: Student radicalism in the early years of the Marcos dictatorship. *Southeast Asian Studies, 46*(2), 175–199.

33 Forbes, A. (2015). Courageous women in media: Marcos and censorship in the Philippines. *Pacific Journalism Review, 21*(1), 195–210. https://doi.org/10.24135/pjr.v21i1.157

34 Hall, R. A. (2018). Civil-military relations: Norming and departures. In M. R. Thompson, E. C. Batalla, & P. N. Abinales (Eds.), *Routledge handbook of the contemporary Philippines* (pp. 144–158). Routledge Taylor & Francis Group.

35 Quitoriano, E., & Libre, E. (2001). Reaching for the gun: The human cost of small arms in Central Mindanao, Philippines. *Kasarinlan, 16*(2), 13–40.

36 Makinano, M. (2001). *Child soldiers in the Philippines.* International Labor Affairs Service. www.childprotection.org.ph

37 Cruz, F. (2010, February 13). The eventual demise of the communist insurgency in the Philippines (report by Brig. Gen. Francisco N. Cruz Jr., Armed Forces of the Philippines). *The Philippine Star.* http://www.philstar.com/letters-editor/548852/eventual-demise-communist-insurgency-philippines

38 Quimpo, N. (2009). The Philippines: Predatory regime, growing authoritarian features. *The Pacific Review, 22*(3), 335–353. https://doi.org/10.1080/09512740903068388

39 Al Jazeera. (2017, May 24). Duterte declares martial law after Mindanao attack. *Al Jazeera.* http://www.aljazeera.com/news/2017/05/duterte-declares-martial-law-mindanao-attack-170523171932275.html

40 Rauhala, E. (2016, November 18). With hero's burial for Marcos, Duterte endorses Philippines' authoritarian past. *The Washington Post.* https://www.washingtonpost.com/world/with-heros-burial-for-marcos-duterte-endorses-philippines-authoritarian-past-/2016/11/18/1b211f20-ad49-11e6-8410-7613f8c1dae8_story.html?utm_term=.e00d4671e7c7

41 Heydarian, R. J. (2018). *The rise of Duterte: A populist revolt against elite democracy* (1st ed.). Springer Singapore : Imprint: Palgrave Pivot. https://doi.org/10.1007/978-981-10-5918-6

42 Adam, J. (2013). A comparative analysis on the micro-level genealogies of conflict in the Philippines' Mindanao Island and Indonesia's Ambon Island. *Oxford Development Studies, 41*(2), 155–172. https://doi.org/10.1080/13600818.2013.789841

History and conflict in Rural Mindanao 65

43 Vellema, S., Borras, S., & Lara, F. (2011). The agrarian roots of contemporary violent conflict in Mindanao, Southern Philippines. *Journal of Agrarian Change, 11*(3), 298–320. https://doi.org/10.1111/j.1471-0366.2011.00311.x

44 Paredes, O. (2018). Between rights protection and development aggression: Indigenous peoples. In M. R. Thompson, E. C. Batalla, & P. N. Abinales (Eds.), *Routledge handbook of the contemporary Philippines* (pp. 341–351). Routledge Taylor & Francis Group.

45 Lasley, T., & Thyne, C. (2015). Secession, legitimacy and the use of child soldiers. *Conflict Management and Peace Science, 32*(3), 289–308. https://doi.org/10.1177/0738894214526541

46 UNICEF. (2016). *Philippines humanitarian situation report* [End of year humanitarian situation report]. United Nations International Children's Emergency Fund. https://www.unicef.org/appeals/files/UNICEF_Philippines_End_of_Year_Humanitarian_Situation_Report_____December_2016.pdf

47 Al Jazeera. (2017, March 11). Hundreds of MILF child soldiers released in Philippines: Moro Islamic Liberation Front, the country's largest armed group, ends recruitment of children as part of peace plan. *Al Jazeera.* http://www.aljazeera.com/news/2017/03/hundreds-milf-child-soldiers-released-philippines-170311064133681.html

48 Keairns, Y. (2003). *The voices of girl child soldiers: Philippines.* Quaker United Nations Office. https://quno.org/resource/2003/1/voices-girl-child-soldiers

49 Ordoña de Ocampo, I. (2006). *The exploitation of children as soldiers in the Philippines: An analysis of issues and challenges in social work practice* [Unpublished MA Thesis, Massey University].

50 UNODC. (2016). *2016 global report on trafficking in persons.* http://www.unodc.org/documents/data-and-analysis/glotip/2016_Global_Report_on_Trafficking_in_Persons.pdf

51 Derluyn, I., Vandenhole, W., Parmentier, S., & Mels, C. (2015). Victims and/or perpetrators? Towards an interdisciplinary dialogue on child soldiers. *BioMed Central International Health and Human Rights, 15*(28). https://doi.org/10.1186/s12914-015-0068-5

52 Kononenko, I. (2016). Prohibiting the use of child soldiers: Contested norms in contemporary human rights discourse. *Nordic Journal of Human Rights, 34*(2), 89–103. https://doi.org/10.1080/18918131.2016.1200293

53 Sampaio, A., & McEvoy, M. (2016). Little weapons of war: Reasons for and consequences of treating child soldiers as victims. *Netherlands International Law Review, 63*(1), 51–73. https://doi.org/10.1007/s40802-016-0054-1

54 Esser, F., Baader, M., Betz, T., & Hungerland, B. (Eds.). (2016). *Reconceptualising agency and childhood: New perspectives in childhood studies.* Routledge.

55 UNICEF. (2017). *Child rights and security checklist.* United Nations International Children's Emergency Fund. https://www.unicef.org/csr/files/Child_rights_and_Security_Checklist_ENG.pdf

56 Swart, M., & Hassen, S. (2016). A comparison between the position of child marriage "victims" and child soldiers: Towards a nuanced approach. *African Human Rights Law Journal, 16*(2), 458–475. https://doi.org/10.17159/1996-2096/2016/v16n2a7

57 Breen, C. (2007). When is a child not a child? Child soldiers in international law. *Human Rights Review, 8*(2), 71–103. https://doi.org/10.1007/BF02881667

58 Rosen, D. (2007). Child soldiers, international humanitarian law, and the globalization of childhood. *American Anthropologist, 109*(2), 296–306. https://doi.org/10.1525/aa.2007.109.2.296

66 *History and conflict in Rural Mindanao*

59 Tiefenbrun, S. (2008). Child soldiers, slavery and the trafficking of children. *Fordham International Law Journal, 31*(2), 415–486.

60 Brett, R. (2002). *Girl soldiers: Challenging the assumptions.* Quaker United Nations Office. http://www.quno.org/sites/default/files/resources/Girl%20Soldiers_Challenging%20the%20assumptions.pdf

61 Brownell, G., & Praetorius, R. (2017). Experiences of former child soldiers in Africa: A qualitative interpretive meta-synthesis. *International Social Work, 60*(2), 452–469. https://doi.org/10.1177/0020872815617994

62 Lee, A. (2009). *Understanding and addressing the phenomenon of "child soldiers": The gap between the global humanitarian discourse and the local understandings of experiences of young people's military recruitment* (Series No. 52) [RSC Working Paper]. Refugee Studies Centre. http://www.rsc.ox.ac.uk/files/publications/working-paper-series/wp52-understanding-addressing-child-soldiers-2009.pdf

63 Stevens, A. (2014). The invisible soldiers: Understanding how the life experiences of girl child soldiers impacts upon their health and rehabilitation needs. *Archives of Disease in Childhood, 2014*(0), 1–5. https://doi.org/10.1136/archdischild-2013-305240

64 Spellings, C. (2008). Scratching the surface: A comparison of girl soldiers from three geographic regions of the world. *International Education, 38*(1), 21–39.

65 Özerdem, A., Podder, S., & Quitoriano, E. (2010). Identity, ideology and child soldiering: Community and youth participation in civil conflict–A study on the Moro Islamic Liberation Front in Mindanao, Philippines. *Civil Wars, 12*(3), 304–325. https://doi.org/10.1080/13698249.2010.509566

66 DOH. (2018). *Philippines health atlas maps.* Department of Health. http://www.maps.doh.gov.ph/

67 Song, S., Tol, W., & de Jong, J. (2014). Indero: Intergenerational trauma and resilience between Burundian former child soldiers and their children. *Family Process, 53*(2), 239–251. https://doi.org/10.1111/famp.12071

68 Haer, R. (2017). The study of child soldiering: Issues and consequences for DDR implementation. *Third World Quarterly, 38*(2), 450–466. https://doi.org/10.1080/01436597.2016.1166946

69 Emmons, K. (2002). *Adult wars, child soldiers: Voices of children involved in armed conflict in the East Asia and Pacific Region.* UNICEF East Asia and Pacific Regional Office.

70 Wessells, M. (2006). *Child soldiers: From violence to protection.* Harvard University Press.

71 Jamieson, N., Maple, M., Ratnarajah, D., & Usher, K. (2020). Military moral injury: A concept analysis. *International Journal of Mental Health Nursing, 29*(6), 1049–1066. https://doi.org/10.1111/inm.12792

72 Bernat, F., & Winkeller, H. (2010). Human sex trafficking: The global becomes local. *Women & Criminal Justice, 20*(1–2), 186–192. https://doi.org/10.1080/08974451003641545

73 Dewey, S. (2014). Understanding force and coercion: Perspectives from law enforcement, social service providers, and sex workers. In K. Hoang & R. Parreñas (Eds.), *Human trafficking reconsidered: Rethinking the problem, envisioning new solutions* (pp. 102–115). International Debate Education Association.

74 UNODC. (2006). *Trafficking in persons: Global patterns* [United Nations Office on Drugs and Crime]. Anti-Human Trafficking Unit Global Programme against

History and conflict in Rural Mindanao   67

Trafficking in Human Beings. http://www.unodc.org/pdf/traffickinginpersons_report_2006ver2.pdf

75 Burke, F. (2015). Innovations in the fight against human trafficking: Advocates' perspectives and proposals. *New York Law School Law Review, 3–4*, 615–622.

76 French, B., & Neville, H. (2016). What is nonconsensual sex? Young women identify sources of coerced sex. *Violence Against Women, 23*(3), 368–394. https://doi.org/10.1177/1077801216641517

77 Tigno, J. (2012). Agency by proxy: Women and the human trafficking discourse in the Philippines. In W. van Schendel, L. Lyons, & M. Ford (Eds.), *Labour migration and human trafficking in Southeast Asia: Critical perspectives* (pp. 23–40). Routledge.

78 Wijers, M. (2015). Purity, victimhood and agency: Fifteen years of the UN trafficking protocol. *Anti-Trafficking Review, 2015*(4), 56–79. https://doi.org/10.14197/atr.20121544

79 Jose, R. (2001). The Philippine armed forces: Protector or oppressor? A historical overview. *Kasarinlan, 16*(2), 73–90.

80 Hilsdon, A. (1995). *Madonnas and martyrs: Militarism and violence in the Philippines.* Allen & Unwin.

81 Holden, W. (2009). Post modern public administration in the land of promise: The basic ecclesial community movement of Mindanao. *Worldviews: Global Religions, Culture, and Ecology, 13*(2), 180–218.

82 Agbola, F., & Acupan, A. (2010). An empirical analysis of international labour migration in the Philippines. *Economic Systems, 34*(4), 386–396. https://doi.org/10.1016/j.ecosys.2010.03.002

83 Englehart, N. (2016). Non-state armed groups as a threat to global security: What threat, whose security? *Journal of Global Security Studies, 1*(2), 171–183. https://doi.org/10.1093/jogss/ogw003

84 Reid, B. (2005). Poverty alleviation and participatory development in the Philippines. *Journal of Contemporary Asia, 35*(1), 29–52. https://doi.org/10.1080/00472330580000031

85 Horner, L. (2013). Networking resources, owning productivity: A post-development alternative in Mindanao? *Globalisation, Societies and Education, 11*(4), 538–559.

86 Le, M., Holton, S., Romero, L., & Fisher, J. (2016). Polyvictimization among children and adolescents in low-and lower-middle-income countries: A systematic review and meta-analysis. *Trauma, Violence, & Abuse, 2016*, 1–20. https://doi.org/10.1177/1524838016659489

87 Farmer, P. (2004). An anthropology of structural violence. *Current Anthropology, 45*(3), 305–325. https://doi.org/10.1086/382250

88 Auyero, J., & Sobering, K. (2017). Violence, the state, and the poor: A view from the South. *Sociological Forum, 32*(S1), 1018–1031. https://doi.org/10.1111/socf.12362

89 Ragsag, A. (2020). *Ethnic boundary-making at the margins of conflict in the Philippines: Everyday identity politics in Mindanao.* Springer Singapore. https://doi.org/10.1007/978-981-15-2525-4

90 Brickell, K., Arrigoitia, M. F., & Vasudevan, A. (2017). Geographies of forced eviction: Dispossession, violence, resistance. In K. Brickell, M. Fernández Arrigoitia, & A. Vasudevan (Eds.), *Geographies of forced eviction* (pp. 1–23). Palgrave Macmillan UK. https://doi.org/10.1057/978-1-137-51127-0

3 Labour and exploitation

Employment and work in Mindanao

3.1 Introduction

> Financially, it's *lisod* [difficult]. *Lisod gyud* [very difficult]. *Lisod*. That's
> why you need to have extra income as well as your job. Aside from my job,
> I need to have another way to earn money, because it's just not enough
> – DonDon (a full-time skilled worker)[i]

One of the defining characteristics of city people-scapes in the Philippines
must be the constant commercial efforts, large and small, from beggars to
ice cream vendors to suited office workers, all going about their business.
In Davao, this labour is often informal, but highly visible such as street
food merchants and the dense public transport options (see Figure 3.1).
One memorable experience in getting around Davao was when a government social worker offered to take me to one of my interviews with a young
woman. Her home was in a poor area of town near the coast. Taxis and
jeepneys could not fit down lanes past the main road, so we took the front
trisikad [tricycle, also known as a pedicab or cycle rickshaw] from the queue
of bored looking men. Our driver was a tiny, wizened man who looked to be
at least.[70] He peddled us slowly along the narrow, paved road, the umbrella
wobbling as it spun unsteadily every time it banged into that of a peddled
or motorised *trisikad* coming in the opposite direction. As we turned off
onto the rough, potholed dirt road, our slow speed reduced considerably as
our driver strained his thin legs to deliver us to the next block. I considered
whether the right thing to do would be to get off and walk, which would
probably not be any slower and reduce the load on our driver. As a young
and able-bodied person, it felt wrong to be sitting ferried by a man of his age
even in return for the 20 pesos he would earn for our ten-minute journey.
I knew, though, that as an older man, most formal jobs would be closed to
him, and so he worked how he could in this informal labour. Without family
to rely on, many older people struggle to survive. Many of the side streets in
Davao would have a large queue of *trisikad* drivers, waiting for a passenger;
the fare was up to ₱10 (\$ 0.30[ii] NZD) per rider depending on the length of
the journey. I do not know what the average number of trips is per day, but
it must have been near impossible to make a living at this rate.

DOI: 10.4324/9781003261049-3

Labour and exploitation 69

Figure 3.1 Wandering anthropologist, street-side as a row of jeepneys pass by.

In discussions of human trafficking, there has been controversy over the degree to which labour trafficking and sex trafficking are related. Some have argued that as sexual labour[iii] is another type of work, making a distinction reinforces the "moral outcry" over sexual labour in general.[1] Others have pointed out the distinctions, such as the specific relationship between sexual trafficking and other forms of gender-based exploitation and violence.[2,3] However, the constraints and pressures in and around work also create conditions that are linked with human trafficking and other types of exploitation and abuse in work and beyond. As such, the focus on sexual labour and trafficking in the second part of this chapter extends the discussion of working conditions to highlight both the gendered aspect of my participants' experiences and the position of workers who are among the most marginalised, stigmatised, and excluded from the formal economy. The factors which make labour, particularly certain types of labour, a point of vulnerability, emerge from conditions beyond the individual workplace to both social and structural conditions. The discussion of choice, coercion, control, and agency emerges from the wider social context.

This chapter gives a deeper understanding of the work and employment conditions in the Philippines. The stories I present from workers and formerly trafficked persons, across a wide range of formal-informal economic positions and degrees of exploitation, reveal complex continuums and relationships between labour exploitation, human trafficking, and the work situation in general. I argue for a theoretical model which can account for the characteristics of both exploitative work and human trafficking, as I contend that both are shaped by social factors beyond the employment/trafficking relationships which must be considered in analysing and addressing

70 Labour and exploitation

these phenomena. The second part of the chapter focuses specifically on trafficking for sexual labour in the context of gendered employment and economic conditions. All my participants who had experienced trafficking for sexual labour were women; within the already challenging and constrained employment realities of the Philippines, women face further social and structural barriers which shape their experience of sexual labour and economic life. Where the previous chapter considered movement from rural-to-rural areas, labour exploitation – alongside labour opportunity – often occurs in the context of rural to urban areas. DonDon, Gabriel, Erica, and Crystal all moved from rural agricultural areas to the city to look for work.

3.2 Part 1: employment, economics, law, and structural violence

Like my *trisikad* driver, significant numbers of people in Davao and Mindanao are struggling to make a living through formal and informal labour. The economic aspects of Philippine society are among the most significant in shaping people's life chances, and the strategic choices that individuals and families deploy to improve their situations. Human trafficking has often been studied as a distinct phenomenon. However, this approach can easily obscure the incidence of related conditions such as exploitative labour, and position human trafficking as unrelated to other forms of exploitation. The aim of this chapter is to explore the processes which contribute to the experience of work as unequal and vulnerable. Gender, social status, education, and age are factors that are magnified in the experience of work and contribute to vulnerability as well as exclusion from opportunities. Access, or lack of access, to sufficient and legitimate employment opportunities is a significant factor in understanding human trafficking both from the side of the perpetrators and from those exploited.

The poverty line set by the Philippine government, at or below an income of ₱60 ($1.70 NZD) per day, is listed as the minimum for food and additional costs, but in real life is not actually sufficient for basic needs and would barely cover one day's meals.[4(p. 125),5] Even the shortest jeepney rides, for example, cost ₱8 or more; a return trip to and from work could constitute, at the very least, over 25% of that ₱60. In context, when I was in Davao, we could get a small rotisserie chicken from a street vendor for ₱100 ($2.80 NZD) for our family's dinner. The World Bank, however, has set the international poverty indicator at $1.90 US, or about ₱98, and Ofreneo suggested that by a measure of $2 US/₱103, as of 2009, half of the population was living in poverty.[iv] This assessment is supported by the vast squatter settlements in Manila that exceed official counts, the fact that 55% of the population was rural as of 2010, and the 2012 USAID analysis of 19.2% of Filipinos living in "extreme" poverty below US$1.25/₱65 per day.[4–6] Low wages and the prevalence of poverty have shaped the multiple economic strategies families use to survive.

Labour and exploitation 71

These economic strategies frequently include work that is highly insecure, variable, and low-paid. The number of *trisikad* drivers parked and waiting, for example, as there were behind the elderly driver I described, demonstrates the limitations of unemployment and underemployment statistics. Although in 2017, the official unemployment rate in the Philippines was 5.7–6.6%, Ofreneo[4(p. 122)] has argued that "more than half of the employed do not actually have adequate and decent work" when accounting for part-time workers, unpaid family workers, and those seeking additional work.[7] According to the Philippines Statistics Authority, as of 2016, 33.5% of the labour force was part time, 8.6% were "unpaid family workers," and an additional 8.1% of full-time workers were actively seeking additional work, making a total of 55.9% of the population unemployed or underemployed in 2016 based on Ofreneo's method of analysis.[8] Additionally, the percentage of "unpaid family workers" is likely underestimated, as, for example, "housewives" are excluded from the labour force statistics. One wage is not sufficient for a family to survive, but as opportunities are limited, many families rely on multiple low-paid income streams such as an informal *tindahan* [small shop] or one member running a *trisikad* [tricycle].

The informal economy also plays an integral role, especially in poorer areas, but as of 2016, estimates indicate that over half of employed workers were also involved in informal economic strategies.[v4(p. 123),7] Small shops and stands sell single packets of coffee and biscuits, and necessities such as charcoal, and cough medicine. Trays of small fresh fish appear in the afternoons once the catch has come in and made its way from the docks to the barangays. Hawkers walk around carrying bunches of second hand shoes, others weave between traffic stopped at lights and in rush hour to vend bottles of cold water, back scratchers, dash ornaments, and snacks, especially to the taxi drivers who might not have had a break. The informal economy is highly visible and entwined with formal day-to-day economic practices.

In navigating structural violence, Clark[10(p. 36)] pointed out that low-wage workers frequently depend on "fragile survival strategies," which often rely on social networks through reciprocal and relational exchanges. This practice extends the integrated and social sense of self in Philippines culture to what McKay[11(pp. 330, 343)] refers to as "relational, rather than individuated, models of economic personhood."[12] McKay,[11(p. 341)] for instance, described how a community in the Visayas[vi] considered people prosperous, not because of their own resources, but because of their relationships with productive family members. Accessing healthcare and other emergency expenses often demands drawing on family/social relationships.[13] Pastors, nuns, and other community leaders play a key role in the informal social economy in terms of redistribution of resources, particularly in times of hardship or distress. One of my language teachers, for example, was also in this role, and on one occasion while I was at a lesson was asking me and her other students for a few lessons advance payment so that she could help a family with the costs of a funeral. A large part of the Philippines economy is

72 *Labour and exploitation*

informal and semi-formal, and is critical to the survival of low-wage workers and those outside of formal employment.

A common wage for full-time, skilled workers such as DonDon and Mariel's husband in Davao was ₱500 ($14 NZD) per day, but participants described how this was not enough to sustain a family of five, particularly given the costs of schooling for children in high school or tertiary programs. Nurses in private hospitals, even with the extensive training and licencing required, have been reported making ₱3,000–8,000 ($84–223 NZD)/month, or ₱100–266 ($2.80–7.42 NZD)/day, while caring for 30 patients in their shift. Legally, all nurses are theoretically entitled to about ₱26,000/month (₱867/day), but this 2002 legislation has never been implemented nor enforced, and efforts have been continually blocked by politicians.[14] The largest employment sector, however, is unskilled labour, and this is true for both men and women.[15] Note the employment advertisement from Davao (see Figure 3.5) which advertised ₱250–500 ($7–14 NZD)/day, offering a pay scale that started well below minimum wage.

The Philippines has robust employment laws which address workers' rights to fair wages, termination and disability benefits, reasonable hours including breaks, overtime, non-discrimination including equal pay, and the right to join unions.[16,17] Further, the labour and anti-trafficking laws prohibit unreasonable child labour, bonded labour, threats and assault including both physical and verbal abuse, and also prohibit employers from firing employees to avoid paying benefits such as maternity leave.[16,17] Despite these laws that should protect workers' interests, however, workers often cannot access the laws' potential as there is limited and ineffective enforcement to the point that non-compliance is the norm.[16,18(p. 184)]

Documented legal cases suggest that companies' power is reinforced by legal structures. Hutchinson[18(p. 185)] traced the limited power of workers and workers' associations to the longstanding oligarchic control despite the ostensible democratic political system. Departing employees, for example, are not entitled to their retirement or severance payments until they have signed a contract releasing the company from further requirements. Financial pressure due to this delayed payment has resulted in employees agreeing to lesser amounts than what was due, and unable to legally challenge their employers once documents were signed.[19,20] As employment standards are not widely enforced while competition for jobs is intense, there is a high level of tolerance of abuse and control under these conditions. Controlling work situations have thus been normalised as part of wage employment, and situations of human trafficking represent the extreme forms of powerlessness among workers.

Women are more often socially positioned as "domestic" and expected to extend their supposedly inherent qualities and abilities to the workplace in jobs that replicate home duties and service, embodying and reiterating social inequalities; at the same time, as for men, the largest employment sector was in unskilled work, which is the lowest paid but also least regulated area, the

Labour and exploitation 73

Figure 3.2 "Wanted 10 girls 18–25 yrs old apply inside."

site of many dubious employment practices (see Figure 3.2 for a "suspicious" job ad).[15,21(p. 277)] A common requirement for women workers is that they have a "pleasing personality" and are "willing to be trained."[22] (see Figures 3.3 and 3.4). Although statistics list women and men as having roughly comparable employment rates, this does not include the fact that only 50.1% of women are considered part of the labour force, but does include the 57% of unpaid family workers who are women.[15] This means that women who are retired or "housewives" are not counted as unemployed, but women working in family businesses or agriculture are counted as employed, despite the fact that neither has any personal income, which suggests that women's rates of employment are significantly overestimated.

The Philippines' employment conditions have become increasingly precarious.[23(p. 26),24(p. 49),25(p. 214)] Irregular and unreliable work hours, underpayment, and underemployment are a few of the trends that have been reported.[9,18(p. 188),26,27(p. 344)] Numerous people told me about how employers would often dismiss and replace their entire staff of service workers every few months; one participant told me about a relative who struggled to survive with jobs lasting for three months only. Workers are often hired on temporary contracts short enough to avoid providing full-time positions and accompanying legal benefits, or hired on contract through an external agency with the same results.[4(p. 126),9(p. 2),18(p. 188),23(p. 26)] Another tactic

74 *Labour and exploitation*

Figure 3.3 Job advertisements in Davao City. Note requirements that include gender, height, "plessing" [sic] personality, and tertiary education for cashier/waiter roles.

employers use is the "trainee" provision where new staff can be paid 25% less than the minimum wage for up to two years; Ofreneo and Hernandez[4(p. 126)] found, for example, that at one electronics company in 2010, about 19,000 of the 20,000 workers were classed and paid as trainees. Other complaints from unions include the per-unit pay where workers are only paid per sale (commission) or unit produced such as in garment factories.[4(p. 127)]

In formal employment, the strict demands and requirements of employers have created a certain "ideal worker" in job application requirements. The shortage of jobs means that the ideal worker has been defined very narrowly – in service sectors, for example, workers are often sought who are female, under about 28 years old, university educated, physically attractive, polite, and deferential. As there is a "labour surplus economy," employers easily discriminate against women/non-males, older people, youth, and disabled people.[9(p. 2)] I would often see and hear job advertisements which included not only details about acceptable gender and maximum age but also height requirements.[vii] The job advertisement for SM with its cardboard cut-out exemplifies this specificity, with their sought female worker being aged 20–26 while having already completed a four-year tertiary course (see

Labour and exploitation 75

Figure 3.4 Job advertisement in Davao City, specifying gender, age, appearance, and "pleasing personality."

Figure 3.3). Once employed, workers must comply with a long list of rules and requirements. Common stipulations that I heard about included the following: workers will be financially penalised for each minute they are late to work; mall stores' employees are forbidden to shop in the mall; workers may not bring a bag along to work (in case of theft); (female) workers must wear prescribed makeup as well as the uniform which often includes a short skirt, nylon hose, and high heels. Local business analysts, for example, recommended closer direct monitoring to increase productivity, to the point that any conversations with co-workers had to be written down.[28(p. 3468)]

Although court cases for employment infractions are often successful, the limitations of the judicial system mean that this process can take years, which benefits the employers; settlements awarded are often less than even the entitled pay without other benefits and court costs that the employee has lost.[18(p. 187),23(p. 29)] Court documents suggest that when employees have tried to sue their employers for unpaid wages and benefits, appeals from employers are common, increasing the costs to wronged employees and limiting their ability to see out the process.[19,20] Employment relationships draw on a history of colonial and patronage relationships where people have simply had to adapt to survive and benefit under those in power.[29(p. 1273)]

76 *Labour and exploitation*

Figure 3.5 Job advertisements. Child attendant must be single, age 18–23; the other ad offers a pay range starting below minimum wage.

The power of employers comes from several sources: the scarcity of jobs overall; the lack of the government's will and/or ability to address workplace rights, contract and payment abuses, or health and safety issues; and the tenuous position of low-wage workers where even a short time without work could mean disaster. One of my participant's children, for example, was forced to drop out of school when her health meant that she, as the breadwinner, could not work for a period. The threat of a nebulous, unending supply of precarious, desperate workers willing to accept poor conditions and low pay further informs the relationship between employers and employees.

Poverty, and its uneven distribution both locally and globally, has been repeatedly identified as a form of structural violence.[30,31] This assessment draws attention to the violence intrinsic to the day-to-day experience of poverty as well as the ever-present risk of catastrophe if unexpected costs arose.[10(pp. 27,33)] Poverty as a social setting rather than individual measurement is implicated in the normal experience of work in the Philippines and creates the context of my participants' stories.

DonDon's story below illustrates a few of the ordinary struggles that workers have to deal with in attempting to benefit from their work. His experience of financial exploitation in his work is followed by Gabriel's story. Gabriel experienced human trafficking in the form of extreme labour exploitation. Although these stories are quite different from one another, they both demonstrate how labour conditions are shaped by employers but

Labour and exploitation 77

also by the wider Mindanao society where both worked. After this, Melissa's story demonstrates how informal labour relationships can also hide and maintain abuse.

3.3 DonDon's story

DonDon was introduced to me by my language teacher, who was also a community worker. She knew about DonDon's workplace experiences and suggested that I meet him. She also suggested that it would be a good chance to test out and improve my language skills by conducting this interview in Cebuano. I was less confident in my abilities than she seemed to be, but I hoped that DonDon would recount his story, as other participants had, without a great deal of prompting, and my teacher would also interpret when needed. DonDon and his family lived in a rough wooden house in a squatter settlement on public land. He and his wife had two children, and his young son sat on the couch to one side and smiled at me shyly during our visit. His wife served us the coffee and cakes that I had brought, and we chatted about our children and laughed, my Cebuano as usual having been a work in progress.

DonDon grew up in an agricultural family, farming and fishing in a rural area not far from Davao. Like many other children, he would help his father with the farming and fishing work. DonDon worked with his family mainly in the school holidays, and he was able to finish high school. After high school, he moved to Davao city to find work. He worked in a number of trades before becoming an assistant to a welder, and had a number of similar positions which gave him apprenticeship experience where he learned the trade himself. "It is difficult to (find a job) if you don't have any skills. But if you have a skill, it is easy."

DonDon had been working as a welder and automotive body builder. He worked at an automobile plant which would import cars from Japan, partially disassembled. DonDon's work was to reassemble the cars to be ready for sale. He worked for a daily rate of ₱500 plus a payment based on the number of cars he assembled in a day or a week. The workers all worked eight-hour days, six days a week. He, like the other men working in the company, was to be paid the daily salary every week, while the commissioned payment built up to be paid less frequently. However, time went on and DonDon waited and kept enquiring, but the commissions owed were never paid. "Their style of giving us money, whatever was our contract – well, just (bad). They pay us every Saturday, only our salary. But then the full payment for our work, they don't actually give us." He worked for months and months like this, not knowing what to do but hoping that if he stayed the commissions owed would be eventually paid properly, as per his contract. By the time he had reached ₱100,000 owing to him, DonDon was despairing. He felt trapped by the situation, knowing that if he left he would be forfeiting whatever chance there was that he would be paid what was owed.

78 *Labour and exploitation*

The day I spoke with him had finally been the breaking point after a long period with *walay bayad* [no payment].

"That's why I decided that – only earlier today, I have decided to stop from work then I asked for an account (of my final pay). So from this day today, I quit from my job there."

DonDon had recently been loaned a vehicle to drive. He hoped that whatever he would be paid out from the company would be enough to buy the vehicle outright. Having transportation benefited his family but also supported the small business that they had been running on the side, selling dried fish, which needed to be sourced and transported. He hoped that the income from this would help see them through his period of unemployment. "We had already started a business, so that will be what we will keep doing daily." After quitting his job, DonDon's immediate intention was to work as a jeepney driver, taking over from his father who was past 70. Although DonDon was sure that with his skills as a welder he would find another job, for the short term this was the plan to keep the family going.

Financially, things had already been very difficult. DonDon had had to run a side business with his wife just to meet the family's basic needs, despite his full-time, skilled employment. DonDon was committed to seeing his children through their studies, but recognised the financial pressure that this placed on him and the family's resources. "I want that they will be able to finish schooling. Whatever profession they want, I will do my best to see them finish their studies, to graduate from college." Like many Filipino families, DonDon and his wife realised that the best chances for all of their futures depended on their children's financial abilities and success.

Despite the exploitation that he has experienced, DonDon was relatively optimistic about the family's future. "In my life, my life is fine because even if it's not (perfect) – even if it is quite tough, at least, we are serving the Lord. Because if you are with God, all things that are in this world, he will add to you. That's why you really must prioritize God. Then, your work next. So, our family is fine, even if it's tough like this, but we are happy. No troubles, we understand each other." In the tiny, rough wooden house in the squatter settlement late that *gabii* [evening], I could feel the warmth of DonDon and his wife's generous hospitality.

The other men who worked with DonDon in the automotive company were all in the same situation of being denied their full compensation, and remained so after DonDon left. Like DonDon, they had little recourse or chance of compensation, and would have needed to make the same decision that DonDon did: to choose between staying with the hope that things would change or leaving to try to find a better job. At the time I spoke with DonDon, there was no legal action pending, no official case against the corporation, and no officials had been notified of the contract violations. DonDon's case, I had been told, was unfortunately common, and reflects social configurations of power relations, entwined with economic inequality.

Labour and exploitation 79

As such, normal employment standards are a significant part of the context for labour trafficking such as Gabriel experienced.

3.4 Gabriel's story

Gabriel was the youngest person I interviewed while in Mindanao. At 17, he still seemed to me a little more boy than man. It was difficult to reconcile his sweet, shy manner to the difficult experiences he had endured. It was clear, however, that his current guardian was a very strong woman who cared for Gabriel and was determined to support him in making his way into adulthood.

Gabriel grew up on a farm in the mountains. He worked hard on the farm and went to school, and for a time stayed with his grandmother on the same family farm as his parents. "We had just enough. I would help out (on the farm) and go to school. Sometimes we could eat rice, or we would also just eat *kamote* [sweet potato] and cassava." He and his siblings grew up witnessing domestic violence at home where their father would beat ["*ginakulata*"][viii] and intimidate their mother. "Us too, sometimes we avoided him, sometimes we didn't go near him, because he abused us." When their mother fled from the abuse, the children continued to live with violence and fear at home with their father. Gabriel continued primary school, but he quit to work on the farm before sixth grade. Finally, Gabriel could not take the conditions and left home at age fourteen to escape.

After a recruiter came through the rural area looking for able workers for manual labour, an older cousin brought Gabriel to Davao and together they were sent to work at a factory. Soon, though, the cousin decided he could not stand the work and moved on, leaving Gabriel on his own. "That was my first real job." At age fourteen, he had little knowledge about employment or life in the city. The men in the factory worked twelve hours a day from 7:00 am until 7:00 pm, seven days a week. Gabriel was paid ₱100 ($2.73 NZD) per day. They were given accommodation where they were expected to live in a bunkhouse area of the factory. The workers were also fed, but mainly only rice, which Gabriel described as being rather awful, "it was free, but it was only that bad-smelling kind of rice." They would also get some dried or fresh fish and occasionally chicken, but it was never enough, and sometimes very little indeed. "It was really lacking, sometimes not enough (for all of us)."

The work was difficult and dangerous. The factory recycled plastic, mostly old plastic sacks, to be used again in manufacturing. Gabriel's job, like many of the others, was to move the sacks and melt them in the open boiler.

The factory was filthy, decrepit, and incredibly hot. The running water for the manufacturing did not have proper drainage, so there was always dirty, stagnant water adding to the smells and hazards. The chemical fumes from the melting plastic from the old sacks were the most intense smell, adding to the sweat, dirt, dust, and mould.

80   *Labour and exploitation*

The fumes from the plastic were not only unpleasant, but the workers were often sick from being exposed to the chemicals and dirty conditions. "It's really dangerous because of the bad smell, and then the others would even get sick." Gabriel showed me the scars on his legs and feet, deep burns from the melting plastic he worked with all day, every day. He was threatened, physically and verbally abused, and humiliated. "I was *ginadaog-daog* [very oppressed]." Gabriel recalled being happy and relieved when the rescuers – including NBI,[ix] social services and more – descended, and he thought, "I will be able to leave." The conditions were such that upon freeing the men, the factory was immediately closed down and the buildings condemned.

He reported that older workers, who were on a slightly higher pay scale, initially had mixed emotions about the raid. "They felt kind of sad and worried, but we could no longer bear it." They were all happy to be free from the horrible working conditions and glad that the employers were being held to account. However, their first thoughts were also about sudden unemployment, and whether they would be paid the wages that were owed. Gabriel told me that older workers had been promised certain wages, but had not been paid properly, and so they were worried that now that the factory was closed there would be no chance of getting the back pay.

The men Gabriel worked with were disappointed that when they were rescued, the social services did not help them to find other jobs in the city, and the owed wages were not repaid. "But in the end, nothing. Because (the former employers) have been imprisoned." At this, most of them took the funds available from the social services to return to their provincial homes, as most of the men like Gabriel and his cousin had been recruited from rural areas.

Gabriel has been assisted under the human trafficking rehabilitation programs which include emergency shelter, psycho-social rehabilitation, education and livelihood programs, and support during legal proceedings. He has had access to a number of support services including counselling and the Alternative Learning System (ALS),[x] and was placed in a caring home while he worked to complete his studies. Gabriel had also been assisted to resume limited contact with various family members, including his mother whom he had not seen in many years.

Gabriel reflected that if his mother had not left the family home, his life might have gone differently. "Maybe if my mother didn't leave us, things would have been better. I could have continued going to school." Gabriel's *lola* [grandmother] and his mother had encouraged him to carry on in his schooling. Gabriel and his siblings were very sad and withdrawn once their mother left as they had been very close to her. Their father was more distant as well as being abusive, and Gabriel attributed the emotional impact of his mother leaving as part of the reason he was not able to carry on beyond primary school – "we were all gloomy and had no more desire to go to school because we really missed our mother." He reasoned that if he had had an education, he would not have ended up at the factory.

Labour and exploitation 81

After this experience had ended, Gabriel had resumed studying with the support of his foster family. He was working towards completing high school through the ALS as well as taking vocational training. He did not have any specific plans about the work he would like to do, but he said that his main ambition was to work to be able to support his family. "Anything as long as there is a job." Despite his struggles in dealing with an absent mother and abusive father, Gabriel's primary goal had become contributing financially to their and his siblings' lives. Like other participants such as Erica, Gabriel's relationships with his family reveal the complex expectations, entanglements, and social obligations, even towards family members who had abused him. Melissa's story, similarly, indicates the role of social relationships in perpetuating abuse.

3.5 Melissa's story

Like DonDon, Melissa's case is also not registered officially with legal or social services, and no action has ever been taken against her abuser.

Melissa's family lived in an urban *barangay* [suburb] and was very poor and socially marginalised. "I would say that we come from a very poor family." Her mother was caring towards Melissa and her many siblings but had not gone past elementary level education. Her father had worked in stable employment, but when he lost his job, he turned to alcohol instead of seeking another position. He became an alcoholic, and her parents were constantly fighting. "He lost his job and instead of trying to, you know, be helpful, he didn't. He was drinking, he would just drink every day – most of the day, and would always fight with my Mom." The family lived together with Melissa's father's family, who were often spiteful towards Melissa's family. As well as her lack of education, Melissa's mother's conversion from Catholicism to Protestantism had left her ostracised by her family and neighbours.

When Melissa was very young and her father was working, they had had food, and the children were in school. When he lost his job, however, he sent Melissa's oldest brother out to work instead of finishing tertiary study, and pressured all of the children to earn money for the family. "It was hard for us to even get rice on our table, and that's the most basic thing for Filipinos, right? We didn't have enough rice. Sometimes we would have to borrow money or ask for rice from our aunt and uncle just so we would have something on the table. We didn't have any meat, so if there was leftover rice from breakfast, we would add sugar and hot water to have as a snack. In the evening, we wouldn't have any more rice, so we would be hungry while we waited for our *kuya* [older brother] to come home from work and bring us some food or some money to buy noodles for dinner."

When Melissa was a child, a neighbour offered her a chance to do some work at their home business in exchange for her jeepney fare to get to school every day. Melissa would get up early to work from 4:00 to 5:30 am in exchange for ₱15 ($0.50 NZD), before going off to school. "It's our

82   *Labour and exploitation*

neighbour's food business. I had to wake up early, for three years, I helped out at this business. For that time, the person I was working for, molested me. So finally I stopped." This situation was already exploitative to some degree, but Melissa was also sexually abused by this employer. Child abuse is a problem in the Philippines and in Melissa's case was closely connected to her work situation. Further, when Melissa attempted to tell her mother what was happening, she was scolded as the abusing neighbour was also a community leader, and not to be disrespected. "My mom, she didn't believe me. She said, don't ever say that about (him)."

As Melissa grew up, she became increasingly angry with the way her mother was treated by the rest of the family. "I remember, I would come home after school and find my mom in the house crying. Really crying, because my auntie just came and said some things, and sometimes they would terrorise her, trying to scare her." The physical bullying, false accusations, and social rejection made it a very stressful home environment for Melissa's mother as well as the children. On one occasion, Melissa took up a bolo knife to ward off her relatives' threatening behaviour, demanding, "So who wants to hurt my mom? Who wants to keep yelling?," and she was proud that she stood up to them and they backed off. As Melissa and her siblings grew up, their ability to support their mother meant that their relatives began to ease off.

Melissa eventually got a position with an NGO, which supported her in going overseas for religious-based leadership training. On her return, Melissa continued to work with the group, using her natural charisma and enhanced leadership skills to contribute to running their programs. They were also able to arrange sponsorship to allow her to enrol in tertiary study, where she obtained a managerial degree in the area of tourism. "I'm the only one who has a degree in my family."

Her oldest brother, as mentioned, was forced to drop out of his tertiary study to become the family breadwinner. He continued to support Melissa's parents and siblings. Melissa's older sister was awarded a scholarship, which she lost due to becoming pregnant while studying. Another brother enrolled in a tertiary course, but even though he had a scholarship for the tuition fees, he had to drop out because he could not afford the materials and transport costs for the required projects. Many of her siblings were working in the informal economy, some supported by other family members.

Melissa was content in her role at the NGO, where she was challenged, made use of her training, and had close friends. Long-term, she had a dream to someday work on a cruise ship. Melissa was one of the most upbeat, high-energy people I have known, and she excelled in sharing her enthusiasm with children and adults alike. I have no doubt that if she got the chance, she would be an ideal cruise director, joining the ranks of the overseas Filipino workers (OFWs).

The man who had abused Melissa still worked at a church in a position of authority and lived near Melissa's family. She had taken an active role in

Labour and exploitation   83

attempting to break ties with him, and to see that he was not permitted to visit their home or be around her younger siblings. He had not been prosecuted, and nothing had been done to stop his re-offending.

Melissa's story illustrates how the informal economy can also be a site of exploitation and abuse. In each of these stories, the workers had little power to change their situation, because of both the employment situation and the social context.

3.6 Structural violence, labour, and human trafficking

The concept of structural violence is useful in considering work as it provides insight into the problem of inequality and abuse in work without drawing firm lines between "normal" work, exploitative work, or human trafficking.[30,32] It also emphasises that the inequalities and constraints are experienced, not as inconvenience or risk, but as *violence* against a person and their life. Working conditions in the Philippines, particularly the job insecurity and low wages, have been fruitfully considered through frameworks including neoliberalism, globalisation, and precarity.[9,23,26,33–35] However, exploitation and abuse go beyond the employer/employee exchanges and implicate the wider legal and social structures which support "*systemic* exploitation."[32(p. 86)] The State and its lack of enforcement and control over labour standards, and the limitations of existing law to prevent abuse and exploitation, are thus heavily implicated in the structural violence against workers. Further, the ongoing and day-to-day condition of uncertainty in employment situations contributes to the *experience* of structural violence which shapes life choices and life chances.

These stories illustrate some of the difficulties inherent to the work and employment experience in the Philippines. Gabriel's story illustrates how the relationship between human trafficking and a person's ability to escape is not always as clear cut as it might appear, as well as the role that family relationships play in shaping a life course. DonDon's story also indicates how getting out of an exploitative situation is not just a matter of being able to leave physically or quit the job; social and financial entanglements can make it extremely difficult to choose to leave. Melissa's experiences also indicate how multiple power imbalances can support abuse and exploitative labour, as do social networks and relationships. Each of these stories indicates that the factors that maintain conditions of exploitation, caused by a person or group exploiting another, include social factors beyond the employment relationship alone.

The economic conditions of widespread poverty, low wages, and unemployment normalise and undermine acknowledgement of the severity of exploitation; degrees of the powerlessness and economic instability that characterise labour exploitation are typical and often expected in employment. Workers are socialised from childhood to be obedient and adapt to the demands placed upon them by parents, teachers, and employers.[36]

84 *Labour and exploitation*

Combined with the overall employment standards and competition for jobs, employment relationships are often characterised by highly unequal power relationships. Not only was Melissa paid a pittance for hours of work early in the morning, but she was sexually abused. The way her employer abused and controlled her during her work time implicates labour exploitation beyond just child abuse. The position of children within society where they are expected to be respectful, subservient, and obedient to elders exacerbates cases of exploitative or abusive child labour and allows few options for escape. Financial and sexual exploitation were made easier by Melissa's age and status, as well as her family's social status, and Melissa's reliance on the fare she earned to get to school.

DonDon's situation is one example of how employees have used money and false promises to control and exploit workers. Leaving his job meant not just finding new employment, but a real possibility of catastrophe when already living close to the bread line. When DonDon left his job, he was also forfeiting any chance of recovering the significant amount of money that the company owed him. This threat helped to keep DonDon compliant and under his employers' control, continuing to work hard in the expectation that he would eventually be paid for his efforts. In the Philippines, debt of this kind has been frequently implicated as the mechanism of control in various types of human trafficking, particularly agent-facilitated labour migration.[37] Gabriel's co-workers experienced a similar situation, which highlights the way that debt can be a secondary violence in controlling against the possibility of objection to undesirable or violent working conditions.

Social networks are important in finding regular employment, but are also used in intentional recruiting for legitimate as well as questionable or illegal, and exploitative work situations. Social pressure can maintain employment standards where official processes fail through relational pressure to behave correctly and save face. I witnessed this process in action where a financial dispute between a landlord and real estate agent was settled, neither in person nor through the courts, but through mediation by a mutually respected friend who pressed both parties to reach an agreement. My husband was also warned repeatedly not to do business dealings with anyone he had not been personally introduced to, as they would cheat him. However, employment through personal connections is not always an option. Gabriel's position in the factory that he initially entered alongside his cousin is an example of how family members help shape employment activities, although in their case the role of the recruiter was also significant. This pattern of family influence was evident in many of the stories I heard, and younger people in particular often got a job – or were exploited or trafficked – through a friend or extended family member. Erica's story, for example, was shaped by existing social relationships as, like Gabriel, she fled from abuse and poverty, and was subsequently trafficked by a friend into the sex industry. Social networks can both facilitate low-wage work and human trafficking and mitigate against its effects.

Labour and exploitation   85

The relational model of economic activity means in practice that there is significant pressure to use resources for consumption rather than investment as those who have money are expected to support those who do not. This is also a social investment and reciprocal safety net, but the relational economic life depends on investment in people and relationships – subsistence, education, health, and reciprocal care. Security that is based on current work and earnings produced by the family overall is ultimately limited in the Philippines' current economy that does not provide enough adequately paid employment for potential workers. The high levels of unemployment and underemployment and inability to access jobs for many people supports the disposability of precarious workers.

These stories suggest that the binary framework of victimhood/agency[xi] is not complicated enough to hold the ways that individual agency and choice is made and constrained by social and cultural factors including the choices between perceived options. When human trafficking has been equated to slavery with its accompanying imagery of chains and physical force, the question is sometimes reduced to a matter of individual control or complicity. There are horrendous cases of chains, violence, and control in all types of trafficking that exist around the world, and particularly disturbing cases involving sex trafficking of minors in the Philippines have been reported.[xii] A focus on the control between trafficker and trafficked, however, can obscure the wider constraints that facilitate exploitation on the one hand, and on the other, prevent a trafficked or exploited worker from being able to leave. Gabriel, in theory, could have run away at the end of a workday. This does not mean that he was not trafficked by his abusive employers, who benefitted from his youth and status which kept him from leaving as well as their threats. However, a wider focus can "go beyond narrow framings of blame to bring social systems into account."[38(p. 621)]

Even in extreme cases, structural violence supports physical violence. A reported case in Mindanao, from one of the NGOs I worked with, involved a young girl who was chained up, beaten, and forced to sell sex by a relative. I do not know whether there were eventually convictions, but a case of human trafficking such as this certainly demands some form of direct action. However, the girl was reported to be in her relative's "care" as both of her parents were overseas as labour migrants as they had been unable to provide for her through work in the Philippines. The girl had been left with this relative – undoubtedly an emotionally violent situation for both parents and daughter – because of the violence of poverty. Further to this, the limitations of social services providers and of prosecuting offenders mean that the power of the state is a less influential protection as a disincentive to trafficking and abuse than is intended by the strong anti-trafficking laws.

Structural violence operates on a social level, is systematic and invisible, but exists alongside a "moral economy still geared to pinning praise or blame on individual actors."[30(p. 307)] A theme running through this book is destabilising the binary conceptions of victimhood in relation to human

86 *Labour and exploitation*

trafficking – victimhood as contrasted with agency, victims as the opposite of perpetrators, and victimhood contrasted with culpability and blame. Blame has been attributed to underage soldiers or removed by designating them as trafficking victims; sexual labourers have been identified similarly. Migrant labourers, similarly, have been blamed for exploitation or abuse they experienced as irregular migrants/workers. The work and employment culture of the Philippines illustrates the individualised responsibility to overcome the barriers that structural violence creates.

In the Philippines, the attribution of individual-level responsibility within the formal economic sector contrasts sharply with the collective sense of identity in wider social relations, supporting the use of individual "shame" to ensure compliance.[39,40(p. 230)] This too is a manifestation of violence, both against a person's sense of self and in transferring the wider constraints that people experience to an *individual* responsibility to overcome them. Employees may be desperately poor and not paid a decent wage; they then are often closely monitored by their employers, so they do not steal. Employees may not be able to afford many transport options, and must work informally to support themselves; they are penalised by the employer if they are late. Employees might not afford makeup and decent clothes; their appearance is stipulated and monitored by the employer. The mistrust and control of workers is an example of the systematic, indirect structural violence which arises from the unequal power relationships between employers and employees, as well as the violence of poverty which is given a second blow through employers' controls. Thus, structural violence is compounding both in general, and in specific areas such as employment.

Structural violence is part of social structures beyond one aspect of life or institutional relationships, but also cumulative and comes from multiple sources simultaneously which maintain oppression.[30] The position of low-wage workers is reiterated and internalised through mechanisms such as the "fatalism" that many Filipinos express about their futures, the essentialising of women as domestic and servile, and the lack of high paying jobs in the Philippines as compared to overseas.[34,39,41] Further, the power of "shame" in this "face"-based culture has been demonstrated as a factor preventing workers from challenging their working conditions, supported by attitudes and practices that reinforce the inferiority and servitude of the poor to the rich and powerful with their origin in colonial relations.[29(p. 1273),39(p. 56)] The lack of informal and formal social mechanisms for addressing working conditions has meant that workers "are left to negotiate structural violence in individual ways, perceiving violations of rights as part of everyday struggles to hold on to their employment or resorting to employment as informal/illegal workers."[32(p. 86)] The normality of low-paid work with substandard working conditions indicates structural violence in employment conditions which maintains the position of the poor in Mindanao.

Although Gabriel's experience of labour exploitation was "officially" recognised as human trafficking, while Melissa's and DonDon's were not, the

Labour and exploitation 87

case that I am presenting is that all of these experiences emerge from the same structural violence by which employers are able to exert a great deal of control over their employees. Exploitative and abusive practices are normalised, hidden, and maintained in this context, and the wider structural violence of poverty and uncertainty press on employees to endure the conditions for the sake of keeping the job, often no matter how undesirable it may be. As Scheper-Hughes[42(p. 14)] pointed out, a significant manifestation of structural violence is the "paralysis and powerlessness among vulnerable populations forced into complicity with the very social forces that are poised, intentionally or not, to destroy them." The position of labourers overlaps with the position of women in society and the economy to shape the experiences of women working in the sex industry.

3.7 Part 2: sexual labour and sexual traffic: women in Mindanao seeking work

"They told me that I would be babysitting, but it wasn't true."
– Crystal, trafficked for sexual labour.

Both domestic and international sex trafficking are significant problems for the Philippines. Although a small amount of high quality research has been conducted with Filipino women overseas who have experienced various forms and degrees of sex trafficking,[37,43] little research has been done in the domestic context. Within the Philippines, issues related to sex trafficking include the forced, coerced, and voluntary sexual labour of minors, the role of shame and stigma in the experiences of sex trafficking or sexual labour, and the limited economic options for women in general. Many researchers who have worked with sexual labourers and trafficked sexual labourers have argued that both sex trafficking and voluntary commercial sex are significantly shaped by women's position in society.[44,45(p. 215)] This section explores the relationship between women's position and options within Mindanao and the experiences of human trafficking in the form of forced sexual labour as part of the wider discussion of labour, employment, and structural violence.

The focus on gender in this section is not intended to eclipse the experiences of men and boys who have been sex trafficked, but to set the context for my participants' experiences as young women, and to explore the fact that the majority of those trafficked for sexual labour are female, including in Mindanao and the Philippines. As of 2016, 95% of convicted trafficking cases were for sex trafficking, and of convicted cases of both sex and labour trafficking overall, 93% of all victims were female, strongly implicating the role of gender.[xiii46] Further, the discussion of human trafficking in the context of the wider sex industry does not mean to conflate forced and voluntary sexual labour, but to highlight the issues that women face generally in Mindanao, and specifically within the sex industry, whether they have initially

88 *Labour and exploitation*

entered through trafficking or not. The domestic market for sexual labour, for example, draws on a history of military colonialism where American bases were serviced by local women who made their living providing sexual services, which has since carried on similarly in catering for sex tourism.[44(p. 227),47] The local context that women inhabit and negotiate is shaped by specific cultural and historic conditions which create unique options and limitations.

Women's access to employment in the Philippines in general is unequal to men's, and although women have statistically higher levels of education, this does not equate to higher wages or more job options.[21(p. 276)] For women in the Philippines without a high school or tertiary education, job options are limited. The jobs that are available tend to be informal, either self-employed or working in a family enterprise, or the lowest paid, lowest status, most unregulated sectors. Agricultural work is one example in rural areas where women are paid significantly less than men for the same work, in a sector which is already notoriously underpaid.[15] Women also comprise the majority of the "pool" of cheap, flexible, and disposable labour, and women have been found to bear the most negative impacts of economic fluctuations.[47(p. 162),48] Even sectors which are dominated by women such as domestic work, find women underpaid compared with men.[49]

The position of domestic workers in the Philippines is significant to understanding the alternatives young, uneducated women have for employment. Sex, care, and domestic labour are aspects of what Boris and Parreñas[50] have termed "intimate labour" which emphasises the demands of physical, emotional, relational, and material labour in attending to others. In the Philippines, as in many other locations, this realm is frequently socially invisible, undervalued, underpaid, and configured by gender where women make up the majority of intimate labourers both domestically and as migrants.[15] As of 2011, at least 1.9 million Filipino households employed domestic staff over the age of fifteen, mainly women.[51] The invisibility of domestic workers, particularly residential ones, supports the recognised prevalence of exploitative or abusive conditions: non- or under-payment, lack of recognition as employees, long hours, controlling conditions such as prohibiting time off for social/cultural/religious participation, sexual/physical/emotional abuse, non-payment or termination if pregnant or sick.[52] Statistics from 2011 list only 9.2% of domestic workers as fifteen to seventeen, but this does not count underage, unreported, unpaid, or "adoption" situations which are common[49]; as of 2001, the Visayan Forum's researchers reported that 60% of domestic workers were under 18.[52] General minimum wages vary by location and sector, but ranged from ₱250 to ₱380 (from $7.20 to $11.00 NZD) per day in 2016.[53] Domestic workers, by comparison, had a monthly minimum legal wage of ₱1800–3500 ($52–101 NZD), or ₱69–134 ($1.50–3.86 NZD) per day, despite also working longer than usual hours.[xiv51,53]

The high proportion of women in sexual labour as well as domestic and care work also reflects an essentialised view that equates women with

Labour and exploitation 89

domestic life, service, and "intimate labour," rationalises, and perpetuates gender-based inequality.[50,54] In acknowledging the multiplicity of experiences and the changeable temporality of questions of consent, coercion, agency, and exploitation, I have used the term "sexual labour" to expand an understanding of such work beyond sex acts alone to include work such as dancing and flirting that occur in Filipino clubs. This usage also links notions of sexual labour with other forms of gendered economic activity, such as domestic and service work, which often demand gendered or even sexualised labour.[55(p. 132)]

In the Philippines, commercial sex is illegal but generally tolerated rather than laws being strictly enforced; government health facilities, for example, require registration of street and club based workers and provide medical services.[56,57] In Davao, the police intentionally turn a blind eye to the position of regular (i.e., not underage) street-based sexual labourers, and the women I knew were not afraid of them and in fact suggested that their occasional drive-bys were more likely for their safety than their illegal activity. In other parts of the Philippines, however, corruption among police, governmental and judicial authorities has been cited as allowing commercial sex and sex trafficking to continue with official cooperation. For example, brothel owners have been required to supply bribes to the police in exchange for allowing their continued operation or withdrawing prosecution.[58(pp. 91–92)] In Davao, there are several sympathetic NGOs across the political and religious spectrums whose aims are to support sexual labourers and provide access to services, social support, and alternate economic opportunities where desired. One program, for example, offers sexual labourers' children an alternate education site which gives them better education support and removes them from the public system where their mothers' work can often leave them stigmatised socially, heavily impacting their attainment at school.

Within the Philippines, sexual labour is socially stigmatised and marginalised.[59(p. 41)] There remains a significant sense of moral judgement, not only around sexual labour, but extramarital sex in general. Many of the sex workers I knew were highly sensitive to their neighbours' perceptions and concerned that people would refer to them in derogatory terms, particularly in front of their children. Thrupkaew[60] cited a young Filipina street-based sexual labourer who explained beginning this work at age fifteen because "my boyfriend took my virginity, and then left me. So what else was I good for after that?" My friends at one NGO were supporting several formerly trafficked women who had been forced into the sex industry in Malaysia, who refused to go to the government authorities or even tell their families what had happened due to the shame and stigma. The sense of shame that women had internalised contributed to feeling that they were not able to continue in "respectable" society, relationships, and employment. Single mothers, similarly, experience both social stigma and time constraints which affect their job prospects.

90 *Labour and exploitation*

Even women trafficked into the sex industry in some of the worst cases, have returned to the Philippines feeling that they were stigmatised for their involvement. Erpelo[61(p. 127)] observed that the women in her research who had experienced international sex trafficking still rationalised and explained their experiences in terms of a strongly conservative, patriarchal view of women's sexuality and virtue, and after the sex trafficking situation, most of the women interviewed "ended up either alone or in abusive relationships, just glad at the fact that somebody still deemed them fit." Women in different forms of sexual labour in the Philippines have also expressed disdain for other "worse" forms and the women who performed them.[62] After exiting sexual labour and/or trafficking, those who had settled in the Philippines have at times experienced social and financial difficulties in reintegration.[37,63,64] The lack of opportunities that pushed them to initially move was exacerbated by the stigma of having done sexual labour, even when forced.

Sexual labour in the Philippines, as in other locations, entails particular risks. However, this varies according to different types and locations of sexual labour. Club positions, for example, mean that women are in a closed environment where it is difficult to leave if necessary, and the arrangement of drinking with customers opens the possibility of drinks being spiked by clients or managers. Commercial sex while either the client or the worker is intoxicated has also been associated with unsafe sex practices and higher rates of STIs.[65,66] Globally, street-based sexual labour has been often identified as one of the most dangerous jobs.[45,67(p. 79)] Clubs may offer some level of protection with other employees around, but if a worker leaves in a client's private vehicle, they are outside of this structure. The street-based women I met recounted that they had had near escapes, and they were alert to signs that the situation might be dangerous. They would text each other to maintain contact when they went with a client, and were conscious of signs that a situation might be dangerous, such as if the client started driving out of town or away from where they had said they were going. I was alarmed, though, when the NGO workers I was with made inquiries about a woman who had not been out recently. "I think she might have gone overseas with her boyfriend?" was the best guess anyone could offer; in a marginalised position, the women were often invisible within wider social networks.

The danger of physical violence compounds the emotional and relational consequences of working in a socially marginal and stigmatised profession. Gill[68] cited the case of a woman who had been part of a livelihood-based rehabilitation program after sex trafficking in the Philippines but dropped out and returned to sexual labour following a particular incident. After taking an illegal drug to terminate an unplanned pregnancy, she needed medical care but was "retraumatized by reproachful, verbally abusive staff who refused her treatment."[68(p. 2)] Particularly for young women in the Philippines who have not completed high school, entry into the sex industry usually also displaces education, which also disrupts their future employment options and continues the cycle of the feminisation of poverty. Participants,

Labour and exploitation 91

including NGO workers and present and former sex workers, confirmed that in the Philippines, there is a large demand for girls under age fifteen for sexual labour (see Figure 3.6 for the club whose name emphasises the youth of its performers), and minors often face heightened risks of violence and social consequences.

Several of the current and former sexual labourers I met had entered the work as minors.[xv] Similar to coerced or forced sexual labourers, those who began as minors have higher risks for HIV and unsafe sexual practices – both linked to less power to "negotiate safe sex."[57] Like soldiers, underage sexual labourers are categorised as trafficked for sexual exploitation as they are not considered legally able to consent to voluntary participation, even where they have entered the trade voluntarily. This designation has led to situations where minors were involuntarily taken into care as "trafficking victims,"[69] as was Joramae, whose story is below. Ideas about victimhood and agency have been central to discussions of sex trafficking, entwined with notions of gender as well as age.

In the Philippines, sexual abuse, sex trafficking of minors, and CSEC (commercial sexual exploitation of children) including online CSEC are all recognised as significant problems. Legally, any commercial sexual activity involving minors can be defined as sex trafficking based on age alone, even in cases of teenagers in voluntary sexual labour. A case in UK international news in 2016 reported how Filipino children heard from their friends how other families were making money via webcams, and suggested this to their family.[70] The parents were not educated, and the thirteen-year-old communicated with English speaking customers. The parents were prosecuted, but the children did not understand how providing a better income for their family had resulted in their parents going to jail. Social workers noted that these children were not traumatised in the same way as other abused children in the shelter.[70] Several social workers I knew, described a recent case in Mindanao where a mother and aunt had been sexually exploiting their children in front of a webcam. The social workers described how heart-breaking the scene in court had been when the mothers and children had been crying upon seeing each other, wishing to be together. This, unfortunately perhaps, made it one of the easier cases to prosecute as it did not depend on the parents' consent to build a legal case.

Legal and social workers described to me how social pressure has been one reason that it has been difficult to prosecute human trafficking including CSEC, as well as other forms of child abuse. Cases are often settled out of court, or dropped entirely, due to pressure which may include harassment of the victims and/or their families, or financial settlements as incentives not to pursue legal action.[36(pp. 199–200)] Court processes do not guarantee a conviction, and demand overcoming any sense of shame and difficulty in confronting individuals in positions of power, as Melissa found.[36(p. 197)] If the case was against a more socially or economically powerful person, a financial settlement would often be offered that was an incentive not to

92 *Labour and exploitation*

prosecute. Social workers reported the families' attitudes in these situations: "Why would we bring charges against them? They are helping us." Going through the courts, in contrast, is expensive in terms of travel and lost income, time consuming and slow, and does not guarantee an outcome, or any material benefit. However, in these cases perpetrators are not being brought to account and are free to continue abusing. I heard about another alleged case of child abuse where the accused had found out the identity of the person bringing charges; subsequently, intimidation and harassment resulted in the case being dropped. Lengthy trials, corruption, and social pressure have meant that all forms of human trafficking have had negligible rates of conviction compared to the numbers of cases.[46,58]

Domestic sex trafficking has received little scholarly attention. West[58] (pp. 76–80) gave accounts from several young women who had been trafficked into clubs and brothels. Most had left impoverished rural communities to take a job offer to support their family, but instead were forced into sexual labour,[58] similar to recruiting tactics Wiss[71] found in rural areas. West[58] also interviewed young women in the Philippines whose parents had attempted to "sell" the girls directly to a brothel. Various NGO workers I met confirmed this practice and described a common situation where impoverished parents or relatives sent young women (usually around age thirteen to sixteen) out on the street to sell sex. NGOs found this a particularly difficult situation, as when social workers would offer the underage girls support and lodging so that they could return to school, the parents would come and pick them up and send them back to work. This further complicates the idea of consent; although the UN has pronounced that minors (and, presumably, their parents) cannot consent to being exploited as a basic violation of their human rights,[72,73] it does raise the question of who ultimately decides about a young person's life in some circumstances.

Both trafficking of women and voluntary paid sexual labour are part of what has been termed "sexual economies,"[74] and represent the most overt manifestations of the way that sex is implicated in many economic and reciprocal exchanges such as tourism, politics, and marriage, in the Philippines and globally. Chapman[44(p. 235)] and David[75] both described the gendered, service-oriented economy that emerged around colonial settlements, such as American naval bases as supporting the ongoing sex industry under the same rationale. Chapman argued that "sex tourism and mail order bride industries...carry with them imperialist ways of seeing Filipina women ... sex tourism to former colonies has not occurred in a vacuum and is reflective of colonial history.[44(pp. 227–228)] In this light, recent estimates that 2% or more of Filipina women aged 15–30 were involved in the sex industry can be considered as a neo-colonial legacy as well as commentary on the levels of poverty that drive women into this stigmatised and marginalised industry.[56]

The three women's stories in this chapter demonstrate some of the local social configurations for women. Particular themes include the role of

Labour and exploitation 93

Figure 3.6 "Baby Face Night Bar" gentleman's club in Davao City.

women in their families and the sense of duty this entails, and the opportunities and limitations for economic success that women face. Erica's life demonstrates how gender-based abuse can take many forms, and how the moral stigma around female sexuality can affect women's lives.

3.8 Erica's story

"We were really poor. My father was a fisherman. My mama was a church worker. We didn't have any money – and my father would drink. Then my mother and father would always fight. My mother went to Manila in order to work as a (domestic) helper. When I was six years old." Erica paused to regain her composure over the tears that were falling. "And then my mama left."

Erica was so excited for a chance to tell us her story. Before we had realised, she had set up chairs in a lovely shaded spot under the trees outside the NGO office where she worked. But no more than a couple of minutes through, she was in tears as she began her account of growing up in a poor rural area of Mindanao.

Being left with an alcoholic father, without the stability and care that her mother had provided, Erica's already precarious family situation deteriorated significantly at this point. After her mother had gone to Manila, Erica's oldest brother began to sexually abuse her. "Then my brother abused me. Sexually abused me. I just tried to ignore it." At six years old, she didn't have the ability to do anything but try to endure the situation. A few months later, her aunt married a businessman in a larger centre. Erica had not yet gone to school, and the rural town did not have sufficient opportunities for the

94 *Labour and exploitation*

children's education, so, Erica and two of her brothers were sent to live with the aunt and her new husband so that they could go to school.

The situation turned out to be less than ideal from the children's perspective. "When we arrived there, my brothers couldn't bear it, so they fled." The boys were older and ran away to escape the strict and punitive treatment of their uncle, leaving Erica on her own to endure the new home life. Now alone with new caregivers, Erica's material situation had improved, but her relational security had not. Erica was well fed, better than at home in the village, and she was able to attend school. Erica's aunt employed a driver who used to drive Erica to school. This man began to sexually abuse Erica, and did so regularly for several years until he left the job. Although after her previous abuse, Erica did not fully understand that this was not normal behaviour, there was a part of her that wanted to confide in her aunt. She was not able to "gather the strength and courage" though, mainly out of fear that she would be scolded or punished.

Graduating from elementary school and beginning high school marked another turning point in Erica's life. Relationships with friends began to consume her attention to the point that she lost interest in studying and getting her education. "Friends, and then a boyfriend." When she was fifteen, she had her first boyfriend which quickly turned to a sexual relationship. Erica related her desire for a sexual relationship to the normalisation of sex following the abuse she had experienced. By this point, Erica had little interest in studying. The school finally called her aunt to report that she had been caught drinking and smoking.

Out of fear, Erica refused to return to her aunt and uncle's house to face the consequences of this report. She asked her boyfriend to help her return to where her mother was, now back in the village. "When I got there, I realised that we are really very poor." In the aunt's house, tinned sardines and ground corn were fed to the dogs; at her mother's home, this was the staple diet. She stayed there for a few months but found the material hardship too much. Erica went to stay with a few different relatives, ending up at her oldest brother's house. "The one who had abused me before." He was by then married and in his own household, but once Erica was there he began to abuse her again. Erica wanted to escape, but didn't want to go back to either her mother or aunt's houses again. At this point, Erica felt she had no other option but to head out away from her family and look for work. She wanted to get away from the abuse from her brother, but she also wanted to be able to help her family who were living in such poverty back in the village. She was sixteen years old at this point.

Erica had been working as a waitress in a *karenderya* [small restaurant] in the town where her brother lived, and the cook there knew that she wanted to leave to seek work. He asked her if she wanted to go to Cagayan, and told her that was the place to earn a lot of money. This man told her that he had previously worked in a bar in Cagayan as a waiter,

Labour and exploitation 95

and he offered to help her get a job there. "He said, 'do you want to go to Cagayan? You will make a lot of money.' That's where the trafficking started." He took her to Cagayan and let her stay with his family for a few days before taking her to the bar, where she suddenly realised that it was not a waitressing job.

"And then, when the first time I saw girls dancing, I told myself, 'No, I could never do this.' Because they danced naked. Everything is seen. Although I was not a virgin, but I said, 'No, I won't, I really could not. This is my first time.' But later on, I had no choice once I was already there."

After this, Erica didn't know what to do. The first week, she could only think about how to get away. She recalled the turmoil she was in, thinking to herself, "'I have no relatives here. I have nothing to eat and I can't feed myself.' It was like survival. It was hardly bearable, (but I believed it would be) only for a few days. I said, 'I will work here for another few days until I find a different job, while I search for a different job.' So then, when I couldn't find any other job, I realised I had been staying there for too long already." It didn't take long for Erica to become entrenched in her new lifestyle and the job which soon was not only dancing but commercial sex as well. "I earned so much money. Lots of money, and then I encountered different guys, handsome guys, different nationalities, like foreigners. Yes, because I had a lot of customers, foreigner guys, then I was really able to help my mother with lots of money."

Before working at the club, Erica had drunk alcohol but had not used drugs. At the club, this changed. "I used drugs, I used alcohol. Every time I would work, every time, I would take drugs, for the reason so I won't be ashamed. Because it is very shameful to dance (naked). It is very embarrassing to show your body. It is so shameful. So, I would use drugs so that I could ignore it. Like when I would look at the audience, it is nothing. It's nothing. It would just feel great to dance."

For some years Erica remained in the club, where she had a top position and a reputation as a star dancer. She began a cycle where she would work, sending money back to her family, until she met a "big time customer." From time-to-time Erica would meet a man like this who would become something of a boyfriend, supporting her financially providing a house, asking her to stop her work. However, these relationships often didn't last. "There are times that it will be gone immediately because sometimes, you know, we get fed up especially if our partner is an old person and there is no love." Erica would return again to working in the club along with the other women.

By the time Erica was 25 she had reached a very low point in her life, and she described how "life became miserable then." The conflicting rollercoaster of emotions between dancing, sexual labour, using drugs, and making "big money" were compounded by her home situation. At that time, Erica was living with a boyfriend who used to *kulatahon*[xvi] [hit and beat] her

96   *Labour and exploitation*

regularly. The chaos in her life escalated. "I realised that I was not content with just one man. Even though I already had a live-in partner, and even when there was a customer as well, I really wanted to find something – I was really looking for conflict. I would have another boyfriend just to have excitement." Erica saw this as a kind of addiction. "So then I realised that it is really *dili maayo* [not good]. It was really not good."

This was a turning point. Erica did not like being in that situation where she was always high and relying on drugs to get through life. However, the money, the excitement of the club and the lifestyle, and the friendships at the club had kept her coming back. There had always been many customers and the money flowed, until she was 25 when things started to change. "Many customers were still coming, until such time that I realised I was already old. If you are (25), customers don't like you anymore."

"I started thinking and realising, I said, 'Why can't I stop this when this wasn't part of the aspirations of my life?' This is not what I dreamed about. I never aspired like this at all when I was still a child. I just wanted to help my family."

Erica was at the club when Anna, a woman from an NGO and regular visitor to the women at the club, began to recruit her. Erica was a good communicator and entertainer, popular with the customers as well as the other women at the club. Anna targeted her as a potential peer mentor, as she could see that Erica would be an excellent leader. She finally convinced Erica to try the work that Anna was suggesting. Erica first attended a Department of Health training seminar for six days, to become a peer educator about HIV and STIs and a peer counsellor to women in the sex industry. "So when I started working on that job, I liked it and then, my worries that I would miss the bar were gone. Gone. I enjoyed it… Especially because you are able to help your peers." The excitement of the club began to lose its appeal as Erica began to identify more with Anna and the other NGO workers and peer educators. She began work as a Department of Health peer educator and counsellor to sexual labourers including the women she used to work with at the club.

"I was able to help and then especially when the ones you've helped tell you, 'Thank you very much *Ate*,[xvii] thank you so much,' it's – what an honour. It's very heavy to take because of their huge gratitude. How great it is if you are able to help others, isn't it? Even if there isn't so much money – my (former) colleagues would tell me, 'You don't make much money, how much is your salary there? Why did you leave – how are you able to sustain yourself now?' Like that, but you know, I could not explain. I said it didn't matter, that it's not the money that matters. It's just the fulfilment of being able to help people. That's what made me like what I was doing then."

At this point, Erica was also immediately enrolled in ALS (extramural high school equivalency program). Prior to this, she had left high school

Labour and exploitation 97

in the third year when she was fifteen. Erica's attitude towards life and schooling had changed significantly in that time. "I went to school in ALS, I passed. I passed straight through. Oh, my God. When I passed ALS, I was able to work for (another local NGO). Yes, my success just continued on and on."

Her new job was working as a community health outreach worker for sexual labourers. Some of the other workers in the NGO were planning to study to become fully qualified social workers, and Erica was offered full tuition through the NGO to study as well. "So, I really prayed for that. 'Lord, Lord, what should I really choose because it's important to me.' Yes, so I really chose to study. When I picked schooling, I worried where I would get money because only the tuition would be paid." However, the NGO also provided room and board, in exchange for Erica working as a manager. In her second year, she also found work with a medical NGO, and the income covered her transport costs for school, and later the tuition when the NGO could not cover her for a period.

Erica worked hard and is very proud of her success. "By God's grace, I did not fail any subjects. Oh, Lord. Thank you so much. I really said that. I could cry, that oh, my, in my old age when it is so difficult...that I really achieved. That I never had a failing mark."

Erica's tenacity has seen her through a number of obstacles over the past few years. The first was finding the remaining funds to pay for the costs of going to school, which she achieved by finding additional work, but she had also had to struggle with her motivation as difficulties occurred. "I had encountered a little problem because I have a boyfriend. Then we had a small conflict between me and my boyfriend. After that I returned to drinking. Drinking only, then I did not do drugs, I have really stopped with them. But yes, drinking. Then, maybe, the others at the NGO saw that I weakened for a while. My determination was weakened because of the conflict with my boyfriend. My mentor would notice when I seemed to have a problem. She would really call me to counsel me. Sometimes problems would make me think that maybe I should just return to my work in the bar. But then I would say, 'oh, all my hard work will just be a waste if I do that. It would just be a waste if I return.'"

Erica is excited about graduating and moving on with her work in the community. She is particularly concerned about the number of young teenagers she meets working on the street, many from twelve or thirteen years old and often working against their will. Her position with the NGOs means that she will likely have stable employment for the near future. However, as a social worker, she will also probably never make "big money" and be able to support her family to the degree she did in the past. Despite this, Erica shared another success – she was able to see her nephew, the son of her oldest brother, graduate from a specialised university degree because of her financial support over the years.

98   *Labour and exploitation*

3.9 Crystal's story

I met Crystal at the NGO office where she worked. Like Erica, she had gone on to support other women in the sex industry after she herself left that world. This particular NGO supported sexual labourers in many ways, from support in accessing medical and prenatal care, to a soup kitchen and safe drop-in centre, as well as longer-term residential and rehabilitative care options for those exiting voluntary or trafficked sexual labour.

Crystal described her family as being very poor. Her father had left when she and her siblings were very small, leaving the already poor family in extreme difficulty. "I didn't have a father – my father had a second family. My father was very irresponsible. So I grew up just only with my mother. So we were a very poor family." Crystal's father was a farmer and fisherman. After he left, her mother would prepare and sell salt to support the family. Her mother had held a piece of land, but once she was on her own with little income, this was the only asset she had access to. The land had to be sold when one of the children was ill and needed medical care. Crystal had attended school up to Grade 4, but eventually had to stop in order to support the family. "In order to survive, I would sell as a sidewalk vendor so that we could buy rice." Crystal also described that in her family, she did not feel that she was considered important because she was a girl. "In the family there was (an attitude) like, 'Oh, you are special, you are my boy child.' That was how I felt then."

Crystal said that this was part of her motivation for leaving home at the age of fifteen. She did not want to stay with her family, but she hoped to be able to contribute more to the family by finding work outside of their area. "A friend of my sister came (to see me), and she promised me a job as a nanny, that I would be babysitting her child in Zamboanga City." Crystal did not tell her mother that she was leaving or where she would be going. "*Ako lang* [just me]. I just left."

"So at the time that I got trafficked, I was transported to the airport. So maybe that's how high tech she was as a trafficker because she had a relationship with someone from the Air Force. So I rode the (Air Force plane), arrived in Davao, had lunch and then we went to Zamboanga City. They told me that I would be babysitting, but it wasn't true. Upon arriving in Zamboanga City it seemed I was staying in a boarding house, but when night came, I was taken to a club. I ended up there in a big club. So it was there the story started that I began my duty, which was to dance as a go-go dancer. So from there I started working in the bar as a prostituted woman. Sometimes, they would make me entertain a customer. I was *bata* [young; literally, a child] then. I had no idea of – of the ways in a bar. So I immediately began using drugs. Using drugs, and drinking alcohol."

Crystal remained in the club for several years from her entry at age fifteen. "So many things happened to my life which were *dili maayo* in Zamboanga.

Labour and exploitation 99

I got more and more addicted to drugs. I couldn't return to my family. It seemed that when a person uses drugs, they are already in a miserable situation. It immediately happened that I got married to a man. There was a man who took me. A few weeks before I turned 18 years old, I got married to my partner, who was Muslim. For Muslims, it is prohibited for the Muslim and Christian to live together if they did not go through matrimony, so we got married."

Crystal and her husband returned to the area where she had grown up. "We lived together for a long time back there in our place. My husband was a security guard. We did not have kids, maybe (because) I was into drugs in my youth." They did, however, adopt one of Crystal's nephews. "When my sibling abandoned him, I took him in." Crystal had later adopted another nephew as well, as she was concerned about their options if they went to another family, as "if you would be a helper or you are a working student, you will be abused."

"Then afterwards, it happened that my husband went missing. I had no means to survive living, (and to support) that child we had adopted. So, I returned again to that situation because it seemed that I already had a guide, I knew how to do that. So, for me and that child to survive, I applied as GRO, guest relations officer. There it started again, that situation, in order to live, was my only thought, just in order to survive living. I was reached out to by (a recruiter) and I was trafficked again to (another city) as a dancer. I stayed there for nine months. It was very clear to me that I would work there as a – in the bar. I was turning 24 that time, I was no longer a minor. So, I cannot consider that as still trafficking. But in the context because of hardship, it was still traffic, right? It was in order to meet my needs to survive, to be able to eat, to be able to send (the children) to school. Because I was still sending (money for) my nephews and nieces at that time. So it was like that, because of hardship on my part, because of hardship is why I worked there."

"When I returned home, I was able to dance at my place. When I often danced, I would dance, work, table a customer, but I was not really any more into the thing called 'outing.' That's to join a customer because of money, because I had a vision and I was afraid to be impregnated by a different person that I did not love. There were occasions that I went out because of money, but also not just about money. Because I also really liked the customer. It was that sort of a situation. My situation was like prostitution because it was the only way I could work for my livelihood. I was there to be able to provide for my child, for my mother then I was able to send my nephews and nieces to school. At least, they finished high school. But sometimes, my mother would scold me because I myself do not have an education. I only finished Grade 4."

"So gradually, (an NGO) reached out to us (at the club). Before, it was only the STI-HIV-Aids, only about condoms. But I discovered that in a situation

100 *Labour and exploitation*

if a woman would equip herself with knowledge, they would have nothing, they cannot abuse (her) any more. It seemed like, I was a fighter. I don't want that in whichever situation, that our rights as women would seem to be abused. Because it doesn't mean that because (customers) gave a ladies' drink worth 210, they can touch our personal, private parts of our body." Crystal was inspired to become an advocate with this group. "So, we would bring (the training course) – we had a (holistic) education, the one on the street. It was also different, the learning group session, there inside the bar. So, for me it was not difficult to reach out among our peers who were still in that situation until now, because whatever is the situation that they have gone through, it would be the same situation that I would have gone through or experienced. I love reaching out to people. For them to be educated. For them not to be victims in human trafficking. As well as the STI-HIV because it is not easy for them when they get sick. So I volunteer with (these organisations)"

"I dreamed for myself that I would be able to finish high school to have a diploma as high school graduate since I finished studying only Grade 4 elementary level. That's why I want to help my nieces, my nephews for them to have a good education, not like me, I don't have education. But now, when they finish their high school, I promised to myself that I need to also finish my high school. Because my two sons now are already college, first year. So maybe for me, that's my dream, and for them to have a good education and also for my peers. I always look forward for them to reach out and encourage them, 'you, go to school. You have to finish your high school in ALS, like I am. Don't be ashamed. Even your age (doesn't matter).'"

"I had really wanted to become a lawyer. But then (I wasn't able to) because of the difficult circumstances that my parents were very poor. But I don't say that I regretted this. Rather, I am thankful that that happened, what happened to me. I've been trafficked, I've been abused. I was thankful for that. Why? Because I can say to myself that I can be a stronger person."

"I grew up only with my mother. In the context maybe if a family, especially parents if they have clear vision for their children, maybe they grow up with enough education. But in our family, nothing. Never. Me, I can say now, I declare I'll be the one who's graduated high school. That's really my (conviction). That's why I'm very passionate about that, right? I have very strong feelings for that. If there is an opportunity then for me, how will I qualify now for the opportunity if I don't have enough education? So, it's better to have an education. In (the NGO) we see that (women) need to venture for a livelihood, to move on from the past, but then nothing (they would do) succeeds. So, we saw that through education a woman could say that this (life) is not good for herself. So, it is her who can decide to stop from the situation of prostitution."

Crystal, like Erica, had found a great deal of empowerment through her NGO connections and exiting sexual labour. Joramae's story, however, is somewhat different.

3.10 Joramae's story

Joramae grew up with her parents and siblings. Her father was a fisherman, and her mother did jobs including manicures and domestic cleaning. Joramae did well in school and was supported by an achievement-based scholarship from her *barangay*. When Joramae's mother died, Joramae had finished two years of high school. At that point, she had to drop out of school in order to help support the family. "I stopped when my mother died, I worked as a dishwasher in a restaurant, and as a (domestic) helper…It's more difficult now. Because when my mom was around, we were ok. I went to school every day because I was sponsored."

Joramae was a young teenager when she became pregnant with her boyfriend. The family was already under strain, and now would have a baby to add to the chores and costs.

A friend, Julia, introduced Joramae to sexual labour as a way to provide for her family and baby. "We were invited by my friends." They were already working on the street when they encountered a foreign woman who offered to arrange jobs for them. When Joramae was 16 and her baby was then two months old, she was given a chance to spend a longer time with a client and travel. Leaving the baby with her partner and her family, she and her friend Julia both went with a foreign man to a bigger city. They stayed in a hotel, entertaining the client, while he provided gadgets, shopping, and trips to the beach. Pia, Joramae's younger sister, had come to visit her and collect some money for the baby's expenses when the hotel was raided. The three young women were taken into protection by social services while the client was arrested.

Although the social workers and police put together a case for human trafficking prosecution, the prosecutors instead chose to proceed as child abuse, hoping for a greater chance of conviction. However, the case was eventually dismissed completely.

Joramae and Julia were taken to the women's shelter for rehabilitation, while Pia returned home. At the shelter, they received counselling, ALS and skills education, and time for exercise. "Our life was great there. We learned many activities there." Handiwork, study, spiritual practices, cooking, cleaning, and learning gardening skills filled the days and gave structure to the women's time.

When I met Joramae, she was seventeen. She did not have immediate plans to finish school. "It depends, because first I have to provide for my child's needs." Joramae's ambitions were centred on her baby, and she hoped that he would get an education and would not be in the position that she is. "Now, my child is first, that's my first priority. I want him to go to school, by God's will, to go to school, to finish it, and not to follow in my footsteps." Her partner was seeking to go overseas with his family. Joramae was working as a domestic helper, mainly doing relief work when the regular workers were absent. "(I work) so that I have money to buy milk and food for my

102   *Labour and exploitation*

child." While she worked her father or siblings would look after the baby. If she could go out in the evenings, she would also work helping her partner with his *trisikad* route.

For the future, Joramae hoped to get a more stable job. "I would like to be able to work at (the mall) as a cashier, even if only like that." She reflected on how suddenly her life and freedom had changed. "It was so different when I was single than now. Now I have many priorities plus I have to think about many things. Now, I have to order my life so that we can eat three times a day. My obligations now are different."

Joramae is Badjao in origin, although her family has settled in Davao permanently. Badjao are known to be poor, transient, and are looked down upon socially. The social worker and I had a discussion with Joramae and her father, who owned the small wooden house by the sea, about their community. They had no running water and would fetch it daily, but their electricity was paid for by Korean Christian organisations who have also helped set up livelihood projects for Badjao groups. Joramae's father noted the improvements in many people's lives such as fishing from boats they had received, and peddling shoes and bags. "They have improved. They have cleaned up. They are not so dirty that you are squeamish to go near."

Joramae's sister Pia was still finishing high school. She hoped to travel, to work, and to help her family as well as the government organisation that supported them. Pia had also stayed a short time in the women's shelter, and enjoyed the experience but also felt bad for some of the women who were in difficult circumstances. She dreamed to work as a flight attendant then return to the Philippines, buy a house, marry and raise a family. She wanted to run a business with her husband, and to have a nice house that would be well maintained. "If I have a house, I want it to be clean." Pia described her dream job: "I want to travel abroad. I want to work as a flight attendant, and go everywhere. Anywhere."

3.11 Choice, coercion, agency

Much of the Western literature on sexual labour and sex trafficking focuses on the distinctions between voluntary or forced sexual labour, and the role of agency.[3(p. 41),45,76(p. 61)] However, scholars working in other contexts have argued that this is a false dichotomy based on Western notions of the individual, which overlooks perspectives from the developing world, and the complex and multiple paths to sexual labour which are not reducible to questions of personal choice alone.[3,45,77] Indeed, in the Philippines, women who entered the sex industry through trafficking are often difficult to distinguish from their "voluntary" co-workers.[47(p. 162),56,66] In these three stories, we can see that neither entering or exiting sexual labour was solely a question of choice, force, or coercion, but a combination of individual and structural factors and pressures.

Labour and exploitation   103

In many locations worldwide, gendered structural violence including poverty, prescribed and limited social roles, inaccessibility of services, racial or other social marginalisation, and violence, have contributed to situations where commercial sex is among the few feasible options available.[44(pp. 225,236),78(p. 187),79] Further to this, sexual labourers have also been identified as bearing additional forms of structural violence in exclusion through stigma, marginalisation, and lack of legal protection.[76,79,80] However, beyond the global continuities, the labour conditions in Mindanao create a unique setting where there are multiple personal and "structural conditions shaping the uneven distribution of agency, subordination, and job satisfaction" as well as employment options for women in the Philippines.[45(p. 215)] Personal agency, choice, coercion, necessity, social context, and relationships all affected these women's paths in intertwining, fluid, and ever-changing proportions over time and through navigating both the exceptional and the ordinary.

In considering human trafficking, choice, and agency, it is the available options as perceived that shape actions. Erica experienced her life at times as chaotic as she navigated the conflicting pressures on her life. She went out to work to earn money for her family, but it was also an escape from abuse and poverty. Erica's life as a young person reveals an increasing trajectory towards insecurity in the financial, social, and relational aspects of her life. When Erica was trafficked into the sex industry, she was personally at a point where there seemed to be few options available to her. Crystal was in a similar position and remaining at home was neither appealing nor financially stable. Both Joramae and Crystal found that as mothers, they had few options that were sufficient or available to provide for their children. Human trafficking has been linked with gendered inequality and the feminisation of poverty, where women have unequal "local access to sustainable livelihoods," and gender-based forms of structural violence that compound the experience of poverty and unemployment.[3(p. 38),80(p. 187)] However, within these constrained circumstances, each young woman made choices to try to find work elsewhere as the known situations were not sufficient. Crystal and Erica left their homes and bore the risk of further, unknown violence in response to the known violences of poverty, abuse, and discrimination.

These stories illustrate some of the issues in defining both age and agency in terms of sexual labour and coercion. Joramae, for example, expressed more control in having chosen sexual labour at about age sixteen than Crystal did at 24 in accepting a second bar position because she felt she had no other options. Crystal saw little difference between being forced and tricked into sexual labour as a fifteen-year-old and having to return later due to hardship, although this also drew on her earlier experiences. Erica and Crystal both acknowledged that their young age was part of the vulnerability as well as trauma in their experiences of trafficking. Joramae's story

104 *Labour and exploitation*

is clearly very different from Erica and Crystal's forced entries to sexual labour; legally, however, there is little distinction. Indeed, the events that led to the designation of Joramae as having been trafficked – having been transported and engaged in underage sexual labour – were described as also having been a lot of fun for Joramae and Julia, and a rare experience of abundant shopping and holidaying. Gardening, although useful, is unlikely to provide these experiences, and there are few, if any jobs domestically, where Joramae will ever earn what she did in sexual labour.

Erica and Crystal's stories indicate that the factors that maintained conditions of exploitation (caused initially by a person or group exploiting another) are complex combinations of individual choice and agency, and social factors far beyond as well as within the employment relationships. Beyond her initial introduction to erotic dancing and sexual labour, Erica was able to walk out of the club and in theory could have moved away, gone home, found other work, or anything else; her experience, however, also included other factors which severely limited her ability to do this. Joramae, Crystal, and Erica's voluntary experiences were all constrained by necessity and lack of options, but hardship does not eclipse the role of agency in evaluating and choosing among the limited options available for survival. Seeing the complexity, social positionality and meanings, and personal agency does not negate recognising the unequal position of women in society, but emphasises the complex and particular context that women navigate in sexual labours. Sexual labourlike other forms of commodification and consumption can be read in more complex ways than simply as a confirmation of male domination... it can be understood as a place of agency where the sex worker makes active use of the existing social order.[81(pp. 29–30)]

Indeed, choosing sexual labour at a young age is one of the points in Joramae's story where she exhibited the most agency and autonomy; leaving trafficking undermined it in multiple ways. Many women trafficked into the sex industry frequently choose to either remain or return even when they have the option of leaving, often from a lack of other economic alternatives, as Crystal did.[61,66] In this way, women like Erica and Crystal have turned their experiences into opportunities that would serve them; these choices, however, were also constrained by other social factors including the stigma attached to commercial sex.

Particularly in this marginalised and moralised industry, for both Erica and Crystal to genuinely leave and pursue new directions required a large amount of effort in constructing new identities, over time and based on relationships. Erica acknowledged that as a non-virgin she was already somehow morally tarnished socially, but she still contrasted this identity with the practice of sexual labour that she was being forced to undertake and the resulting "moral injury," as discussed in Chapter 2. The position of sexual labourers in society as "bad" may be intended to deter some from embarking on this path, but also makes it difficult for people to transition out of it

Labour and exploitation 105

as a result. In the context of conscripting underage soldiers, Wessells[73(p. 94)] commented:

> Rape is a powerful means of subjugation since it profoundly violates girls' sense of safety and bodily integrity and can lead girls to see themselves as impure and damaged. Rape also casts a large stigma on the survivors, who may be shunned or otherwise treated badly by others, including people from whom they need support.

This is often true in the Philippines where sex and sexual labour is heavily moralised and stigmatised, and particularly so, when rape or forced sexual labour is the entry to the sex industry. Indeed, "bad" is part of how the *Mama-san* street worker I knew described her job to me – "I am the manager for the bad girls." Once the women had internalised and accepted on some level that they were outside of legitimate society, it created a chasm between their work, relationships, and position in society and the rest of "good" society and work. Moral injury goes beyond the internal trauma and sense of self to an injury of the moral social identity.

Relationships were significant throughout these women's stories. Erica liked dancing and enjoyed her relationships with the other women at the club, and she also formed relationships with men over this time. Erica and Crystal found that financially dependent relationships with men they met at the clubs allowed them to exit that lifestyle, at least for a time. However, both expressed a combination of financial reliance and their own choices in forming these relationships. Like other Filipinas who had been trafficked into the sex industry, the women initially left home to pursue work because of their relational responsibilities and hopes for their families.[61(p. 125)] Both experienced various forms of hardship and rejection from their families; however, both ultimately ended up willingly and happily supporting the same family members. Joramae began commercial sexual labour for the sake of her baby; now, she is highly dependent on other family members, and her relationships are positive but financially uncertain. In Erica and Crystal's lives, long-term and involved relationships were key to being able to leave the sex industry many years after having been trafficked. Relationships enabled identity shifts as the women became part of different communities, began to pursue their educations, and saw themselves in other roles and identities. Crystal found that as she became involved with women's and sexual labourers' activist groups, she was presented with ideas about womanhood and women's rights that profoundly altered her sense of self, and subsequently, the way she acted in the world.

A common question in the literature is, what do trafficked persons as well as sexual labourers need – is it rescuing or something else? Perhaps at the very beginning when they were forced into sexual labour Erica and Crystal might have benefitted from rescue; beyond this, what they needed was significantly more complicated. Brennan[82(pp. 493–494)] described how after exiting

106 *Labour and exploitation*

trafficking, with no social networks or significant skills, formerly trafficked people in the USA often remained in extreme poverty and precarious labour, while anti-trafficking GOs and NGOs would most often discuss the emotional and psychological needs after exiting trafficking. Brennan[82(p. 490)] described decision-making and planning for the future as central to rebuilding a life after trafficking, but this was difficult when basic needs were not being met.

There is a clear contrast between Pia's long-term planning and Joramae's focus on immediate, day-to-day needs. Joramae had immediately adopted the cultural role of sacrificial mother, and she compared the freedom she had when she was *single* rather than before motherhood. I cannot help but see the deeply ingrained gender norms as a limiting form of structural/symbolic violence, where at age seventeen, Joramae had mostly abandoned her ambitions for her own life – and where her "rescue" had not given her a stable path for the future. Erica and Crystal, in contrast, had renewed hopes and plans despite their significant family responsibilities over the years – supported by long-term relationships, they had chosen and navigated their own paths forward. These women's paths reveal complex interplay between choice, coercion, and agency at every stage. Agency is closely related to a sense of temporality, and to the sense of hope that links present agency with future direction.

3.12 Structural violence, labour, and gender

As is evident in these stories, human trafficking is often closely connected to other events in a person's life history that led to their vulnerability to exploitation – poverty, lack of education, abuse. What is often not discussed is how it can also be related to the subsequent events and choices that a person faces. For Erica, the point of trafficking as an entry into sexual labour turned out to be – financially speaking – a success for her. But it also set a chain of events in motion that she had not intended, and she had to find new ways to deal with life and make choices within this situation. Like Erica, Crystal turned to drugs and alcohol to endure the forced sexual labour, but once she was addicted it became even more difficult to leave or even imagine alternatives. For them, drug use corresponded to Coy's[83(p. 112)] findings with British sexual labourers as a "dissociative mechanism that begins as an emotional survival strategy." Crystal chose marriage as a way out of the sex industry, but after having spent her teen years there, she had no education or marketable skills which could have sustained her after her husband vanished. The compounding effects of the trafficking experiences continued to affect people's life paths.

The real-life context and experience of voluntary sexual labourers in the Philippines is far more complex than its legal or illegal status, and is significantly shaped by gender-based inequalities and socio-economic conditions. In the Philippines context, there is no way to know whether legalised commercial sex would have benefitted Erica and Crystal either long-term or in

Labour and exploitation 107

escaping initially, or whether it would have enabled those who trafficked them. The context for sexual labour, coercion, power relations, and sex trafficking is not limited to the law. A case where human trafficking of minors into sexual labour was successfully prosecuted in the Philippines raises further questions about power structures and accountability: a young woman was charged for recruiting others to a private club for sexual labour, but no charges were brought against the business owners who had directed her and most likely hired her initially as a minor and therefore made her, under legal definitions, a trafficking victim herself.[44] The law did not address the power structures that maintain the marginalisation of sexual labourers, and in this case, the State's operation reinforced and compounded them.

As has been observed in Manila, women trafficked into the sex industry worked alongside others who had entered voluntarily, suggesting both the prevalence of human trafficking and the invisibility of even voluntary sexual labourers in the Philippines.[66,71] The violences and risks associated with sexual labour in the Philippines include the abuses and non-payment of clients, the control or abuse of managers, the continuums of control, force, and coercion that lead to women and men entering or continuing in sexual labour out of force or necessity, as well as the social marginalisation in the wider community.[56,71,84] Sexual labourers in the Philippines who were initially trafficked have demonstrably worse health outcomes than those not trafficked;[57,66] violence is compounding, and they have begun with more violence against their life and person. "Why doesn't she just leave" is often implicitly asked of women in this industry who say they would prefer not to be there – as did all of the street workers that I met – but this question assumes there are other options, there is somewhere they could go where this type of work would not be necessary for survival.[67]

Joramae's story complicates the idea of rescue as the solution to underage sexual labour (generally considered trafficking under legal definitions). The social workers had taken Joramae from the world of sexual labour, with justifiable rationale according to her young age, but in doing so they have taken away her livelihood without providing a viable alternative. Her partner's work as a *trisikad* driver is minimal and can fluctuate; Joramae and the baby are again primarily dependent upon her husband's and father's abilities to provide for them. Sex workers rights groups have argued that the criminalisation and removal of their livelihood is a form of oppression.[85(p. 5)] At the same time, sexual labour can be a dangerous and volatile profession, and the older street-based women that I met were finding it more and more difficult to make a living[xviii]; without other skills to fall back on, the future did not seem bright. Like domestic labour, sexual labour does not provide career progression or skill development[52]; in fact, the opposite can be true as these intimate labours are highly dependent on youth, and over time workers' labour often becomes less rather than more valuable.

The women's stories presented in this chapter challenge the dominant anti-trafficking narrative of "rescue, rehabilitation, reintegration" and

108　*Labour and exploitation*

similar variations. Joramae was most clearly rescued, but while the experience was positive and supportive, it has not "rescued" her from the financial constraints and lack of options that initially supported her decision to undertake sexual labour. Erica and Crystal, in contrast, were given support from NGOs that did not remove them from their environments, but offered long-term, relationship-based support, and realistic additional choices.

Women's inequality, in terms of physical violence, economics, and social position, is a form of structural violence that is multifaceted but ubiquitous on a global scale.[47,67,79,80] The Philippines context shares the unequal position of women within society but configured according to its unique culture and history, including labour conditions. As Anderson[86(p. 61)] found with women who sold sex in Malawi, despite deep inequality, "injustice is not experienced passively." The women I met navigated the constraints and obstacles to achieve their own aims, even in situations of exploitation. Many[xix] found sexual labour to be an unrivalled opportunity to succeed financially and support their families. However, most voluntary and formerly trafficked sexual labourers I met expressed the same desire – an economically and practically viable alternative that would allow them to provide for their families. As yet, labour opportunities, particularly for women, and even more so for women without tertiary education, are not sufficient to displace sexual labour as a uniquely lucrative option, even as it is an option that directs the structural violence of poverty and gender inequality into direct risks of violence, social exclusion, and future hardship.

3.13　Conclusions

Work in the Philippines is highly precarious, not only in its uncertain duration but also in the exposure of workers to financial and physical risks. Unemployment, underemployment, and high levels of poverty constrain workers to accept and endure the work that is available; the inadequacy of labour standards enforcement allows employers to set their own conditions and stipulations without consequence when they exploit their workers. Participation in the informal economy is a necessary strategy for survival, but informal labour relationships can also hide abuse, exploitation, and child labour. The significant control exerted by employers is a form of structural violence in itself, and it is also a secondary structural violence in terms of preventing the wider social constraints from affecting employees' labour through further controls. Structural violence is thus compounding in the experience of labour, in that it comes from multiple sources which increase its effects, and that the risks that it creates are directed back to individuals in employment relationships and working conditions.

Gendered poverty and gendered unemployment are both forms of structural violence that affect women's entry into sexual labour; they also contribute to the vulnerability to trafficking for sexual labour where women, particularly young women, have limited and risky options by which to fulfil

Labour and exploitation 109

their familial obligations. The illegality of sexual labour and treatment of workers are often experienced as forms of structural violence from the state, and more so in parts of the Philippines where the law is abused by corrupt officials to extort and control sexual labourers. Coerced and forced sexual labour is supported by gender inequality and limitations for women's labour opportunities, as well as the stigma and marginalisation of women once involved. The violence that these women experienced went beyond the trafficking events, as structural violences created vulnerability and blocked escape.

Current economic configurations do not present rural labour migrants with sufficient opportunities for them to pass up dubious recruitment offers, despite the accompanying risks of exploitation and abuse. Domestic labour trafficking emerges from the same context where employers are enabled to wield a great deal of control over their workers with little government intervention. Migration is a strategy to escape the uncertainty and unemployment in the Philippines, but it has become a self-perpetuating necessity as the reliance on migration for economic development has stalled the expansion of the domestic economy and local jobs.[4(p. 114)] Migration, and the corresponding potential for trafficking and abuse of migrants, is also significantly shaped by the local employment situation. The lack of decent jobs is experienced as violence which pushes people towards risky or undesirable options, both in the Philippines and overseas. The following chapter begins by exploring the movement from the urban Philippines to overseas locations as the context for experiences of trafficking or exploitation among migrants.

Notes

i   Interview was conducted in Cebuano; this phrasing "*lisod...*" is presented as spoken to retain the repetitive emphasis.

ii   All currency conversions are correct at the time of publication; however, they are often rounded figures.

iii See Section 7 for discussion of this term.

iv   I was unable to find more recent comparable data; most of the PSA's poverty and income measures are based on family income, which obscures the individual incomes of family members.[5]

v   The statistics Ofreneo cites suggest that up to 77% of employed workers are also involved in the informal economy as of 2006; the statistics I located from the PSA are comparable, but list one fewer category which likely accounts for the discrepancy between the figures. I have used Ofreneo's method of calculation, which includes "unpaid family workers" (8.6%), self-employed (27.6%), and running a family business or farm (3.2%), as well as the underemployed (18%) who are presumably currently relying on relational or informal economic strategies, for a total of 57.4%.[7,9]

vi   The Visayas is the neighbouring region to Mindanao, which shares a common first language. Cebuano and Visayan are among the many terms which refer to the primary language of the southern Philippines.

vii For example, I heard a radio advertisement for male and female security guards requiring that females were at least 5'0 (152 cm) tall and males 5'6 (167 cm).

110 *Labour and exploitation*

viii See Chapter 4, Section 8 for further discussion of this word.

ix National Bureau of Investigation.

x High school equivalency program that could be completed extramurally.

xi The discussion of structural violence in this section is not intended to eclipse the role of agency, choice, hope, and resilience in Melissa, Gabriel, and Don-Don's stories, but to set the backdrop of economic conditions. See Chapter 6 which explores the relationship between agency and structure in participants' lives.

xii See Chapter 1, Section 3 for an overview of the human trafficking situation in the Philippines.

xiii Ninety five percent sex trafficking and 7% labour trafficking, indicating that some cases spanned both; also, note that some cases had multiple victims/perpetrators. 54% of all victims were minors.[46]

xiv Lower wages do in part reflect the expectation of included room and board. For domestic employees in 2011, the average weekly working hours were 52 for "private home workers" but 66 for live in domestic workers.[51] The average working day was 10.3 hours, and almost 80% (78.1) worked 9 hours or more (9.8% 13–16 hours/day; 68.3% 9–12 hours/day).[51] Almost a third of live in female domestic workers (32%) normally work at least 11 hours/day.[49]

xv See Chapter 2, Section 5 for a discussion of childhood and age as a factor in defining human trafficking.

xvi From the root word *kulata*; see Chapter 4, Section 8 for further discussions of this term.

xvii Older sister, a term of respect.

xviii See Susan's story for further discussion; Susan is a street-based sexual labourer in her forties who has been working in this industry for many years.

xix As above, younger women found sexual labour more lucrative than women over about age 40.

References

1 Bettio, F., Della Giusta, M., & Di Tommaso, M. (2017). Sex work and trafficking: Moving beyond dichotomies. *Feminist Economics, 23*(3), 1–22. https://doi.org/10.1080/13545701.2017.1330547

2 Efrat, A. (2016). Global efforts against human trafficking: The misguided conflation of sex, labor, and organ trafficking. *International Studies Perspectives, 17*(1), 34–54. https://doi.org/10.1111/insp.12097

3 Turner, J. (2012). Means of delivery: The trafficking of women into prostitution, harms and human rights discourse. In M. Coy (Ed.), *Prostitution, harm and gender inequality: Theory, research and policy* (pp. 33–52). Ashgate.

4 Ofreneo, R. (2015). Growth and employment in de-industrializing Philippines. *Journal of the Asia Pacific Economy, 20*(1), 111–129. https://doi.org/10.1080/13547 860.2014.974335

5 PSA. (2016). *Poverty incidence among Filipinos registered at 26.3%, as of first semester of 2015* (No. 2016–318). Philippine Statistics Authority. https://psa.gov.ph/content/poverty-incidence-among-filipinos-registered-263-first-semester-2015-psa

6 Dy-Liacco, G. (2014). *Extreme poverty in the Philippines*. USAID. https://www.usaid.gov/frontiers/2014/publication/section-1-extreme-poverty-philippines

7 PSA. (2017). *Employment situation in October 2016 (Final Results)* (No. 2017–114). Philippine Statistics Authority. https://psa.gov.ph/content/employment-situation-october-2016-final-results

Labour and exploitation   111

8 PSA. (2017). *Philippines in figures 2016*. Philippine Statistics Authority. https://psa.gov.ph/sites/default/files/PIF%202016.pdf

9 Edralin, D. (2016). Good work through decent work: Practises of sixteen unionized firms in the Philippines. *DLSU Business & Economics Review, 26*(1), 1–16.

10 Clark, E. (2014). Anthropological theories of low-wage work. *Journal of Human Behavior in the Social Environment, 24*(1), 26–37. https://doi.org/10.1080/10911359.2014.844599

11 McKay, D. (2009). Performing economy differently: Exploring economic personhood and local economic diversity. *The Australian Journal of Anthropology, 20*(3), 330–346.

12 Milgram, B. (2014). Remapping the edge: Informality and legality in the Harrison Road night market, Baguio City, Philippines. *City & Society, 26*(2), 153–174. https://doi.org/10.1111/ciso.12038

13 Luu, K., Brubacher, L. J., Lau, L. L., Liu, J. A., & Dodd, W. (2022). Exploring the role of social networks in facilitating health service access among low-income women in the Philippines: A qualitative study. *Health Services Insights, 15*, 117863292110689. https://doi.org/10.1177/11786329211068916

14 Badilla, N. (2016, May 15). 200,000 registered nurses are jobless. *The Manila Times*. http://www.manilatimes.net/200000-registered-nurses-are-jobless/262211/

15 PSA. (2016). *Women and men in the Philippines 2016 statistical handbook*. Philippine Statistics Authority. https://psa.gov.ph/sites/default/files/kmcd/WAM%20Women%20and%20Men%20Handbook%20in%20the%20Philippines%202016.%20Final.pdf

16 DOLE. (2011). *The Philippine labor & employment plan 2011 – 2016: Inclusive growth through decent and productive work*. Department of Labor and Employment. https://www.dole.gov.ph/fndr/bong/files/PLEP-26%20April%20version.pdf

17 DOLE. (2013). *Labor codes of the Philippines*. Department of Labor and Employment. https://www.dole.gov.ph/labor_codes

18 Hutchison, J. (2016). The state and employment relations in the Philippines. *Journal of Industrial Relations, 58*(2), 183–198. https://doi.org/10.1177/0022185615617958

19 Bersamin, J. (2015). Radio Mindanao Network, Inc. V. Michael Maximo R. Amurao III. *UST Law Review, LIX*(1).

20 Mendoza, J. (2013). Benigno M. Vigilla, et al. V. Philippine College of Criminology, et al. *UST Law Review, LVIII*(1).

21 Yap, D., & Melchor, M. (2015). Beyond parity in education: Gender disparities in labour and employment outcomes in the Philippines. *Journal of Asian Public Policy, 8*(3), 276–296. https://doi.org/10.1080/17516234.2015.1050752

22 San Beda. (2017). *Admissions—College of nursing: Admission policies*. San Beda College, Manila. http://www.sanbeda.edu.ph/admissions.php#undergraduate

23 Bitonio, B. (2008). *Labour market governance in the Philippines: Issues and institutions* (ILO Asia-Pacific Working Paper Series) [ILO Asia-Pacific Working Paper Series]. International Labour Organisation.

24 Gonzaga, E. (2009). *Globalization and becoming-nation: Subjectivity, nationhood, and narrative in the period of global capitalism*. University of the Philippines Press.

25 Oabel, P. (2015). Last of the labour aristocrats: Restructuring of the Philippine sugar industry and the exportist labour market. *Journal of Contemporary Asia, 45*(2), 195–218. https://doi.org/10.1080/00472336.2014.953193

112 *Labour and exploitation*

26 Ofreneo, R. (2013). Precarious Philippines: Expanding informal sector, "flexibilizing" labor market. *American Behavioral Scientist, 57*(4), 420–443. https://doi.org/10.1177/0002764212466237

27 Sale, J., & Sale, A. (2014). Changes in Philippine labour relations policy: Convergence or divergence of productivity, flexibility and welfare? *The Economic and Labour Relations Review, 25*(2), 327–352. https://doi.org//10.1177/1035304614537173

28 Portus, A., & Martinez, I. (2015). Identifying characteristics of jobs of front-line personnel that affect abnormal idle time: A case study on a popular amusement center in the Philippines. *Procedia Manufacturing, 3*, 3463–3469. https://doi.org/10.1016/j.promfg.2015.07.574

29 Seki, K. (2015). Capitalizing on desire: Reconfiguring 'the social' and the government of poverty in the Philippines. *Development and Change, 46*(6), 1253–1276.

30 Farmer, P. (2004). An anthropology of structural violence. *Current Anthropology, 45*(3), 305–325. https://doi.org/10.1086/382250

31 Vogt, W. (2013). Crossing Mexico: Structural violence and the commodification of undocumented Central American migrants. *American Ethnologist, 40*(4), 764–780. https://doi.org/10.1111/amet.12053

32 Kodoth, P. (2016). Structural violence against emigrant domestic workers and survival in the Middle East: The effects of Indian emigration policy. *Journal of Interdisciplinary Economics, 28*(1), 83–106. https://doi.org/10.1177/0260107915609824

33 McKay, S. (2006). *Satanic mills or silicon islands?: The politics of high-tech production in the Philippines.* Cornell University Press.

34 Oh, Y. (2016). Oligarchic rule and best practice migration management: The political economy origins of labour migration regime of the Philippines. *Contemporary Politics, 22*(2), 197–214. https://doi.org/10.1080/13569775.2016.1153286

35 Tremlett, P. (2012). Two shock doctrines: From Christo-disciplinary to neoliberal urbanisms in the Philippines. *Culture and Religion, 13*(4), 405–423. https://doi.org/10.1080/14755610.2012.728139

36 Velayo, R. (2005). A perspective on child abuse in the Philippines. In F. Denmark, H. Krauss, R. Wesner, E. Midlarsky, & U. Gielen (Eds.), *Violence in schools* (pp. 191–205). Springer-Verlag.

37 Parreñas, R. (2011). *Illicit flirtations: Labor, migration, and sex trafficking in Tokyo.* Stanford University Press.

38 Benson, P. (2008). El campo: Faciality and structural violence in farm labor camps. *Cultural Anthropology, 23*(4), 589–629. https://doi.org/10.1111/j.1548-1360.2008.00020.x

39 Rutten, R. (2007). Losing face in Philippine labor confrontations: How shame may inhibit worker activism. In L. Joseph, M. Mahler, & J. Auyero (Eds.), *New perspectives in political ethnography* (pp. 37–59). Springer.

40 Teng-Calleja, M., Baquiano, M., & Montiel, C. (2015). From "good day" to "sign here": Norms shaping negotiations within a face culture. *Negotiation and Conflict Management Research, 8*(4), 228–242. https://doi.org/10.34891/9tye-3882

41 Aligan, R. (2016). God and the concept of death and suffering in the Philippine context. *Catholic Theology and Thought, 77*(Summer 2016), 66–97.

42 Scheper-Hughes, N. (2006). Dangerous and endangered youth: Social structures and determinants of violence. *Annals of the New York Academy of Sciences, 1036*(1), 13–46. https://doi.org/10.1196/annals.1330.002

Labour and exploitation 113

43 Hilsdon, A. (2007). Transnationalism and agency in East Malaysia: Filipina migrants in the nightlife industries. *The Australian Journal of Anthropology, 18*(2), 172–193. https://doi.org/10.1111/j.1835-9310.2007.tb00087.x

44 Chapman, L. (2017). "Just being real": A post-colonial critique on Amerasian engagement in Central Luzon's sex industry. *Asian Journal of Women's Studies, 23*(2), 224–242. https://doi.org/10.1080/12259276.2017.1317917

45 Weitzer, R. (2009). Sociology of sex work. *Annual Review of Sociology, 35*(1), 213–234. https://doi.org/10.1146/annurev-soc-070308-120025

46 Visayan Forum. (2016). *Facts & figures.* Visayan Forum Foundation. http://visayanforum.org/facts-figures/

47 Samarasinghe, V. (2008). *Female sex trafficking in Asia: The resilience of patriarchy in a changing world.* Routledge.

48 Lim, J. (2000). The effects of the East Asian crisis on the employment of women and men: The Philippine case. *World Development, 28*(7), 1285–1306. https://doi.org/10.1016/S0305-750X(00)00023-1

49 ILO. (2011). *Domestic workers in the Philippines: Profile and working conditions.* International Labour Organisation. http://www.ilo.org/wcmsp5/groups/public/@ed_protect/@protrav/@travail/documents/publication/wcms_167021.pdf

50 Boris, E., & Parreñas, R. (Eds.). (2010). *Intimate labors: Cultures, technologies, and the politics of care.* Stanford Social Sciences.

51 BLES. (2011). *Profile of persons employed in private households.* LABSTAT Updates, *15*(27). Bureau of Labor and Employment Statistics. https://psa.gov.ph/sites/default/files/vol15_27.pdf

52 Pacis, R. (2009). *Consolidation of island-wide consultations on decent work agenda for domestic workers in the Philippines.* Visayan Forum Foundation.

53 PSA. (2017). *Minimum wage rates by sector and region, Philippines: As of January 6, 2017* (Table 21; pp. 29–35). Philippine Statistics Authority. https://psa.gov.ph/sites/default/files/attachments/cls/Tab21_2.pdf

54 Parreñas, R. (2008). *The force of domesticity: Filipina migrants and globalization.* New York University Press.

55 Boris, E., Gilmore, S., & Parreñas, R. (2010). Sexual labors: Interdisciplinary perspectives toward sex as work. *Sexualities, 13*(2), 131–137. https://doi.org/10.1177/1363460709359228

56 Bagley, C., Madrid, S., & Simkhada, P. (2017). Adolescent girls offered alternatives to commercial sexual exploitation: A case study from the Philippines. *Dignity: A Journal on Sexual Exploitation and Violence, 2*(2). https://doi.org/10.23860/dignity.2017.02.02.08

57 Urada, L., Silverman, J., Tsai, L., & Morisky, D. (2014). Underage youth trading sex in the Philippines: Trafficking and HIV risk. *AIDS Care, 26*(12), 1586–1591. https://doi.org/10.1080/09540121.2014.936818

58 West, C. (2014). *The migration-trafficking nexus: An investigation into the survival strategies of the Philippines' poorest migrants.* [MA Thesis, Massey University]. http://mro.massey.ac.nz/handle/10179/7263

59 Urada, L., & Simmons, J. (2014). A collaborative methodology for investigating the ethical conduct of research on female sex workers in the Philippines. *Journal of Empirical Research on Human Research Ethics, 9*(1), 41–45. https://doi.org/10.1525/jer.2014.9.1.41

114   *Labour and exploitation*

60 Thrupkaew, N. (2009, October 26). Beyond rescue: The campaign against forced prostitution works when it addresses the needs of victims. *The Nation*. https://www.thenation.com/article/beyond-rescue/

61 Erpelo, M. (1998). Eight women, one story: A synthesis. In D. Jose & M. Erpelo (Eds.), *Halfway through the circle: The lives of eight Filipino women survivors of prostitution and trafficking* (pp. 123–132). Women's Education, Development, Productivity and Research Organization.

62 Mathews, P. (2017). Cam models, sex work, and job immobility in the Philippines. *Feminist Economics, 23*(3), 160–183. https://doi.org/10.1080/13545701.2017.1293835

63 Jose, D., & Erpelo, M. (Eds.). (1998). *Halfway through the circle: The lives of eight Filipino women survivors of prostitution and trafficking*. Women's Education, Development, Productivity and Research Organization.

64 Tsai, L. (2017). Family financial roles assumed by sex trafficking survivors upon community re-entry: Findings from a financial diaries study in the Philippines. *Journal of Human Behavior in the Social Environment, 27*(4), 334–345. https://doi.org/10.1080/10911359.2017.1288193

65 Chiao, C., Morisky, D., Rosenberg, R., Ksobiech, K., & Malow, R. (2006). The relationship between HIV sexually transmitted infection risk and alcohol use during commercial sex episodes: Results from the study of female commercial sex workers in the Philippines. *Substance Use & Misuse, 41*(10–12), 1509–1533. https://doi.org/10.1080/10826080600846284

66 Urada, L., Halterman, S., Raj, A., Tsuyuki, K., Pimentel-Simbulan, N., & Silverman, J. (2016). Socio-structural and behavioral risk factors associated with trafficked history of female bar/spa entertainers in the sex trade in the Philippines. *International Journal of Gynecology & Obstetrics, 132*(1), 55–59. https://doi.org/10.1016/j.ijgo.2015.07.004

67 Price, J. (2012). *Structural violence: Hidden brutality in the lives of women*. State University of New York Press.

68 Gill, M. (2017). Improving health outcomes in trafficking survivors through core skills development in the workplace: Experience from the Philippines. *Dignity: A Journal on Sexual Exploitation and Violence, 2*(2). https://doi.org/10.23860/dignity.2017.02.02.02

69 Perkins, E., & Ruiz, C. (2017). Domestic minor sex trafficking in a rural state: Interviews with adjudicated female juveniles. *Child and Adolescent Social Work Journal, 34*(2), 171–180. https://doi.org/10.1007/S10560-016-0455-3

70 Holmes, O. (2016, May 31). How child sexual abuse became a family business in the Philippines. *The Guardian*. https://www.theguardian.com/world/2016/may/31/live-streaming-child-sex-abuse-family-business-philippines.

71 Wiss, R. (2012). 'No minors allowed': Outsider bar-girls and trafficking in a Philippines sex tourism industry. In U. Eickelkamp (Ed.), *Online proceedings of the symposium 'Young Lives, Changing Times: Perspectives on social reproduction,' University of Sydney 8 – 9 June 2011*. University of Sydney. https://www.researchgate.net/publication/308071138_'No_Minors_Allowed'_Outsider_Bar-girls_and_Trafficking_in_a_Philippines_Sex_Tourism_Industry

72 Swart, M., & Hassen, S. (2016). A comparison between the position of child marriage "victims" and child soldiers: Towards a nuanced approach. *African Human Rights Law Journal, 16*(2), 458–475. https://doi.org/10.17159/1996-2096/2016/v16n2a7

Labour and exploitation 115

73 Wessells, M. (2006). *Child soldiers: From violence to protection.* Harvard University Press.
74 Piscitelli, A. (2016). Sexual economies, love and human trafficking – new conceptual issues. *Cadernos Pagu, 47.* https://doi.org/10.1590/18094449201600470005
75 David, E. (2015). The sexual fields of empire: On the ethnosexual frontiers of global outsourcing. *Radical History Review, 2015*(123), 115–143. https://doi.org/10.1215/01636545-3088180
76 Walker, R. (2017). Selling sex, mothering and 'keeping well' in the city: Reflecting on the everyday experiences of cross-border migrant women who sell sex in Johannesburg. *Urban Forum, 28*(1), 59–73. https://doi.org/10.1007/s12132-016-9284-x
77 Schwarz, C., Kennedy, E., & Britton, H. (2017). Aligned across difference: Structural injustice, sex work, and human trafficking. *Feminist Formations, 29*(2), 1–25. https://doi.org/10.1353/ff.2017.0014
78 Beckerleg, S., & Hundt, G. (2005). Women heroin users: Exploring the limitations of the structural violence approach. *International Journal of Drug Policy, 16*(3), 183–190. https://doi.org/:10.1016/j.drugpo.2005.03.002
79 Khan, S., Lorway, R., Chevrier, C., Dutta, S., Ramanaik, S., Roy, A., Bhattacharjee, P., Mishra, S., Moses, S., Blanchard, J., & Becker, M. (2017). Dutiful daughters: HIV/AIDS, moral pragmatics, female citizenship and structural violence among Devadasis in northern Karnataka, India. *Global Public Health,* 1–16. https://doi.org/10.1080/17441692.2017.1280070
80 Basnyat, I. (2017). Structural violence in health care: Lived experience of street-based female commercial sex workers in Kathmandu. *Qualitative Health Research, 27*(2), 191–203. https://doi.org/10.1177/1049732315601665
81 Chapkis, W. (1997). *Live sex acts: Women performing erotic labor.* Routledge.
82 Brennan, D. (2017). Fighting human trafficking today: Moral panics, zombie data, and the seduction of rescue. *Wake Forest Law Review, 52*(2017), 477–496.
83 Coy, M. (2012). "I am a person too": Women's accounts and images about body and self in prostitution. In M. Coy (Ed.), *Prostitution, harm and gender inequality: Theory, research and policy* (pp. 103–120). Ashgate Publishing Limited.
84 Davis, J. D., & Miles, G. M. (2021). "Strive harder and don't lose hope": Sexual exploitation of male youth in the sex trade in Manila. *International Journal of Sociology and Social Policy, 41*(5/6), 689–706. https://doi.org/10.1108/IJSSP-05-2020-0189
85 Saini, A. (2016). What do sex workers need to better control their working conditions? *World Policy Journal, 33*(4), 5.
86 Anderson, E. (2015). *Gender, HIV and risk; navigating structural violence.* Springer.

4 Migration and globalisation
Migrant experience and multiple violences

4.1 Introduction

> "Work overseas the legal way! Take the free Pre-Enrolment Orientation Seminar (PEOS) online!"[1]

I was on my way home from fieldwork, relieved and excited to be reunited with my family after the final two months that I had remained in the Philippines on my own. I started chatting with the man sitting next to me, Sam, a long-term Filipino migrant worker. He was on the first leg of his journey, flying from Davao to Singapore, on his way back to the UK and away from his family. The stress of migration had led to his marriage breaking up years ago, Sam told me, and he returned to the Philippines as often as he could to visit his nearly grown children. Returning to the UK was a difficult and emotional moment for him, and after two months of mothering from afar, I could only begin to imagine the constant feeling of distance between migrants and their loved ones. I told Sam about my research, which included understanding the place of migration in Filipino society. "You want to know about migration?," he replied, "I'll tell you. It tears families apart."

Sam's comments reflected what others had told me about the difficulty of migration, but contradict the image of migration as the epitome of success in the Philippines. Researchers agree that human trafficking is a migration problem, and particularly a problem for low-skilled labour migrants.[2-6] In the Philippines as in other areas, there are also established links between irregular migration facilitated by an agent ("human smuggling") and subsequent trafficking.[7-9] The processes that drive migration also create the possibility of human trafficking.

In the Philippines, migration is commonly seen as a positive strategy to access greater opportunities and diversify family income sources. However, from the angle of human trafficking, any point of mobility also appears as a significant point of risk for deception and abuse. The local labour situation feeds the flow of migrants who do not have access to local jobs, and as the numbers of migrant workers have increased, the domestic labour market growth has declined.[10(p. 388)] The effects of remittances are often

DOI: 10.4324/9781003261049-4

Migration and globalisation   117

Figure 4.1 Migration agents' advertisements around Davao City – "Good life awaits you."

highly visible, particularly in close communities and family groups where everyone's income levels are known.[11(p. 53)] Poverty, unemployment, and low wages are factors beyond people's control. Migration, however, means access to more and better opportunities. Migration, in turn, deprives the nation of many of its workers, particularly skilled workers, who could otherwise contribute to developing the local economy.[12] While unemployment remains high, employers have also reported shortages of skilled workers.[13(p. 1279)] Women in particular experience a lack of jobs domestically, while female care workers are in demand internationally. Migration is a strategic way to access better paid employment and to transfer wealth into the local economy. Migration and migrant labour are also sites where power relationships are acutely felt, and labour migrants have often found that they had few rights in their overseas employment.[14,15] Human trafficking and other forms of abuse and exploitation demonstrate the extreme side of this process that affects many migrants, particularly temporary, unskilled, and irregular labour migrants.

The trafficking of migrants is difficult to measure or define, and it has often been difficult to legally distinguish between contract infringements, migrant abuse, and trafficking. Filipinos are commonly employed in the Middle East, Europe, and other parts of Asia as low-skilled manual labourers.[16] Filipinas in particular migrate in response to the "care gap" where the demand for caregivers including skilled workers such as nurses in the developed world with an aging population exceeds the family, government, and private resources available.[17,18] For some, migration is an opportunity

118   *Migration and globalisation*

to earn foreign currency and send home remittances. However, it can also be a place of abuse, exploitation, and deception, where the accommodation, working conditions, hours, freedom of movement, or payment received do not align to that promised. Migrants, particularly temporary labour migrants, often have different or no access to minimum wage and working condition rights, medical care, and labour laws as compared to citizens.[15(p. 124),19–21] The marginalisation, invisibility, and tenuous legal status of overseas workers on temporary contracts have contributed to the exploitation of migrant workers. The ratio of migrants to trafficked persons is unknown, but evidence from government and NGO reports suggest that the numbers of trafficked or otherwise abused and exploited migrant workers go far beyond those officially documented.[7,22,23]

The experience and prevalence of human trafficking emerges from local systems whose cultures and societies are increasingly affected and shaped by global pressures. On a global level, the Philippines is frequently a source of natural and human resources used by more affluent nations. Locally, call centres, coconut plantations, and fisheries serve the needs of many overseas locations.[24,25] Overseas, Filipino labour migrants are most commonly temporary and unskilled workers, while skilled workers have also found their labour undervalued and underpaid overseas.[26–28] Within the Philippines, offshore companies have been known to take advantage of the Philippines' lack of laws/enforcement around labour standards, such as factories that used short contracts to avoid paying benefits.[29] Reliance on the global market has increased instability of work duration, wage levels, and working conditions, both at home and in migrant labour, built on the reality that every exchange is made through unequal power relations in which the Philippines and Filipino workers are often unfavourably positioned.[15,18,30] The focus on "destination" countries and migration management, and the lack of attention to "source" locations for human trafficking, suggest that global inequality as it is experienced has been considered less important than border security issues. However, the close links, in the Philippines and globally, between migration and human trafficking demand analysis of the processes by which certain populations are made more at risk within international systems.

Human trafficking of migrants is often conceived as the (exploitative) control of migrants. However, imagining a concrete distinction between free, autonomous migrants and those under some kind of control is a false dichotomy. In this chapter, I will describe the ways that human trafficking relates to, mirrors, and extends the controls and restraints that migrants from the Philippines frequently experience. Migrants are willing to run the risks associated with migration, which include human trafficking, because they are pushed to do this by multiple factors beyond their control. From poverty and lack of opportunity for education or jobs, to the pressure to support immediate and wider family, and the government's policies on migration, there are multiple pressures which shape migration decisions

Migration and globalisation 119

and experiences. Migrants are under employers' control to varying degrees; human trafficking can represent the worst end of a spectrum of practices rather than a discrete event or occurrence. The fact that the employers' rights, and the migrant labourer's lack of rights, are often maintained by law suggests that the control in human trafficking and exploitative labour practices can be an extension of the controls exerted by the state.[5]

The "culture of migration" and government policy of migration in the Philippines which codifies migration as the path to success, while legally denying migration to many of those who most desperately need a better financial opportunity, pushes irregular migration as much as it does regular migration. The demand for smugglers and migration agents, both within and outside of official government regulations, is an outcome of the same official processes. Agents offer credit which places migrants in debt and contractual obligation, and even relationships with legal agents can resemble situations of trafficking and debt bondage.

This chapter is an attempt to engage seriously with the proposition enunciated most clearly by O'Connell-Davidson,[5] that if the objection to human trafficking is on the basis of it being a form of control and exploitation, this demands analysis of the other forms of control and exploitation that shape migrants' lives, and how these relate to the controls in trafficking. O'Connell-Davidson[5] suggested that rather than seeing trafficking as slavery, a better metaphor is to compare irregular migrants from developing or conflict-ridden countries with historic escaping slaves who were outside of the law and vulnerable to exploitation. Parreñas,[6,31] similarly, has identified human trafficking of Filipinos as a problem of the lack of migrants' rights, where the law maintains their vulnerability and social exclusion. In the context of structural violence, the multiple "goads" and "fences" at various levels of society represent macro-level coercion and control in the processes of migration. I argue that the structures around the Philippines' labour migration inherently support and contain the possibility of negative outcomes including abuse, exploitation, and human trafficking, as well as less extreme but common outcomes such as failure or exclusion.

4.2 Migration in the Philippines: state control and social norms

The Philippine government's policies on migration, as well as the availability, resources and powers of embassy and consulate services, shape, constrain, and control the experiences and decisions related to migration. Remittances are taxed by the Philippine government, and there are tight controls over who may and may not migrate. "Suspicion of human trafficking" has been used as an excuse to detain travellers, primarily women, who are suspected to be planning to leave the Philippines to work illegally and as such are a danger to themselves in becoming vulnerable to trafficking.[32(p. 132)] Legal migrants must go through the Overseas Workers' Welfare Association

120 *Migration and globalisation*

(OWWA) programs, paying for transport and membership, before securing a job offer prior to leaving. Female domestic workers under age 23, anyone over 45 in most cases, and anyone without proper medical certification as fit to work, as well as an approved job offer through an officially recognised agent, is not permitted to travel for work.[20(p. 37)] The observation that the majority of documented migrants do not come from the poorest households also indicates the effects of restrictions to legal migration.[33(p. 104)]

At the same time, the government continues its dependence on migration and remittances, supports training programs for overseas work such as nursing and seafaring, and legitimates and codifies the desire for better paid work through migration.[34(p. 200)] For those outside of the official programs, this is a contradictory pressure both to migrate and to not migrate – or, to not migrate legally. Despite the multiple legal and practical measures to support migration, the Philippines government has been hesitant to admit the degree to which the economy is dependent on this strategy.[10(p. 388)] Similarly, the government has also denied the link between widespread migration and human trafficking. Success stories are reported and celebrated, overseas Filipino workers (OFWs) lauded as heroes. On the other side, the extreme cases of abuse and human trafficking arouse outrage and sympathy. However, there is little effort to connect the two, or to tell some of the more ordinary stories, of workers who have lost their jobs, been unable to repay their debts, or experienced everyday harassment and discrimination as Filipinos abroad.

Local gender inequalities have been continued and magnified in migration. Migrant mothers in particular have been vilified in the media as abandoning their children and contributing to social problems.[13(p. 1271),35,36] Remittances are shaped by inequality, where women have been found to remit less earnings despite their greater numbers and higher levels of education overall.[37] Available work options have been based on racialised conceptions of gender, such as domestic work and caregiving for Filipinas, and low-level manual labour for Filipino men.[13,17,22,38] Nursing, for example, is a sector which is overwhelmingly female, and one of the Philippines main skilled migrant sectors.[26,27,39] Nursing training includes socialisation to a certain feminised persona and aesthetic, which my friend Wanda, a nurse, described including requirements about both demeanour and physical appearance; for example, anyone not meeting height[40] or physical appearance requirements, such as "to be physically fit (without deformities/abnormalities)"[41] or to not have any tattoos,[42] may be excluded from training and access to these job opportunities.

The rhetoric and practices relating to the human trafficking of migrants have also been heavily shaped by gendered ideas. Men in situations of forced labour may not be recognised where the working definition of human trafficking is thought to include only women. Migrant women have often been conflated with trafficked persons or labelled "vulnerable" and as such subject to further controls by the state, as has happened to Filipinas stopped

Migration and globalisation 121

before boarding their flights.[32] The social pressures and constraints based on gender have been codified to extend gender-based controls in the labour migration experience.

Agents extend and transform the control by the Philippine government, and by government policies overseas, and exert their own controls on migrants. Under Philippine law for safeguarding migrants' welfare, potential labour migrants must have an agent secure an offer of work before they will be permitted to depart[9,34(p. 199)]; see Figures 4.1 and 4.2 for examples of the abundant advertising for migration agents. Agents can complicate the migration process as well as adding costs, but can also offer security within the migration process. Legitimate agents who comply with government requirements, such as registration as a migrant with official support agencies and with the migrant insurance program, and provide ongoing support can fulfil the intentions of the law which requires the use of agents. Legal migration under government or registered independent agents provides many safety nets but can be costly, time consuming, and complicated, and does not guarantee a job offer at the end of the process.[43(p. 186)] Migration through an unofficial agent (smuggler) is faster and cheaper, and often comes with the promise of a job, or can be the fastest way to access a known job opportunity. However, there are few safeguards against human trafficking, abuse, or exploitation including underpayment outside of legal channels.

Even legal agents can leave migrants trapped by their debts and contracts, unable to leave an abusive employer without forfeiting their earnings and unable to repay.[6,7,31] Migrants in this situation can both resemble and not resemble trafficking cases. Migrants may have been deceived as to the type of work or are not free to leave their jobs in cases of abuse or exploitation, but it can be the agent through financial debt and/or the state through the limitations of visa requirements rather than the employer who exerts this control. Agents, whether registered or not, can also perpetuate human trafficking, exploitation or abuse if they do not support workers in exiting these situations to prosecute or find new employment. In irregular migration, the difference between smuggling and trafficking can at times be the payment plan – those extending payment plans have ongoing power over the migrant which can result in debt bondage or human trafficking.[44] The relationship between the agent and the migrant is endorsed by the state as a legal requirement, but not controlled once overseas, and debt bondage in particular is difficult to measure or regulate.

Traffickers have controlled victims through the threat of violence posed by the destination state, if they were to be found as illegal migrants, for example, by taking passports to prevent escape.[44(p. 145)] Indeed, the consequences for illegal migrants in common labour migration destinations for Filipinos have ranged from huge fines (e.g. in China, Italy, Japan), to detention or imprisonment (e.g. in Australia, USA) or even caning (e.g. in Malaysia).[19(p. 66),44,45(p. 30)] In Sabah, Malaysia, large numbers of irregular Filipino migrants are regularly deported, but the well-documented human

122 *Migration and globalisation*

Figure 4.2 "Work as a Factory worker in South Korea." Note the requirements of minimum high school graduate and age 18–36 years.

trafficking problems are not recognised by local authorities.[44(pp. 147–148)] Migration is controlled and shaped by the laws and practices in the destination country, control which impacts at every level from decisions about migration to the day-to-day relationships with overseas employers.

Overseas racialised perceptions shape the position and options of migrants, such as where "Filipino women's racial, national and gender identities are connected to their opportunities for mobility."[46(p. 9)] The image of Filipinas as docile and submissive is particularly pernicious and has been implicated in cases where Australian men have sought Filipina brides, and used this idea to justify domestic violence against their wives who did not conform to this image.[47,48(p. 20)] Migrants have often been paid less for the same work based on migration status or country of origin rather than skills. The limited job options also goes beyond government policy to racialised status, and in Japan and Rome, Filipinas have reported being denied access to any opportunities other than domestic and caregiving work.[38,49] Research with Filipino labour migrants overseas has revealed that degrees of control, abuse, and exploitation are ubiquitous, particularly for unskilled

Migration and globalisation 123

workers.[27,46,50–53] In several countries, it has also been noted that "Filipina" has been used synonymously with "domestic helper."[14(p. 59)] Domestic workers, labourers, and others who live at their work site may not have access to social relationships outside of the household or labour site, which further reinforces their status and prevents outside influences or context for the labour conditions. Where migrants have been looked down on and rejected from normal social relations including work, these conditions have significant effects on the experience of migration as well as limiting the possibilities for success.[15,17,26,53,54]

As with other migrants, government and private organisations explicitly prepare and market Filipino seafarers to the demands of the international industry. The government markets Filipinos as English-speaking obedient workers, a value that is also integrated into Philippines Overseas Employment Administration (POEA) training programs where "obedience is equated with being a patriotic Filipino."[52,55(p. 195)] Ruggunan[55] describes the conditions of Filipino seafarers' employment which are arranged and negotiated by a local "union" (AMOSUP – Associated Marine Officers and Seamen's Union of the Philippines), which is actually a family profit-making business rather than a member-controlled entity. Wages have been set at higher than non-union members, but lower than international standards to maintain Filipino competitiveness. Benefits provided for seafarers are generally only valid during active contracts, usually about nine months, and the fee for membership can be $100 USD (₱5064; $137 NZD) per month while on contract – which contributes to the profits of AMOSUP.[55(pp. 196,198)] Despite the good wages paid in US dollars, fees and contract durations contribute to the fact that seafarers on average return similar remittances as other OFWs.[i56(p. 65)]

The intersection of gender discrimination and Filipino migrant status has resulted in skilled nurses and medical professionals often having been employed in positions with lower status and pay than those from other locations. At the same time, even lower status positions overseas are often more lucrative than opportunities at home.[13,26,27,39] Even fully trained medical doctors in the Philippines have sought nursing opportunities primarily in the Western world, and nurses have accepted "unskilled" caregiving positions.[13(p. 1279),26] Filipinos in the Middle East and the Western world have generally been relegated to lower-paid, lower-status medical roles with little opportunity to advance.[13,26,27,39] The underpayment of skilled migrants illustrates how international political and migration status has real and monetary consequences in the global economy, and is an extension of the same processes where unskilled migrant workers are subject to exploitation, unsafe conditions, low pay, and abuse because of their status.

Bianca was formerly one such "unskilled" migrant worker that I met in Mindanao. She was a quiet woman but always quick to laugh. Her story contributes to understanding the relationship between migration and human trafficking, and to viewing a more complete picture of a migrant's life cycle.

124 *Migration and globalisation*

4.3 Bianca's story

I had known Bianca through friends for a few months before I met her in the restaurant where we sat down to have lunch together and conduct the interview. She had done some childcare for us, and I arranged the interview through younger friends who stressed that she did not need to participate, but Bianca was happy to talk about her life. Although I have not included most of our banter, we had a lot of fun and joking during the interview, particularly when I asked Bianca whether she hoped to get married someday. It was also interrupted by my – unsuccessful – attempts to get a watermelon smoothie without any sugar added to it, Filipino food tending to be much sweeter than what I was used to. Bianca spoke English well as a result of her overseas work, and hers was the only interview I conducted without an outside support worker present in some capacity. However, she also did some work with an NGO I was familiar with, and after knowing her for some time, and the significant time that had passed since her migrant trafficking experience, I felt confident that we could conduct the interview and that she had significant support systems in place already. I was, however, prepared with the same strategies of being attuned to her emotional state, making sure she knew her rights as a participant, and offering to arrange follow-up support if she wanted it, which she declined. Although these safeguards are important, the fact that Bianca had no concerns about relating her story highlights the fact that a trafficking event does not necessarily or permanently cause a person to adopt an identity of "victim."

Bianca was raised by her grandmother through her elementary school years. "I really did grow up with my grandmother, and I was with her for a long time. It's like half of my life, until I was a teenager I was with her, all through elementary school. And I love her so much. She's my dear grandmother like that. I always say this that I always like my grandmother more than my mother, because I was with her all the time. And growing up with my grandmother was so much fun." When Bianca was a teenager, she returned to her parents' home. There was a lot of fighting, arguing, and domestic violence where Bianca's mother would begin beating her father. Eventually her father moved out to a house nearby. "It was a sad story because they broke up." Bianca tried to persuade him to come home, saying that the family missed him. "I said, 'pa, come home. Come home already. We miss you at home. Come on, go home already. We want you to stay with us in the house.' And then, he wasn't coming home. 'No, I won't because I'm angry with your mother.' And then he said, 'no, I can't. I'm not living there or else, if you force me to stay in the house maybe I will kill your mother.'"

Bianca struggled with this domestic situation while progressing through high school. Her first year, she was paying for her schooling by boarding as a domestic helper in exchange for school fees and room and board. "I was working in the house of my landlady. Fetching water, and doing her

Migration and globalisation 125

washing and cleaning her house, just to have my allowance for school and to get my boarding free because I'm working. She was a nice lady." Bianca had enjoyed living with the landlady and her two children, helping around the house and studying.

At this point, Bianca's family instructed her to quit school, and not even finish the last four months of her first level. "In the middle, they wanted me to stop – they didn't want me to continue school, because (they said) they can't support me anymore. I said, 'you are not supporting me. I'm supporting myself.'" Bianca was concerned about her parents and siblings, so she finally agreed and returned home to try to help. "But I couldn't do anything about it." There turned out to be no chance of her parents' reconciliation. Bianca's aunt, the sister of her mother, suggested that the family move to Davao, away from her father. So her mother sold the three farms and the big house that they owned. Everything was sold. Bianca recalled, "I didn't see the money, what they did with the money. We didn't even buy *slippers*,[ii] no new clothes. I don't know what happened with that money that they received from the house...I would think to myself, what are these people doing? They don't even care that they have children. There are five of us, I am the second child. My youngest brother, he was only two or three at that time. I was quite shocked at what they did."

A visit back to the rural area turned out to be the last time Bianca would ever see her father. While they were there, Bianca would sneak out to see him as her mother would not allow her to go. Once, however, she was caught. "I went home, she really beat me badly, really, really bad, that I don't know where her hands went on my face that all the blood came out from my nose. She saw it (bleeding a lot). She saw the blood on the floor. She cleaned it, then I went to one corner, sat there and cried. 'I want my Dad.' But I don't know why I didn't have the strength to go and run. I just stayed there and cried under the table. That was more anger building in my heart." Bianca had been close to her father and missed him badly over the years to come.

Back in Davao, Bianca's aunt helped her enrol in school again, and she finished high school while doing most of the housework for her mother and siblings. "I was working, every chore in the house, I was doing it. And at night, I was doing night school. I wasn't doing it in daytime, it was from 4 pm to 8 pm until I finished high school. Then after I finished high school, my uncle wanted me to go abroad. He said, 'I'd rather choose you to go abroad and help your mother and your siblings than keep schooling. I said 'okay. I'll go abroad instead, maybe after 2 or 3 years, I'll come back and finish my college.' That didn't happen, I stayed abroad for the longest time."

The agency that Bianca's family used arranged work for her as a domestic helper. It was only after she had gone that Bianca realised the agency was operating illegally, and had sent her overseas without a proper work contract or travel documents. "They didn't have their proper papers and documents, and they wrote on the contract that I will have my salary for $200 (USD/month), but when I got there, I only got $100."

126 *Migration and globalisation*

"Only $100. They don't give a day off. They don't give the salary properly and they were keeping my passport. It is not allowed that your employer keep your passport. And those people, that's what they were doing to their helpers. They were keeping the passports, they were not giving a day off and even the salary, they didn't really give it monthly. Sometimes they give it, very late, after 2 months, after 3 months. And then most of their families were waiting to be sent their money." The employers took Bianca's passport, and she was forced to work seven days a week. "I missed (home) a lot. I really cried. I said, 'I want to go home.'" The woman who employed Bianca would also beat her to force her into compliance. "The worst thing, she beat me, that employer. That employer, she really did hit me."

Nine months passed, and Bianca was working hard without a day off, and she had not yet been paid. First, she began to inquire about her passport. She was informed that the employers had lost it. The employers promised to help her get a new passport, and that she would be paid, but time went on without any change. After another month had passed, Bianca realised that she needed to escape. "It was ten months already; the salary and passport were still not there. I said, 'okay this is it. I need to get out of this house.' I had a strong conviction to run away, because she already hit me. So, I ran away from that house. It was very far out in the countryside." Bianca left and ran away, on foot and without even her passport.

She eventually found her way to the city. First, she sought out the agency that had placed her in the home and was supposed to take care of her. When she got to their office, though, the guard told her that they were not there anymore. The agents had fled to the USA after having been found as an unscrupulous and illegal operation, and were being sought by the police. Bianca was at a loss, but other Filipina domestic workers she had met told her to go to the Philippine consulate and report her employer for being violent.

The officer at the consulate demanded a medical certificate as proof of the violence Bianca had experienced, which she could not provide. "He said, 'where's the bruise?,' because they want to get the medical certificate. I said, 'how can I show it to you? Because she slapped me. There is no bruise because she slapped me yesterday and today I went to the consulate and there is no mark anymore.'" Previously, Bianca had never had a day off where she could have sought medical verification of her bruises. The agent did, however, accompany her back to the employer's home to help her collect her things. With his support, Bianca did this and received only $500 USD, which included the reimbursement for the passport. Even at the reduced wage rate, she should have received $1,000 USD plus the costs of getting a new passport. The Philippine consulate supported Bianca in renewing her documents. Bianca did not have the money to return home, and her family expected her to be sending money. She sent them most of what she had received, and looked again for work.

She found a new employer, and this time they were "very nice people" and she enjoyed working for them. However, she was still not paid the expected

Migration and globalisation 127

minimum salary, and received $100 USD per month. This time Bianca did not mind, as the conditions were so much improved, and she was also given a day off on Sundays. Her employer would often drive her to attend church on this day, which was a valuable source of connections with other Filipinos and emotional support.

Bianca remained in the Middle East and had five employers over the first ten years. She had to change employers periodically to obtain the correct documents for her to legally work, and she was continually trying to find higher paying positions. After ten years working, Bianca still had nothing for herself. All of her wages were sent back to the Philippines to support her family and her siblings' educations. "I had been there for a long time already and still didn't have anything for myself. Everything would go to my family, and my siblings and their schooling. My mother, she didn't work. And she had a problem. With her sister, they had a gambling problem."

At this time, Bianca found an ideal position. "After that, I found these very nice people. They were from America and they were working there at a private company. They had an adopted child." Here, she was well paid, and even got to travel with the family, including returning with them to travel through the USA. "I got the opportunity to travel with them to the US and go lots of places in the US. I was looking after the child, and that was my big adventure to travel." There, Bianca met other Filipino migrants who urged her to stay and not return to the Middle East with her employing family. Although Bianca had ambitions to work in the USA and hoped to go back again, she returned to the Middle East and continued working for the same family. "I was with them for ten years, and they were giving me a salary of $300 a month." She continued to support her family at home, who particularly depended on her when a sister needed an operation, and sent an allowance for her mother who was still without an income. Bianca's position ended when the girl in her care was eleven years old, and she went home to the Philippines. She was now about 40.

The family from the USA continued to support Bianca financially. They paid for her to attend two years of Bible College, and they continued to send Christmas and birthday presents. They are past retirement age now, and still lived in the Middle East, where Bianca hoped to visit them again one day. "We still keep in touch on Facebook. I'm very thankful and grateful for them. They are a very nice little family. That's the memories I have of them."

Since she has been back in the Philippines, Bianca does not support her family financially anymore. "Now that I'm here in the Philippines, I don't have much work. I don't have much income anymore and I don't send them anything." Now the other siblings support each other and their mother, who lives rurally again with one of Bianca's sisters, and Bianca visits with them and her nieces and nephews. Bianca has been working as a *katabang* [domestic], taking work as she can find it, and volunteering at church and in various religious organisations.

128   *Migration and globalisation*

Bianca would love to move overseas and have better work opportunities, and after 20 years abroad, she has few social networks in Davao anymore. Her friends have moved on, and her overseas friends are still in the Middle East. "I feel very sad and alone (missing my friends)". Facebook has allowed Bianca to continue some friendships, but it is not the same as having people around her. I asked Bianca if she would like to get married someday. "I'm waiting. I'm happy enough, but you know, there is still a need."

While Bianca was overseas, she missed out on her family and friends growing, living, and even dying without Bianca getting to be part of it. "My father died, because he got sick. I never saw him, I never heard anything from him. He didn't know how to write, so I couldn't get a letter from him. I had a dream that we were together in a boat, talking and holding his hand. I really missed my dad. I asked my sister about him...and I heard that he died." The death of her beloved grandmother who raised Bianca as a child struck her hard when she read of it in a letter from her sister. "I loved my grandmother so much, I love her so much." Bianca credits God for bringing her dreams where she vividly experienced moments of connection with both her father and grandmother even though she was so far away. She also credits God's kindness and her time at Bible College with enabling her to forgive and let go of the anger she had held towards her mother and her uncle for many years. "Time goes by, years go by, and I started to realise how it's not really good to hold anger in your heart for a long time. Because whatever you do, you are not happy."

The church Bianca attended in the Middle East was predominantly Filipino and provided a sense of community and a chance to develop close friendships with other domestic workers. "Lots of Filipinos go there and people are very close. After church...you have food, fellowship, chatting and sharing, until the night, and it's fun. They meet other Filipino people and they can speak their own language and do their own thing, have fun. They even have karaoke. For the girls that are new, it's a comfort for them. When they feel that somebody is taking care of them, talking to them in Tagalog, comforting and praying for them, they like it. They don't miss their family so much in the Philippines. It helps them recover from their longing for their families." This was an important source of strength and rejuvenation. She also described how on Sundays she and some friends would sometimes drive for long distances to a river oasis area that reminded them of the Philippines. "There are nice trees, even banana trees there, and vegetables that are here in the Philippines." These strategies helped Bianca to recover from the stresses that she had experienced and to endure long and lonely years away from her family and home.

Now, Bianca is in her late 40s. She has not had her own children, nor has she yet had a marriage or intimate partnership. She has no savings or assets to show for her years of work overseas, everything having been sent back for her family to live their lives. Bianca has had to rebuild her life in the Philippines, making new friends and reconnecting with family who do not live close at hand, and without skills beyond domestic and caring work.

Migration and globalisation 129

Older people in the Philippines must generally rely on family for support; unless things change, Bianca will need to rely on her siblings' families and her local church networks when she gets older. She still has hope that her former employer or friends might support her to move overseas, and she also hopes to find a husband. At the same time, Bianca is deeply involved in local religious organisations who, along with her family, provide her current support and sense of meaning and community.

4.4 Jasmine's story

"I have encountered so many problems."

Jasmine was a former migrant, a friend of my friend Nina, the NGO worker who introduced us. For our interview, I met Jasmine in a food court in Davao. I had heard from our mutual friend Nina that Jasmine had been having second thoughts about doing an interview with me as she was feeling rather depressed in the period of grief after losing several family members in the past year. I was concerned about the ethical and practical concerns over interviewing someone who might be depressed or traumatised, but I trusted Nina's judgement and her presence as a support person.

Jasmine was a slight woman, even by Philippine standards, with a tiny voice. But she was clear and direct, speaking straightforwardly and with control in her high-pitched, quiet way. The food court was quiet in the mid-morning under the fluorescent light. Nina ate and waited nearby with her children, so we could join her when we were done. Jasmine was struggling with depression and grief but wanted to tell her story. Through her narrative, I forgot my initial impression of her small stature as she gave the sense of being in control and determined as she described what she had endured in her life and even in recent history.

Jasmine grew up in a large town in Mindanao and was the youngest among her brothers and sisters. Jasmine had a stable family life and she was able to complete high school in the Philippines. She married a Filipino man, Ken, who farmed in a rural area. They had a son together, but rural life did not provide much economic opportunity for their future. Jasmine's ambition was to work to be able to contribute to her family.

Jasmine and a Filipina friend travelled to Lebanon to work. They went over with forged documents via Bangkok to work as domestic labourers. Jasmine found a job, "even though I didn't have papers, I worked for two years in a hotel as a housekeeper." The hotel's beauty spa needed a therapist, and Jasmine's employer assigned her to be trained and work in the spa. Jasmine worked for a year as a therapist, using her new skills, but still did not have a valid work permit. Although government officials would conduct regular checks of the hotel and employees, normally the employers would be aware of when they were expected. One day, though, the immigration officers turned up unexpectedly and "everybody was surprised that time."

130 *Migration and globalisation*

In the raid, the officials caught Jasmine in the lobby and asked her to show them her permit. Her employers, though, had prepared Jasmine for this event. "I said, 'I don't have any, sir, I'm a runaway (illegal migrant).' I told him directly, 'I'm a runaway,' because if I didn't it would have been a big problem for my boss. When they asked me, 'Are you working here?' I said, 'No. I only came today.' So, I told a lie for them. I needed to do it because they were the ones who had been paying me. They promised me that if the police caught me, they would buy my ticket to go back to the Philippines. But no. They didn't buy anything, and they didn't have to because they wouldn't admit that I had been working there. So, that was my mistake when I told the immigration officials that I wasn't working there. If I would have told them, I could have gone home the same month. But nobody would be responsible for buying my ticket, so I stayed for two years in the jail."

Jasmine ended up imprisoned as an illegal migrant for two years while she waited for the Philippine government to provide her ticket home. "So even though I told the immigration later that I had been working there at the hotel, they didn't believe me because of what I said when they caught me." Jasmine felt she owed her employers and needed to cover for them because they had given her a job for so long as well as her specialist training. "They didn't help me like they said they would. It's the only thing they did wrong to me, but it's ok because I learned a lot from them."

Finally, she returned to the Philippines, but after five months she wanted to leave again to get better work overseas. She travelled back and forth to several locations in the Middle East between work and returning home for her mother's funeral. During this period, she would spend time with Ken, her son, and other family members while making arrangements to return overseas. Jasmine would send money back for their son as often as she could, and supported Ken as well.

Back in the Middle East, Jasmine found a job as a domestic helper. She was responsible for looking after three pre-school children. The work turned out to be gruelling, and much worse than Jasmine imagined. "I would go to sleep at one o'clock in the morning, and then I would need to wake up at five o'clock in the morning. It felt like 24 hours a day I was working, without a salary." Besides the constant child care duties, Jasmine was made to toil all hours. Her employers made her do all the cooking, laundry, cleaning the swimming pool, yard work, cutting the grass, and heavy labour. "That is work for a man, but I did all of it." On top of this, Jasmine was not paid anything for her work even as the days and weeks passed. Finally, after two months of the abuse, Jasmine could take no more. Although she feared the consequences if her employers would pursue her or report her to immigration, she escaped and ran away.

Jasmine was running away from this abusive employer when she met her future second husband, Ali. "I was in the street when a man passed by in his car." He stopped to ask if she was a runaway and offered help. She was frightened but weighed up her options and went with him, getting in his car.

Migration and globalisation 131

Although still married to Ken in the Philippines, she ended up getting married to Ali, under Islam which was quite foreign to Jasmine. She was with him in Dubai for four years, but in that time, she became increasingly sicker with a chronic health issue. "So I was always in the hospital." Ali supported her in full, paying for her medical costs as well as her living costs. The doctors in Dubai finally advised her to return to the Philippines to seek help.

Jasmine did return to the Philippines and stayed for three years, spending time with her family. Ali continued to support her financially and pay her medical costs. Jasmine reunited with her husband Ken, although he was living in the mountains and she was in the town, and Jasmine became pregnant with her second child. She started to pursue business opportunities in the Philippines, supporting her son who was nearing the end of high school. However, this stability was short-lived.

Six months before I met Jasmine, her father had died. Left without both parents, she and her siblings were grieving and coming to terms with their loss. Jasmine did have her siblings and son with her for support through this time of grief which coincided with the birth of her baby. Three months later, Jasmine's new baby daughter also died. "So, it's all a problem," Jasmine mused flatly on the events that had contributed to her feelings of depression over the past few months. The relationship with Ken was also over. "I'm alone" she reflected. Everything had been difficult with stress from every side.

Jasmine's health had also worsened in the last few months as she had been dealing with more trouble. She was a guarantor for a loan as a business venture, but her partners did not pay. "I was the one to guarantee everything. So, I need to go out from this country again because the Muslim who is our financier for that money is after me. Even now, they keep on searching for me, because they want to kill me. So that is why I decided to run here to Davao. And then, maybe, later this month or early next month, I am going to travel again to Dubai. But I - I have encountered so many problems, right now I don't know what I should do. I need to run (away) for myself, to save myself. But what about my family?"

Jasmine was responsible for debt of over ₱100,000 ($2665 NZD) after the others ran out on her. She has been making payments, but the lenders would not accept her payment plans and have been threatening to kill her unless she pays the full amount, straight out and in cash. Jasmine has been through many trials in her life. "But this time, I don't know if I can get through this problem."

Jasmine is about to return to Dubai, all going well. "Just now, I plan to go out from this country to earn money and to pay (Ali) despite everything that's happened. I need to repay him, and then I need to stay there, in the Middle East because this man has helped me so much. He has helped me financially and for these three years he has given me everything. So, I need to go back, to say thank you for everything." When Jasmine lived with Ali in Dubai previously, he would not permit her to work because as a Muslim

132 *Migration and globalisation*

wife she was expected to remain at home. She also had helpers to do the cooking and cleaning, although she would occasionally do a little as well. "He is a good husband" she reflected. Her life in Dubai, and her marriage to Ali, had been quite different from her family arrangement in the Philippines where she was the breadwinner not only for her husband and son but for her extended natal family as well. "They are both good, my husband here, he is good too. But not in every way, because he doesn't know how to look after his own family, especially financially. He doesn't know how, I am the one (providing) everything. So, it's not like in the Middle East, (the men) are the ones who earn money."

Despite the cultural differences, Jasmine was planning on finding work in Dubai to repay Ali's generosity to her over the years. She had worked on and off in beauty therapy and spa treatment, drawing on her training she received in Lebanon many years ago. She did not want to return to domestic work but hoped to find work in the spa industry. Jasmine was also planning on bringing her son with her to Dubai shortly, after his high school graduation. She did not see much hope for him staying in the Philippines.

In the Philippines, she described, even when people have jobs, "you work only for your food, right? The salary in the Philippines cannot support any of your other needs. It's nothing. Maybe if some people have a really good job, maybe then they can. But with people like us, it's very hard."

4.5 Coercion, consent, control, and agency: trafficking of migrants in context

Jasmine and Bianca's stories reflect common themes in terms of non-payment and abuse that Filipino migrants have experienced, and migrant labour as shaped by gender.[14,15,22,27,50,51] However, they also demonstrate the uniqueness and personal life contexts of migration and human trafficking. Jasmine considered her current situation, with regard to her stress over the debt contract, to be the most difficult problem that she has faced. Her experience of trafficking exists in the context of a life where she has experienced and strategically navigated many opportunities and challenges. Bianca was ultimately a very successful migrant; however, her migration success has not provided her personally with a secure future. Human trafficking in the form of migrant abuse was only one aspect of the constraints and pressures that Filipino migrants face in trying to succeed.

Although in general, poverty and lack of education are considered key indicators for vulnerability to human trafficking, both Jasmine and Bianca had stable if not wealthy family circumstances, and both were able to complete high school. Although some of my participants who had experienced trafficking and exploitation did have very little formal education, there are also stories like Mariel's. She was trafficked while trying to access overseas low-skilled work, as her college degree and past highly skilled work experience did not translate into a job at home. Although education can play a

Migration and globalisation   133

protective role in some ways and circumstances, education that does not correspond to the actual jobs available will not affect either migration or the risks that people must take to access better opportunities.

A key aspect of Bianca's ability to control her experience was in continually looking for better paid employment with acceptable working conditions, and she changed jobs regularly until she found her long-term position. Researchers, and NGO workers I met, have confirmed that this is a common strategy for Filipino migrants, regularly seeking higher paid and more secure work or even a second migration to a more desirable destination.[9,43] The experience of trafficking denied Bianca this ability, not only in the wages she was not paid but the potential earnings if she had been free to look for other work. Bianca's goal was to send sufficient money back to her family. Researchers have highlighted that formerly trafficked people have often maintained this primary aim even after abuse[57–59]; programs to address trafficking need to as a minimum reduce the financial impact that human trafficking has on migrants. Detention or even rehabilitation programs that do not concurrently support migrants in getting back to paid work, if that is their aim, are extending the impact of human trafficking on the person's holistic well-being, and denying them agency and control of their situation.

The responses that the women had to their trafficking situations reveal much about the agency and active role that each played in determining the course of events in their lives. Both weighed their options until they were sure that the pay and conditions were not going to change, and that they would not lose wages by leaving. Once this decision had been made, both escaped and fled. Bianca then sought help to recoup her owed wages, and then looked for a better job. Although she had been constrained and exploited, in taking these actions. she still retained a great deal of agency and made strategic choices within her circumstances. Neither woman saw herself as a victim, and their response to trafficking was to pursue other opportunities rather than return home. Neither was "rescued" as such, but they considered and chose the help that was available. Both, however, expressed anger and a sense of injustice towards the employers who had mistreated them, particularly about the back pay which was lost. Not only the difficult working conditions but the fact that such intensive labour was unpaid was the primary issue, a reaction that reiterates the women's agency in seeking control over the outcomes of their work.

Where legal requirements such as visas tie workers to individual employers, the threat of force posed by the state can compound the unequal power relationship and control that employers have over migrants. Jasmine, like other trafficked migrants,[44] feared leaving an exploitative situation because of her migrant status. Bianca's employers, similarly, kept her passport and wages to stop her from leaving. Even in more positive working environments, Bianca continued to be underpaid for her work. Despite promises to the contrary and the support that they had shown her, Jasmine's first employers did not support her once she was discovered to be working without a permit,

134   *Migration and globalisation*

and she was jailed. Even in amicable working relationships, there is a power imbalance between employer and employee that is exacerbated by the social rights and status ascribed to migrant workers.

The control by the state through the threat of force to irregular migrants is extended by the experiences with government agencies. Bianca's and Jasmine's experiences were highly shaped by the actions of the government representatives they encountered. Bianca's experience of trafficking was followed by support from the consulate which enabled her to find better work opportunities and remain in the country despite her initially dubious papers. Jasmine's positive work experience was followed by arrest and detention for two years because the embassy did not have the capacity to repatriate her at that time. After this experience, she was unlikely to have sought help from official channels in the wake of her later trafficking experience. As will be discussed, Mariel's experience of human trafficking was also heavily shaped by her interactions with official agencies.

Bianca's account shows the importance of social relationships in the migrant experience. Connections gave Bianca not only support and kin-like relationship ties, but a place to compare experiences and determine what "normal" working conditions were. Researchers with Filipino workers have identified community support as a key source of resilience, while isolation has also been identified as part of maintaining control and exploitation of workers.[14,22,27] It is significant in Bianca's trafficking experience not only that she was made to work seven days a week without a physical and mental break for herself, but without a day off she was also unable to form any outside relationships which could have further helped her to challenge her working conditions. Jasmine likewise found that security, in terms of finances as well as migration status, was ultimately found in her second marriage rather than employment. Seafaring migrants have one of the more secure forms of migrant labour as many are represented by a Philippines-based union, demonstrating again the role of social support in employment.[55] Social ties build security and resilience but can also be a source of coercion in relation to migration.

4.6 Social pressures and the culture of migration

The pressure to migrate in the Philippines is not only from the so-called "push" factors such as economics but actual people who are sending family members as migrants, complicating measures of consent and coercion. Children, for example, often do not have control over their future career path.[39(p. 269)] The intersection of traditional familial interdependent relationships, including obedience and obligation to one's parents, with the current "culture of migration" means that young people leaving school or college are often expected to become the family's breadwinner through labour migration. Neither Bianca nor Jasmine went to university because of this family strategy. Bianca was denied her own ambitions because of

Migration and globalisation   135

her family's decision about her migration. Jasmine, like many others, grew up taking it for granted that once she finished school she would migrate to support her family. For parents, seeing their children finish high school and university can appear the only way to offer a better future for the children and family. The pressure of education fees which require higher wages, combined with the local lack of jobs particularly for people past their 20s, can also make the parents' migration the only viable option for the family's future.[60(p. 61)] Mariel and other migrants I met explicitly sought migration to pay for increasing education costs for their families. The need for income beyond what the local economy often provides has combined with the government's endorsement of migration and contributed to the so-called "culture of migration."

Migrants have been called heroes since President Corazon Aquino famously addressed overseas domestic workers as such in 1988. She referred to them as *"bagong bayani"* [modern-day heroes], acknowledging not only their provision but the endurance, suffering, and sacrifice that went into their labour and separation from their families.[61] The government continues to depict migrant labourers as heroes who sacrificially offer their lives and their labour, including emotional labour of absence and endurance, for the sake of the family and the nation.[62–64] This political framing has been widely adopted into popular and private use. Indeed, migrants are heroes not only to their own families, but to the Philippines as a nation whose economy relies on the remittances for income and for taxes. "When migration is discussed, whether by migrants or in popular culture, it is cast as a duty and a personal sacrifice, a form of deferred gratification for the collective national good."[13] Migration is no longer only a sacrifice, but a duty and marker of Filipino identity and value.

As such, this "culture of migration" is not only a descriptor but a normative pressure that shapes Filipino migrants' decisions and life ambitions. Ronquillo,[39(p. 263)] in an ethnographic study of migrant nurses from the Philippines, described that "the popularity of immigration for Filipino nurses is not driven solely by economic motives but is also fuelled by cultural pressures, the desire for status and an internalised desire to migrate." Migration is central to many cultural narratives about success and the life course in the Philippines, and the plan and desire to travel for work is assumed without needing to be rationalised in Filipino culture, as in Jasmine's story.[39,65] Overseas employment and sending remittances is not only about economic capital but cultural capital for the migrant as well as their family at home.[65] Successful migration as a form of local cultural status, however, is often contradictory to the position that migrants occupy in their overseas work, limited to the lowest-status jobs and social standing.

The idea of a "culture of migration" has been used to explain the "risky" behaviour of migrants, particularly poor migrants, creating vulnerabilities to human trafficking as well as other negative outcomes.[65–67] However, this premise suggests that there is an inherent cultural tendency to want to

136 *Migration and globalisation*

migrate regardless of the situation, rather than a strategy in response to real economic problems. The idea of a culture of migration is contradictory, although it draws on traditional ideas about family roles and responsibilities, primarily because it separates families. The Philippines is known for close family and social ties, and a communal sense of identity. Sam, the migrant I met on a plane, characterised his own migration – financially, very successful – as having had a negative impact on his life through disrupting his family relationships. Migration contradicts this more fundamental aspect of culture and of holistic well-being and personhood. Galam[67(p. 155)] explored the imagined aspects of migration from the perspective of family left behind in the Philippines and observed that "the cultural value placed on migration is fundamentally linked to a consideration of the family." Migration also disrupts the traditional life course, family and gender-based responsibilities, and the transmission of family and cultural knowledge.

Everything I had read and heard about the Philippines prior to entering the field suggested that the so-called "culture of migration" was deeply entrenched at every level of society, and considered the best way to provide for one's family and succeed financially. What I found in Davao, however, puzzled me as many of the people I spoke to said that they had no desire to leave Davao or to migrate. "It's very safe here," is what they told me, "not like Manila." I found this surprising and contrary to what I had read: first, that so many people had no interest in migrating, and second, that their reason was not financial or related to job opportunities, but to the perceived physical safety of Davao City, as compared to the levels of violence in Manila and other parts of the Philippines. One such man was a taxi driver who had grown up as an irregular migrant in Malaysia, and he cited the constrained access to legal employment and state services his family had experienced overseas. Another service worker, most likely earning less than 500 pesos ($10 US) per day to support his family of four, told me that he had moved from Manila to Davao because it was safe, and he went so far as to express his belief that in Manila he would have died young. He hoped that his children would stay in Davao, and cited the call centres and retail as opportunities which meant they would not need to leave the country to look for work. If perceived physical safety and the opportunity to find a low-paying job can be enough to negate the drive to migrate, at least for some of the people I spoke to, this suggests that the "culture of migration" can be a response to violence, whether direct, structural, or symbolic.

Migration is described as self-sacrifice, but can also be considered the sacrifice of people by the state. Bautista[62] described the state's role in fashioning "export quality martyrs" as labour migrants based on the idea of self-sacrifice, revealing a symbolic violence in the process of labour migration and the production of risk in migrants' lives. The government has directly manufactured several migration categories including nurses; it has created a market for Filipino seafarers based on low wages and "ideal" workers.[52,62] McKay[52] reported that migrant seafarers were proud of their hero

Migration and globalisation 137

status and of helping their family, but expressed bitterness at the way the government presented them as heroes but then left them vulnerable within the structure of seafaring labour. One seafarer commented that instead of *bagong bayani* [modern heroes], "we should be called '*gagong bayani*' [stupid heroes] because, even if we contribute significantly to the country, the government fails to help unemployed seamen."[52] The government's official policy and rhetoric has contributed to fashioning migrants as sacrificial, docile, transnational workers based on corporeal sacrifice, control and deployment of the body, as well as the emotions.[62,68] In this way, it is not only families and individuals but the state that has sacrificed Filipino workers for global development.[68]

4.7 Global pressures and local lives: history, stories, and migration

The extent to which migration is integrated in Philippine society demonstrates how global processes and forces are inseparable from and often hidden in local lives and decisions. At the same time, global ideas are interpreted within deeply held and socially shared local cultural systems. Globalisation is a reality which cannot be escaped, even in the supposedly "less modern" developing world. Indeed, the presence of luxury air-conditioned malls adjacent to makeshift open air *tindahan* [shops][iii] and rough corrugated iron houses makes the global influences – and accompanying inequalities and contradictions – highly visible, and creates overt and concrete representations of the outside world. Globalisation and the new images and narratives that accompany it are increasingly part of the Philippines' cultural imagination and experience.

In the context of international inequality, globalisation finds concrete expression in local lives and actions. It shapes the social and shared cultural narratives which create and answer fundamental questions about identity, norms, and values, and the place of people in the world. Images of the Self, as Filippino, and the Other, as the West and the rest of the world, narratives about what constitutes success (and failure), and the relationship between the Philippines and the global make up parts of the imaginary and embodied landscape which also includes the known risks of human trafficking, exploitation, and abuse of Filipinos. Bianca and Jasmine's stories fit within official definitions of trafficking, but also overlap with "ordinary" stories of migrants' hardships abroad rather than exceptional accounts. Globalisation contains and creates fundamentally contradictory narratives as it finds expression in local lives and experiences. As Pocock et al.[69(p. 12)] pointed out, "in the face of increasing global labour migration, there has been growing recognition that a substantial proportion of individuals will end up in highly exploitative, violent and sometimes fatal circumstances."

In a local-level analysis, the central aspects of global inequality are the ways that actual people experience and navigate the challenges that global

138 *Migration and globalisation*

pressures create. The multiple flows and processes of globalisation defy a local and global dichotomy in actual experience, which disintegrates and combines diverse forces. Lindio-McGovern[70(p. 199)] pointed out that macro-level legal and political struggles are often embedded in personal (unequal) relationships; she has cited Filipino domestic workers, located in invisible and subservient positions, and often situated along macro-level lines of inequality in terms of gender, colour, and nationality, as particularly embodying the pain of global inequality. The majority of people, particularly those in developing countries, find that there is frequently a gap between globalisation's messages and "promises" and the reality.[71]

Participation in the global economy has personal and real consequences, the experience of migration being a point where the structural violence of global processes finds embodied expression. Many researchers have commented on the multiple financial, emotional, social, cultural, physical, and political costs to Filipinos seeking work overseas.[6,15,54,72] Jørgensen[73(p. 2)] argued that in the global system, migrants and their experiences are pivotal in making sense of "precarity and the process of precaritisation." Precarity is appropriate in considering the ways that the Philippines, and specifically Filippino labour, is positioned in the global economy as temporary, often unprotected by law, and subject to disproportionate risks both physically and financially.[30,48] Continuums of exploitation and precarity within the global economy have shaped the Philippine experiences of human trafficking, as Filipinos' position within the global marketplace is based on certain power relations which inherently include the potential for exploitation.[48]

Despite the personal and national reliance on OFWs and their remittances, there are contradictory narratives around OFWs and their place in society, particularly for women. Migrants are lauded for their sacrifices for their families and nation. At the same time, absent migrant mothers in particular have often been blamed for social problems caused by "abandoned" children, or considered morally suspect.[11(p. 53)] Lindio-McGovern[72(p. 221)] described this internalised script of being both hero and villain where her participants, Filipina domestic OFWs, displayed deep emotions and pain from wanting to be with their families, but bearing this as they would not be able to provide for them financially in the Philippines. For Hannah, a former migrant worker, migration came at a cost of bearing loneliness, pain, and fear that giving her children a better chance and an education might result in the breakdown of her marriage: "Even when I was working, I would be crying... Sometimes, I would have a dream, and I would cry because of the pain in my heart." Nevertheless, the mythology of prosperous migrant families is powerful and pervasive, and reinforced by informal and official social processes including government and media campaigns to promote migration. This narrative is a significant part of the Philippine perspective on the relationship between the local and the global.

Globalisation is often imagined as exchanges, and some of the things being exchanged are stories, narratives about how the world is and how it

Migration and globalisation 139

could be. With Appadurai,[74(p. 5)] I locate the pertinent aspect of globalisation as the creation of new and modified social imaginations which shape human life and social narratives. In the Philippines, a central part of the global mythology is the wealth of many overseas countries, and migration as a way to access it; the power of these "imaginations" in local society goes far beyond the experiences of people who actually migrate.[75(p. 254)] Narratives about Filipinos in the global world, although often hopeful, also suggest a hegemonic power to move people to enact these stories. People often migrate to trade their labour for that narrative, but sometimes find that the trade is not a fair exchange.

A concrete and "official" part of the social narrative on mythology was the annual "Ideal Migrant Family" media campaign. A family was chosen as the Ideal Migrants representing success and a model of migration for others to follow. However, many factors which enable and constrain migrants in achieving success are beyond personal control. The past winners of the contest that I met, for example, had unique circumstances from childhood which enabled them to get their educations and stable jobs overseas. The family breadwinner was also a seafaring migrant who had much more stable, long-term and secure, union-supported employment than the majority of labour migrants on temporary contracts.

Presenting an ideal which is fundamentally out of reach for many Filipinos, even those who were able to attempt labour migration but without the promised success, reiterates the exclusion and inequality of the poor. The opportunity to migrate seems so available and present, but still is so closed by often insurmountable obstacles. I met migrants who had begun the process of labour migration but could not meet the costs for training programs and agents; one former migrant lost her contract due to a health problem that in New Zealand would be considered minor, common and easily resolved but was an insurmountable obstacle due to the financial cost of treatment. The women I knew who were street-based sexual labourers would frequently talk about wanting to migrate, but knew that they could not meet the requirements. One or two would half-jokingly inquire whether my family had a *katabang* [(domestic) helper] already, and did we need a nanny or a cook back in New Zealand? Migration is presented as accessible and lucrative. The reality is that beyond even the actual migration experiences which can include every possibility from success to abuse or human trafficking, migration is not accessible for everyone.

Migration to unskilled work is supported by symbolic violence where it is legitimated by the state, and sought as self-sacrifice, for a better future. However, Gardiner Barber[76(p. 213)] questioned the validity of this expectation as for migrants,

> what they imagine that future to be and the role they play is linked to institutional and social relations sustained through national colonized subordination ... How long will national and personal reliance upon

140   *Migration and globalisation*

migration endure as a protracted yet still temporary set of arrangements through which migrants tolerate dreadfully exploitative labour and living conditions?

Gardiner Barber questioned the premise of migration which is built upon fundamentally unequal and exploitative international relationships and has never become a sustainable path to local economic development. In this way, the sacrifice of migration has only a tenuous relationship to the imagined reward. Migration on an individual, social, and national level reflects the structural violences of global inequality and the Philippines' unique history.

4.8 History and colonial legacy: structural and symbolic violences

Us Filipinos, we can adapt, you know, to different cultures. We are flexible to cater to different ones, I guess with our backgrounds as being controlled by the Spanish, by the Japanese, and also by the Americans in our history. Like we are trying to adapt to just survive the different treatments that we have experienced. So I guess – I know that it is still happening right now. Like when we partnered with (an international organisation) you know, they're the ones in control. They have the money so, you just go with it, whether you like it or not
-Melissa (NGO worker; see Chapter 3 for her story).

Although the focus of this chapter has been on contemporary manifestations of globalisation and international exchange as they relate to local, lived realities in Mindanao, memories and legacies of the colonial era are still very much alive. The violence of the past is invisibly etched into day-to-day life in both structural and symbolic forms of violence. Gabriel used the verb *kulata* [to beat (someone)] to describe the way his father used to beat his mother and the children ("*ginakulata*," past tense). The word is taken directly from the Spanish, *culata*, which refers to the wooden butt of a soldier's rifle which could also be used as a weapon, to club with rather than shoot. In Cebuano, *kulata* means to beat or assault and implies a significant degree of violence (as in "to beat someone to a pulp," my *maestra* [teacher] explained, "until they were black and blue"). The "colonial mentality" was not just something that developed in comparison to the rich *Katsila* [Spanish] and *Amerikano* [American] colonisers. Submission was beaten into Filipinos' ancestors' bodies, language, and culture, and this colonial legacy is invoked symbolically through language.

Researchers have argued that globalisation and global economic strategies have not had the desired effect of improving the economy, but on the contrary, have harmed local industry, agriculture, and traditional

Migration and globalisation 141

livelihoods, maintained high rates of unemployment, and increased local inequality.[71(p. 85),77(p. 29)] As such, the NPA's violent rebellion,[iv] and the support of Duterte's violent response to insurgent groups, can be traced to common points of origin in resisting these manifestations of globalisation. Globalisation, as experienced in the Philippines, has been a violent process since the Spanish colonisers arrived; the post-colonial period has continued to be shaped by powerful global processes and unequal relationships. International powers have reoriented the Philippine economy and society towards export, which has been experienced as violence against the environment, the poor, and the families who are separated by migration. The global trade in low-skilled workers, while it can be strategic for workers, is inherently structurally violent and exploitative, relying on poverty as a lever which forces certain populations into the lowest status jobs. Further to this, is the social violence where migrants are recruited but then treated as lower class beings, looked down on, and given the worst working conditions, pay and benefits. Images of the outside world can also be symbolically violent in reiterating the gap and poverty between the outside portrayed world and the Philippines.

Politically, the Philippines has been identified as one of many emerging sites of resistance to globalisation in electing Duterte who espouses strong nationalist views and is critical of even traditional international "allies."[78,79] Duterte's 2016 presidential win has been analysed as a backlash against the globalised economics which have seen the wealthy prosper without corresponding improvements in employment quantity or quality for most Filipinos.[79(p. 40)] One of Duterte's first acts, in fact, was to publicly and angrily criticise Obama, then the president of the USA which has for many years been the Philippines' most powerful ally.[80(p. 7)] Duterte commented of the USA:

> If there is anything to gripe about, it is me griping: Why did you invade my country 50 years ago? They sat on this land and lived off the fat of the land. And you expect me to be happy?...You treat me as if I am your colony still? You must be kidding. Why would I allow it? Why would I allow you to treat me as if I am your representative here, as your colonial governor? We are an independent country. We will survive, we will endure, we can go hungry. But this time I want my country treated with dignity."[78]

Despite significant controversy, my friends from NGOs had reported that within the Philippines initially at least, Duterte appeared to be having a significant effect on crime and government corruption, and his popularity remained high. I witnessed the election campaign period, which was clearly a boon for signmakers, and strong feelings were very evident (see Figure 4.3). Globalisation has led to not only economic inequality and dependency, but also eroded "traditional forms of authority" and "the sovereignty of

142 *Migration and globalisation*

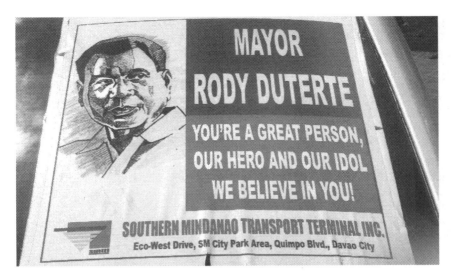

Figure 4.3 Supporter of Duterte displaying a sign on a car during the 2016 campaign period.

nation-states," resistance to which is also suggested in Duterte's comments and the popularity of this strong leader claiming national authority outside of global influences.[74,79(p. 39)]

The idea of globalisation in the Philippines has contradictory implications; it has opened up new possibilities through migration and remittance flows, for example, but it has also encompassed a long history of colonial exploitation and international inequality. Symbolic violence in language, social pressures, and normative narratives continues to shape the violences of global relationships into direct consequences for people today. Local mythology surrounding migration and foreign affluence has a significant impact on migration practices, despite the inherent contradictions and multiple risks that range from financial failure to exploitation and physical violence.

4.9 Conclusions

The dependence on migration is just one form of structural violence in the Philippines, contributing to macro-level underdevelopment as well as the vulnerability of individual migrants. Human trafficking of migrants is bringing or trapping people into abusive, exploitative control. However, there are also other types of control, pressure and coercion that shape migration, from economic pressures and family demands to government restrictions and requirements. The push to migrate, whether safely or unsafely, regularly or irregularly, is another form of coercion by the local government,

Migration and globalisation 143

family, and culture. Government controls mean that exploitation, control, and abuse by employers is enabled and even enforced by these policies, and represents structural violence. Human trafficking is one extreme form of the controls that can shape migrants' lives through unbalanced or exploitative power relationships, and often extends or relies on other controls such as the government's migration policies.

The "culture of migration" where labour migration is often part of the expected and sought life path is a very real part of Filipino understanding, but it exists alongside other cultural narratives that conflict with the individual and social experiences of migration. The narratives about migration are enforced at every level from family decisions to government policy, demonstrating the workings of structural and symbolic violence in producing and deploying migrants. Once overseas, many migrants experience further pressures and constraints that can enable and maintain the trafficking and exploitation of migrant workers. The processes driving migration can be considered forms of coercion to migrate, and constraints on potential migrants. The Philippines is unique in that many migrants do not wish to relocate permanently, but they are still seeking an escape from impoverished conditions for themselves and their families. However, temporary labour migrants often have little power within their employment conditions and migration status, which extends and supports the ability of employers to exploit these workers.

Despite the cultural significance of narratives, decisions about economics and migration are not made uncritically, nor with an uninformed acceptance of the multiple risks which include exploitation and abuse. If there are no jobs, and the family is hungry, the question often becomes, among the limited options, which is the most likely to make things better. Staying and doing nothing is often the only choice where the future is easily predicted; if this is not acceptable, then people must consider other options. The interpretation of risk becomes a force that shapes people's lives and their movement.

The structural and direct forms of violence that migrants experience come from both local and global pressures. The inequality of migrants in the global system in terms of the frequent exploitation, low pay, and relegation to the lowest status, reflects structural violence on a global level. Migration is not the only, but perhaps most direct, way that Filipinos interact with the global economy, and local lives are increasingly shaped by global forces. Rather than viewing human trafficking of migrants as a distinct category, I argue that it sits within the normal and structurally supported outcomes within the possible range of migrant experiences. The risk inherent to migration is supported by structural violence including overt laws in the Philippines and overseas which limit migrant labourers' rights and power, and symbolic violence where official and unofficial social narratives push people to take on the known risks of migration. The global landscape is thus heavily implicated in local understandings of risk, as will be discussed in the following chapter.

144 *Migration and globalisation*

Notes

i   In 2014, 21.9% of OFWs were seafarers, and they returned 22.9% of remittances; high levels of union participation, however, mean that seafarers are also more likely to remit funds that are recorded and taxed officially through the POEA.[55(p. 195),56(p. 65)]

ii   "Slippers" is the local English word for jandals (inexpensive plastic thong sandals); I preferred to refer to my jandals as mga tsinelas (Cebuano) instead while I was in the Philippines to avoid confusion.

iii A small street-side shop, usually just a table.

iv   Insurgency in the Philippines having been linked to massive inequality and widespread poverty in rural areas, refer to Chapter 2 for a more detailed discussion.

References

1 POEA. (2016). *Philippine overseas employment administration*. Government of the Philippines. http://www.poea.gov.ph

2 Cho, S. (2015). Human trafficking, a shadow of migration – Evidence from Germany. *The Journal of Development Studies, 51*(7), 905–921. https://doi.org/10.108 0/00220388.2015.1010158

3 Duong, K. A. (2020). Human trafficking and migration: Examining the issues from gender and policy perspectives. In J. Winterdyk & J. Jones (Eds.), *The Palgrave international handbook of human trafficking* (pp. 1819–1833). Springer International Publishing. https://doi.org/10.1007/978-3-319-63058-8

4 Leun, J., & Schijndel, A. (2016). Emerging from the shadows or pushed into the dark? The relation between the combat against trafficking in human beings and migration control. *International Journal of Law, Crime and Justice, 44*, 26–42. https://doi.org/10.1016/j.ijlcj.2015.04.001

5 O'Connell Davidson, J. (2015). *Modern slavery: The margins of freedom*. Palgrave Macmillan.

6 Parreñas, R. (2011). *Illicit flirtations: Labor, migration, and sex trafficking in Tokyo*. Stanford University Press.

7 Aronowitz, A. (2003). *Coalitions against trafficking in human beings in the Philippines: Research and action final report* [United Nations Office on Drugs and Crime]. Anti-Human Trafficking Unit Global Programme against Trafficking in Human Beings. http://www.unodc.org/pdf/crime/human_trafficking/coalitions_trafficking.pdf

8 Guevarra, A. (2010). *Marketing dreams, manufacturing heroes: The transnational labor brokering of Filipino workers*. Rutgers University Press.

9 Renshaw, L. (2016). Migrating for work and study: The role of the migration broker in facilitating workplace exploitation, human trafficking and slavery. *Trends and Issues in Crime and Criminal Justice, December 2016*(527), 1–18.

10 Agbola, F., & Acupan, A. (2010). An empirical analysis of international labour migration in the Philippines. *Economic Systems, 34*(4), 386–396. https://doi.org/10.1016/j.ecosys.2010.03.002

11 Yu, X. (2015). The sociocultural effects of returnee overseas Filipino workers in the Philippines. *Norsk Geografisk Tidsskrift - Norwegian Journal of Geography, 69*(1), 47–58. https://doi.org/10.1080/00291951.2014.995216

12 Portes, A. (2013). Migration and development: Reconciling opposite views. In S. Eckstein & A. Najam (Eds.), *How immigrants impact their homelands* (pp. 30–51). Duke University Press.

Migration and globalisation 145

13 Gardiner Barber, P. (2008). The ideal immigrant? Gendered class subjects in Philippine–Canada migration. *Third World Quarterly, 29*(7), 1265–1285. https://doi.org/10.1080/01436590802386385

14 Briones, L. (2009). *Empowering migrant women: Why agency and rights are not enough.* Ashgate.

15 Parreñas, R. (2017). The indenture of migrant domestic workers. *WSQ: Women's Studies Quarterly, 45*(1–2), 113–127. https://doi.org/10.1353/wsq.2017.0031

16 PSA. (2015). *Distribution of Overseas Filipino Workers by Sex and Region 2015* (Statistical Tables on Overseas Filipino Workers (OFW): 2015 1.1; Statistical Tables on Overseas Filipino Workers (OFW): 2015). Philippine Statistics Authority. https://psa.gov.ph/sites/default/files/attachments/hsd/article/TABLE%201.7%20%20Distribution%20of%20Overseas%20Filipino%20Workers%20by%20Type%2C%20Sex%20and%20Area%20%202015.pdf

17 Lopez, M. (2012). Reconstituting the affective labour of Filipinos as care workers in Japan. *Global Networks, 12*(2), 252–268. https://doi.org/10.1111/j.1471-0374.2012.00350.x

18 Parreñas, R. (2008). *The force of domesticity: Filipina migrants and globalization.* New York University Press.

19 Abella, M. (2005). Social issues in the management of labour migration in Asia and the Pacific. *Asia-Pacific Population Journal, 20*(3), 61–86. https://doi.org/10.18356/189c379b-en

20 Oishi, N. (2017). Gender and migration policies in Asia. In D. Tittensor & F. Mansouri (Eds.), *The politics of women and migration in the global south* (pp. 27–48). Palgrave Macmillan UK.

21 Piper, N. (2004). Rights of foreign workers and the politics of migration in South-East and East Asia. *International Migration, 42*(5), 71–97. https://doi.org/10.1111/j.0020-7985.2004.00302.x

22 Bernardo, A., Daganzo, M., & Ocampo, A. (2016). Abusive supervision and well-being of Filipino migrant workers in Macau: Consequences for self-esteem and heritage culture detachment. *Social Indicators Research, 2016*, 1–16. https://doi.org/10.1007/s11205-016-1446-7

23 Parreñas, R. (2000). Migrant Filipina domestic workers and the international division of reproductive labor. *Gender & Society, 14*(4), 560–580. https://doi.org/10.1177/089124300014004005

24 Adam, J. (2013). Land reform, dispossession and new elites: A case study on coconut plantations in Davao Oriental, Philippines. *Asia Pacific Viewpoint, 54*(2), 232–245. https://doi.org/10.1111/apv.12011

25 Ferolin, M., & Dunaway, W. (2013). Globalized fisheries, depeasantization and debt bondage in Philippine seafood exporting. *International Journal of Humanities and Social Science, 3*(13), 45–54.

26 Ball, R. (2004). Divergent development, racialised rights: Globalised labour markets and the trade of nurses—The case of the Philippines. *Women's Studies International Forum, 27*(2), 119–133. https://doi.org/10.1016/j.wsif.2004.06.003

27 Choi, S., & Lyons, L. (2012). Gender, citizenship, and women's 'unskilled' labour: The experience of Filipino migrant nurses in Singapore. *Canadian Journal of Women and the Law, 24*(1), 1–26. https://doi.org/10.3138/cjwl.24.1.001

28 PSA. (2016). *Women and men in the Philippines 2016 statistical handbook.* Philippine Statistics Authority. https://psa.gov.ph/sites/default/files/kmcd/WAM%20Women%20and%20Men%20Handbook%20in%20the%20Philippines%202016.%20Final.pdf

146 Migration and globalisation

29 McKay, S. (2006). *Satanic mills or silicon islands?: The politics of high-tech production in the Philippines.* Cornell University Press.

30 Piper, N. (2010). All quiet on the eastern front?—Temporary contract migration in Asia revisited from a development perspective. *Policy and Society, 29*(4), 399–411. https://doi.org/10.1016/j.polsoc.2010.09.007

31 Parreñas, R. (2010). The indentured mobility of migrant women: How gendered protectionist laws lead Filipina hostesses to forced sexual labor. *Journal of Workplace Rights, 15*(3), 327–339. https://doi.org/10.2190/WR.15.3-4.f

32 Hwang, M. (2017). Offloaded: Women's sex work migration across the South China Sea and the gendered antitrafficking emigration policy of the Philippines. *WSQ: Women's Studies Quarterly, 45*(1–2), 131–147. https://doi.org/10.1353/wsq.2017.0017

33 Ducanes, G. (2015). The welfare impact of overseas migration on Philippine households: Analysis using panel data. *Asian and Pacific Migration Journal, 24*(1), 79–106. https://doi.org/10.1177/0117196814565166

34 Oh, Y. (2016). Oligarchic rule and best practice migration management: The political economy origins of labour migration regime of the Philippines. *Contemporary Politics, 22*(2), 197–214. https://doi.org/10.1080/13569775.2016.1153286

35 Lam, T., & Yeoh, B. (2016). Migrant mothers, left-behind fathers: The negotiation of gender subjectivities in Indonesia and the Philippines. *Gender, Place & Culture*, 1–14. https://doi.org/10.1080/0966369X.2016.1249349

36 Parreñas, R. (2013). The gender revolution in the Philippines: Migrant mothering and social transformations. In S. Eckstein & A. Najam (Eds.), *How immigrants impact their homelands* (pp. 191–212). Duke University Press.

37 Semyonov, M., & Gorodzeisky, A. (2006). Labor migration, remittances and household income: A comparison between Filipino and Filipina overseas workers. *International Migration Review, 39*(1), 45–68. https://doi.org/10.1111/j.1747-7379.2005.tb00255.x

38 Lindio-McGovern, L. (2003). Labor export in the context of globalization: The experience of Filipino domestic workers in Rome. *International Sociology, 18*(3), 513–534. https://doi.org/10.1177/02685809030183004

39 Ronquillo, C., Boschma, G., Wong, S., & Quiney, L. (2011). Beyond greener pastures: Exploring contexts surrounding Filipino nurse migration in Canada through oral history. *Nursing Inquiry, 18*(3), 262–275. https://doi.org/10.1111/j.1440-1800.2011.00545.x

40 FEU. (2017). *BS nursing.* Far Eastern University. http://www.feu.edu.ph/manila/index.php/academics/institute-of-nursing/in-program/bs-nursing/

41 San Beda. (2017). *Admissions—college of nursing: Admission policies.* San Beda College. http://www.sanbeda.edu.ph/admissions.php#undergraduate

42 PLMAT. (2010). *General information for freshman admission.* Pamantasan ng Lungsod ng Maynila. https://www.plm.edu.ph/downloads/OUR/PLMAT%202010%20General%20Information%20for%20Freshman%20Admission.pdf

43 Paul, A. (2017). *Multinational maids: Stepwise migration in a global labor market.* Cambridge University Press.

44 Saat, G. (2009). Human trafficking from the Philippines to Malaysia: The impact of urbanism. *South Asian Survey, 16*(1), 137–148. https://doi.org/10.1177/097152310801600109

45 Asis, M. (2005). Recent trends in international migration in Asia and the Pacific. *Asia-Pacific Population Journal, 20*(3), 15–38.

Migration and globalisation 147

46 Constable, N. (2006). Brides, maids, and prostitutes: Reflections on the study of "trafficked" women. *PORTAL Journal of Multidisciplinary International Studies, 3*(2), 1–25. https://doi.org/10.5130/portal.v3i2.164

47 Cunneen, C., & Stubbs, J. (2000). Male violence, male fantasy and the commodification of women through the internet. *International Review of Victimology, 7*(1–3), 5–28. https://doi.org/10.1177/026975800000700302

48 Tigno, J. (2014). At the mercy of the market?: State-enabled, market-oriented labor migration and women migrants from the Philippines. *Philippine Political Science Journal, 35*(1), 19–36. https://doi.org/10.1080/01154451.2014.914999

49 Ball, R., & Piper, N. (2002). Globalisation and regulation of citizenship—Filipino migrant workers in Japan. *Political Geography, 21*(8), 1013–1034. https://doi.org/10.1016/S0962-6298(02)00084-7

50 Constable, N. (2003). Filipina workers in Hong Kong homes: Household rules and relations. In B. Ehrenreich & A. Hochschild (Eds.), *Global woman: Nannies, maids, and sex workers in the new economy* (pp. 115–141). Metropolitan Books.

51 Huang, S., & Yeoh, B. (2007). Emotional labour and transnational domestic work: The moving geographies of 'maid abuse' in Singapore. *Mobilities, 2*(2), 195–217. https://doi.org/10.1080/17450100701381557

52 McKay, S. (2007). Filipino sea men: Constructing masculinities in an ethnic labour niche. *Journal of Ethnic and Migration Studies, 33*(4), 617–633. https://doi.org/10.1080/13691830701265461

53 van der Ham, A., Ujano-Batangan, M., Ignacio, R., & Wolffers, I. (2014). Toward healthy migration: An exploratory study on the resilience of migrant domestic workers from the Philippines. *Transcultural Psychiatry, 51*(4), 545–568. https://doi.org/10.1177/1363461514539028

54 Domingo-Kirk, M. (1994). Victims' discourses: Filipina domestic workers in Germany. *Journal of the American Association for Philippine Psychology, 1*(1), 24–36.

55 Ruggunan, S. (2011). The role of organised labour in preventing a 'race to the bottom' for Filipino seafarers in the global labour market. *African and Asian Studies, 10*(2), 180–208. https://doi.org/10.1163/156921011X587022

56 PSA. (2017). *Philippines in figures 2016*. Philippine Statistics Authority. https://psa.gov.ph/sites/default/files/PIF%202016.pdf

57 Brennan, D. (2010). Key issues in the resettlement of formerly trafficked persons in the United States. *University of Pennsylvania Law Review, 158*(6), 1581–1608.

58 Dahal, P., Joshi, S., & Swahnberg, K. (2015). 'We are looked down upon and rejected socially': A qualitative study on the experiences of trafficking survivors in Nepal. *Global Health Action, 8*(1), 1–9. https://doi.org/10.3402/gha.v8.29267

59 Tsai, L. (2017). Family financial roles assumed by sex trafficking survivors upon community re-entry: Findings from a financial diaries study in the Philippines. *Journal of Human Behavior in the Social Environment, 27*(4), 334–345. https://doi.org/10.1080/10911359.2017.1288193

60 Asis, M. (2006). Living with migration: Experiences of left-behind children in the Philippines. *Asian Population Studies, 2*(1), 45–67. https://doi.org/10.1080/17441730600700556

61 Encinas-Franco, J. (2015). Overseas Filipino workers (OFWs) as heroes: Discursive origins of the "bagong bayani" in the era of labor export. *Humanities Diliman, 12*(2), 56–78.

148   *Migration and globalisation*

62 Bautista, J. (2015). Export-quality martyrs: Roman Catholicism and transnational labor in the Philippines. *Cultural Anthropology, 30*(3), 424–447. https://doi.org/10.14506/ca30.3.04

63 BBFI. (2017). *About us: Bagong Bayani Foundation, Inc. (BBFI)*. Bayong Bayani Foundation. http://bbfi.com.ph/about-us/

64 Bordadora, N. (2011, December 2). Outstanding overseas Filipino workers get Bagong Bayani awards. *The Philippine Daily Inquirer*. http://globalnation.inquirer.net/19879/outstanding-overseas-filipino-workers-get-bagong-bayani-awards

65 Nititham, D. (2011). Migration as cultural capital: The ongoing dependence on overseas Filipino workers. *Malaysian Journal of Economic Studies, 48*(2), 185–201.

66 Alipio, C. (2013). Young men in the Philippines: Mapping the costs and debts of work, marriage, and family life. *The ANNALS of the American Academy of Political and Social Science, 646*(1), 214–232. https://doi.org/10.1177/0002716212467946

67 Galam, R. (2015). Through the prism of seamen's left-behind wives: Imagination and the culture of migration in Ilocos, Philippines. *Asian and Pacific Migration Journal, 24*(2), 137–159. https://doi.org/10.1177/0117196815579953

68 Tyner, J. (2004). *Made in the Philippines: Gendered discourses and the making of migrants*. Routledge/Curzon.

69 Pocock, N., Kiss, L., Oram, S., & Zimmerman, C. (2016). Labour trafficking among men and boys in the greater Mekong subregion: Exploitation, violence, occupational health risks and injuries. *PLoS One, 11*(12), 1–21. https://doi.org/10.1371/journal.pone.0168500

70 Lindio-McGovern, L. (2010). The global structuring of gender, race, and class: Conceptual sites of its dynamics and resistance in the Philippine experience. In R. Dello Buono & D. Fasenfest (Eds.), *Social change, resistance and social practices* (pp. 191–206). Brill.

71 Piquero-Ballescas, M. (2009). Tungod sa kawad-on: Filipino working children's health and globalization. *International Journal of Mental Health, 38*(3), 66–87. https://doi.org/10.2753/IMH0020-7411380305

72 Lindio-McGovern, L. (2004). Alienation and labor export in the context of globalization: Filipino migrant domestic workers in Taiwan and Hong Kong. *Critical Asian Studies, 36*(2), 217–238. https://doi.org/10.1080/14672710410001676043

73 Jørgensen, M. (2016). Precariat—What it is and isn't—Towards an understanding of what it does. *Critical Sociology, 42*(7–8), 959–974. https://doi.org/10.1177/0896920515608925

74 Appadurai, A. (2008). *Modernity at large: Cultural dimensions of globalization*. University of Minnesota Press.

75 Bal, E., & Willems, R. (2014). Introduction: Aspiring migrants, local crises and the imagination of futures 'away from home.' *Identities, 21*(3), 249–258. https://doi.org/10.1080/1070289X.2014.858628

76 Gardiner Barber, P. (2004). Contradictions of class and consumption when the commodity is labour. *Anthropologica, 46*(2), 203–218. https://doi.org/10.2307/25606195

77 Lindio-McGovern, L. (2007). Neo-liberal globalization in the Philippines: Its impact on Filipino women and their forms of resistance. *Journal of Developing Societies, 23*(1–2), 15–35. https://doi.org/10.1177/0169796X0602300202

78 Russia Today. (2017, May 21). 'West is just double talk, I want more ties with Russia & China' – Duterte [Television Broadcast]. In *Russia Today World News*. https://www.rt.com/news/389105-duterte-west-russia-visit/

79 Heydarian, R. (2017). Asian fury: Rodrigo Duterte and the populist backlash against globalization. *Harvard International Review, XXXVIII*(2), 37–41.

80 Winger, G. (2021). Alliance embeddedness: Rodrigo Duterte and the resilience of the US–Philippine alliance. *Foreign Policy Analysis, 17*(3), 1–7. https://doi.org/10.1093/fpa/orab013

5 Risk and violence

Producing and reproducing vulnerability

5.1 Introduction

> At that time (after my father died, when I was fourteen), most of my family were expecting me to just get married. It's a dilemma back in our hometown, most of the girls there get married at an early age...Well, I cannot imagine it, you know. Thank God for rescuing me. There was a guy there that people said, "you could marry him," but I was like, "Oh, gosh." In my mind, I thought, "what if I get married?" First, (I thought), "it's okay, I will end up married, and then have kids," and then I thought – "I do not have work. If I stay in [the rural village], how am I going to support my kids?"... I mean, it's kind of like a cycle. That's how I see it back in my place. If you're not going to try your best to do something good for your family, like to send your kids to study or to finish their education, it's just like a cycle. They end up marrying and having kids and then the kids would finish grade school but not (even high school). So that was one of my dreams that I wanted to get out. I'm not looking down (on people) but somehow I want to, you know, step out from that.
> -Wanda (NGO worker and fully licenced nurse)

Risk is culturally and socially constructed, and woven into day-to-day decision making, as in Wanda's analysis of her life when she was considering marriage. Risk is a major theme in the human trafficking literature, as discussed in Chapter 2, where it is considered in terms of both the general statistical likelihood and of people or groups who are particularly "at-risk." In my participants' experiences, risk was also central to making choices in their lives and responding to the events and realities that they were facing. People make sense of risk, factors to consider (or ignore), and what kinds of social support are available in what kinds of situation, through a socially constructed narrative which is specific to a raft of particular social and cultural conditions and contexts. Risk is imagined in the ongoing cultural conversation between individuals and groups, history and shared memory, values and practical realities. In this context, I define risk as primarily an evaluation of uncertainty.[1(p. 167)] In the Philippines, widespread poverty,

DOI: 10.4324/9781003261049-5

Risk and violence   151

joblessness, lack of education and opportunities, all contribute to the experience of risk.

Risk has multiple connotations, from concrete quantitative measures of likelihood to the social meanings including moral evaluations of why certain events happen at certain times. The dominance of statistical analyses of risk, such as that often applied to human trafficking, requires an individual model of risk that is conducive to quantitative measurement. In human trafficking literature, the concept of "at-risk" has been closely linked to conversations about culture, where culture has, at times been blamed for giving rise to any personal attributes or social categories which correspond to greater incidence of trafficking, reflecting an individualist orientation.[2,3,4(p. 73),5] Indeed, cultures shape the underlying logic by which decisions relating to risk are made, decisions which are mainly small, daily choices which together shape the experience of life where risk is ingrained in the routine of meeting basic needs.[6(p. 43)] However, the calculation of risk goes far beyond a personal expression of cultural values to wider questions about society, that is, who is at risk and why.[7]

This chapter seeks to understand how risk is created and managed in the context of human trafficking and my participants' lives in Mindanao. To achieve this, I explore risk as it relates to human trafficking through the framework of structural and compounding violence. The violences that people experience, and the ways that people interpret and navigate this setting, are both significant to an understanding of risk in these terms. In discussing risk, I would first like to query the idea of "at-risk," particularly as it is typically used in the context of human trafficking. The idea of compounding violence suggests that violent events – whether structural or direct – damage a person's life-world in a way that makes them more likely to experience further violence. The idea of "at-risk," then, can be considered a euphemism for compounding violence as it erases, or neglects to take into account, the violence that has occurred – and may still be occurring – in an individual's life and focuses instead on the future. Precarity, risk, and vulnerability generally refer to the likelihood, and unequal likelihood, of negative outcomes; structural, compounding violence instead emphasises that future risk emerges from some form of violence that is *already* present.

5.2 Susan's story

Susan was a smiling, motherly woman. I met her on a street corner one evening, where I had accompanied women from an NGO who would regularly visit her. Susan had been working in the sex industry on and off for over 25 years. The regularly spaced street lights seemed to be missing from this patch; we could easily see each other, but it must have been the darkest spot in the city. I had been struggling to sleep with the city lights, and entertained a brief fantasy of setting up a hammock under one of the trees. Susan shared that her youngest child had recently had a birthday, and the family had been

152 *Risk and violence*

celebrating. We chatted about our families for a few minutes before Glenda, the local NGO worker and my interpreter for the evening, reintroduced me and checked if Susan was still happy to do an interview. Susan was happy to talk straight away, and I was glad to take the opportunity before business picked up as the evening wore on. She complained of a backache, so we found a spot under a tree to sit down on the curb beside the wide, quiet road. At this hour, in the dark of the evening, I was only just comfortable with the heat.

Susan grew up in a rural area of Mindanao. Her family were farmers, like many rural villagers. She came from a large family; her parents had twelve children, and providing for them was a constant challenge. When Susan was young, her family sent her to Davao City to work as a house maid. "When I was eight years of age, I was here in Davao already. I was sort of adopted by a man. Someone from here and someone from my place took me to her employer. I was their helper until I got older. I grew up in their household." Susan wanted to carry on going to school, but her employers did not allow her to continue past elementary. "I really was *nagsakit* [sick][i] for some time because I begged that I want to go to school, but they didn't want to send me."

The family she worked for sent money back to Susan's family, but Susan was dependent on her employers for her daily needs with no money of her own. She worked long days, seven days a week, doing cleaning, cooking, and washing laundry by hand. "In the morning, sweep outside, then, go back inside. Clean up, wash dishes, just like that. Wiping again and again. Laundry, ironing. It was like that. Hard work." She worked there for seven years, until she was fifteen. By this point, the neighbours' maids were telling her that she should not stay, because she was not being treated properly without a day off or being allowed to attend school. "Why do I suffer there. I was becoming an adult already. We will look for a job." Finally, Susan joined a neighbouring domestic worker in fleeing their employers. Claiming to go for a walk to Rizal Park, they left and did not return.

The young women found work in a *karenderiya* [small restaurant], "I was a server there." They earned 30 pesos ($1NZ) each per day, barely enough for their daily needs, but this was the first time Susan had received her own wage. Susan had never had any independence before this. She stayed working at the *karenderiya* for three years, but did not manage to fulfil her hope of returning to school. "I worked there a long time. I had a good employer and I liked it, they were kind. But it was like the desire to go to school had left me." Working seven days a week from the age of eight meant that her relationship with her employers had been more like that of child and parents, where everything she did and had was through them. Even while working at a very low wage at the *karenderiya*, the freedom she had was significantly different.

While working at the *karenderiya*, she met a man and formed a relationship with him. She was about 17; he was in his 30s. "At that time, I had no

Risk and violence 153

knowledge about men. I had never had a boyfriend. He was like my first love. When he (asked me), I went with him." She talked about her relationship mainly in terms of how her work changed, rather than love: "I met that man there, who became the father of my three children. Then he took me from there (working at the *karenderiya*)." They had three children together in quick succession – "I was *sundanon* [prolific]." But her husband[ii] had been spending less and less time at home, while she was left at home with the children and no money to buy food. It got to the point where he was only home once a week, adding to the pressure on her of having hungry children to care for. She would question him about it, but he told her that his work had assigned him to a different place. She was not satisfied with his answer, but did not yet realise what was happening. Eventually Susan began to hear people talking, telling her that he was actually married to someone else. Even a friend told her that she was "pitiful" and needed to open her eyes to the fact that her man was already married. At this point, Susan left. "That's why I left, I took my small little children with me. They were still small, but I could no longer stand it because the man was married and then he comes and goes. We were all very hungry sometimes."

Susan took her children and returned to her rural home where her family was from. However, things did not improve, and the rural location offered even fewer opportunities to earn money to support her children. Her children were hungry, and Susan was growing increasingly desperate. One of Susan's friends saw her conditions and began to recruit her to work. "She said, 'Money is so easy, money is easy for me. You will only entertain customers, and you will get money immediately.'" Susan finally agreed, and her friend helped Susan dress up and do makeup, and took Susan there. "It was a club. I was shocked. I said, 'what are we going to do here?' She said, 'you know, just to dance. You will earn money instantly.' I said, 'I don't think I can do it. Not like this, oh no.' But the manager (brought me in). She made me drink something. She said, 'drink so that you will not be inhibited. I thought you needed money? We don't want to pressure you.'" The first day, Susan was made to drink alcohol spiked with drugs before she was to dance. Then a customer went to the manager and requested Susan for sex. The manager sent her from the club with the man, but she was afraid. She appealed to him that she was new and not used to the work, and the customer instead gave her money anyway and took her home, advising her to find a better way to raise her children.

The 3,000 pesos (about $90 NZD) she received could not last forever. Susan had never seen this much money and bought a lot of food and infant formula. Susan's friend was continually pestering her, telling her that what the man said was wrong, and after all she had made money just by going there. "That's why, of course, the money easily gets spent. So I returned again." Back in the club, she was again given drinks. "I also drank, so I lost any inhibitions. I do not know what they mixed with my drinks." She felt faint and out of reality when the club manager asked her if she would dance,

154   *Risk and violence*

and she agreed. From there the work quickly turned into sexual labour. "So that's it. I got used to it. I got used to it. I got used to the, you know."

From there, Susan was recruited to Manila to work in a brothel through a friend's sister. Her children were very small at this time, and Susan paid a local woman in Davao to look after them. "So I had so much money. I was very in demand. I was always hired. The Japanese would give me a tip. I had so much money. Lots of money." Such was Susan's favour with her clients that when she finally needed to return home after only a month, one man totally paid for her flights.

When she was working in Manila, Susan would regularly phone the babysitter to check in. One day, though, the lady looking after the children was shaking as she told Susan that her son was ill, and she needed to come home straight away. Susan rushed back to find that the situation was far worse than she expected. "My suffering that time was so bad. I cried so hard because that child of mine, he got bitten by a dog. He was having chills and salivating." She took the child to the doctor, and they told her that the child would likely die, but there was medicine that did have a chance of helping. "His mouth could not open, and his eyes were already closed. That medicine is the only one that might save his life." Susan searched from pharmacy to pharmacy, finally found one which had it in stock, and spent most of the money she had saved buying it. The child lived, and the doctors gathered around and told her that it was a miracle, and the Lord must love her child.

After this, Susan did not return to Manila as she had intended; instead, she tried to get out of the sex industry. "I didn't want to go back to Manila because I pitied my children. But there was no one to turn to. I applied for a job, but they asked for many things which I don't have. So I had nowhere to go." Susan found that she was unable to compete for jobs without the education to even qualify to apply. She was able to obtain the medicine only because the event happened after she had been working in Manila; buying it saved her child's life but caused further strain as she suddenly had little to show for her time away. Susan went in to great detail describing this event, down to the hour she had to be on the plane to return home from Manila. It seemed to represent a turning point for her in that she acted on her desire to get out of sexual labour by attempting to apply for other jobs, but in doing so also proved to herself concretely that she really did not seem to have other options. This story also seemed to indicate Susan's awareness of the precarity of life and of the family's situation.

Instead of returning to Manila or a club, Susan would instead go out on the streets of Davao with a group of young women. Money came easily. Men would drive past and pick one of the group to hire. "So I went back to work. We worked again the same as that (but) I did not go back to the club. My companions and I would stay in corners of the road there in (Davao) – money came easily. At first, there were six of us. We would be walking along here. Then we would be chosen immediately."

Risk and violence 155

There she met a man as a client who offered her a different path. "He reformed me. He said, 'Leave that because you have no future there. Do not worry about your children because I will feed you. Those three children, I will feed them.'" Susan saw this as an ideal opportunity. "So there I met the father of my child, and he changed me too. I was thankful. I said 'thank you' because I would finally reform this time, because there was a man who really was interested in me. We really got married. He married me." It seemed like a dream come true for Susan, and the couple soon had a child. But a few years later, after the birth of their second child (Susan's fifth), strain began to show. Susan was not working, and the children were getting older. "My eldest, he was already going to college. Then we were always fighting. He would recount all the favours he did for us. 'Your children, I work, and you all do not have jobs.' Like that. 'You can no longer send your children to school, because what (more) can I do?' 'You are always asking from me. You all ask from me. You all do not have work.'"

The financial strain showed in the couple's relationship, and in the power imbalance between Susan as the dependent "rescued" party and her husband as the financial earner. "Then we had the child, and then he changed. His attitude was different. That's why we were always fighting. (And then) he had another woman...So that's why he said, "find a house, because I want to have this house rented out...In order to earn money and so that I have something to give you because you are so wasteful. You all have no jobs."

The degree to which Susan consented to her induction into sex work is ambiguous. She went along to the club the second time, naively hoping she might be able to repeat the experience of earning money without engaging in sex work, but with an underlying hesitation. She drank to decrease her inhibitions, but she was also drugged without her awareness. She was an adult, but very inexperienced in the world of labour and of men. Structurally, she did not see or have access to any other options within her sphere; it is impossible to say how things might have looked if she had had wider experience in labour and finding work. Her early child labour experiences, which would meet the UN definition of trafficking, undoubtedly contributed to this sense of having little control over her circumstances. Her fragmented social network after this also played a role in shaping the options and support available to her.

It seems clear that Susan's experience of human trafficking as a child labourer shaped her life course in numerous ways. Her mindsets about work, relationships, money, and every other choice had been influenced by that important period of her childhood. The fact that she was not able to get an education significantly altered and limited the trajectory of her life. Susan has been resourceful and active in working within the limited probabilities and chances, to get out of a relationship, to relocate her family, to take an opportunity in Manila, to return. At the same time, her life reflects the fact that exploitation creates risk, and often the risk of further exploitation.

"It is making my heart ache. Sometimes I would wonder when I will be able to leave this place..." Susan desperately wanted to get off the streets.

156 *Risk and violence*

She did not see any opportunities for herself that would not require an education. Her children would ask her for things, gadgets and treats, that their friends and schoolmates had, but she has had to explain to them that she did not have much money. Indeed, it was much harder to make a living in her late 40s than when she was young; school fees and living expenses for herself and her 5 children placed significant demands on Susan and her financial capability. When she was younger, on the street the first time, money was easy to come by; now, things are harder. Back then, "we'd get hired instantly. We would charge a high price. It's difficult nowadays."

Susan's marginal social status, as a single mother, a sex worker, and without a secure income, is continually reiterated in her social relationships. Her children in particular want mobile phones and "electronic gadgets," the growing social desire and norm, and to socialise with their friends at the same level and financial cost, which Susan often cannot afford. Several women on the street would tell us about having been verbally abused and harassed by neighbours and community members for their occupation. They have also reported close calls and violent customers, and they know to be wary if the client starts to drive away from the city or the place they said they were going. It is impossible to compare these types of risks and experiences: the risk of being an older sexual labourer and not making much money, the risks and costs that come from pursuing other jobs which have proved to be out of reach, other risks of death or ill health from violence or STI. Finding legal employment, though, is very risky with high competition for few jobs, and low pay even for the better jobs. Going overseas to work, again, comes with known and unknown costs and risks about the chance of success.

Susan considers her lack of education to be the biggest reason she has ended up in street-based sexual labour, why she struggles financially and cannot see any way out of her current situation. Educating her children is her top priority and hope for the future. She is well aware that work is becoming less lucrative as she gets older, and will not be viable indefinitely. Her children's education means they might be able to provide for themselves, and possibly Susan as well one day. Now, her ambition for education herself has turned into seeing her children through school. At a number of points during our interview Susan reflected on having been "ill" and heartsick at not being able to attend school, and feeling the regret later on. "Lately, just the past few days, I was *nagsakit* [ill; suffering]. (I wondered), why did that happen, when I really dreamt that I could go to school." Her experience with her husband reflected that he did not understand how limited her options were, or what it was like to be in that situation with all sorts of invisible doors closed around her. Susan had looked into going overseas, but even working as a domestic helper has many qualifying requirements and application costs that seemed far out of reach. To her, however, there was a simple explanation. "I did not finish grade 6. That's why I'm here now."

5.3 Risk and compounding violence

The idea of risk is central to considering human trafficking within local and global contexts. Risk, and the ways that it is conceptualised and managed, have interested anthropologists since Evans-Pritchard[8] illuminated how an understanding of danger, how and why bad things happen, is shaped in culturally specific ways. Anthropological perspectives have always emphasised the social determinants of risk. Mary Douglas[9] brought risk to the forefront of analysis in many of her works. Douglas[10(p. 204)] suggested that "the anthropology of risks...is about the social pressures to avoid or take risks." Douglas built an understanding that although human life is physically vulnerable in the natural world, the risks that people face are expanded and complicated by the social meanings, influences, and approaches to risk. Risk, then, is not merely a probability of certain outcomes, but a "cultural and symbolic product of community" embedded and expressed in everyday living.[6(p. 192)] An exposition on risk has led to an understanding that the risks that people face are not spread evenly through the population but that certain segments experience more or less protection, risk, exposure to hazards, and measures that offset risk and danger.

Susan's story perhaps illustrates most clearly how across a life path, violence can lead to further violence. Her early experience of child labour, which would meet the UN definition of human trafficking (although she had never been formally identified as trafficked), was a result of structural violence in terms of her rural family's poverty. In an already unequal social dispersal of risk, it is clear that risk also creates more risk. Susan's story shows that before she experienced trafficking, she was already experiencing structural and slow violence in several ways. Being one of twelve siblings meant the family was under economic strain. Being in a rural location, fully dependent on agriculture, meant another set of constraints and risk factors such as challenging growing conditions and a lack of alternative income sources or community resources and support. However, the violence of exploitative child labour compounded these effects, not only placing her in an exploitative and dependent situation, but creating a further set of risks in terms of her lack of education and experiences with money, employment, and social relationships. This set a trajectory and limited range of possibilities in Susan's life, which she still experiences.

Poverty is the main reason cited for the risk of trafficking, as it was for Susan being sent to the city, but poverty goes beyond income levels to the day-to-day realities as well as social connotations. The experience of lack, the present hunger, and the future uncertainty all combine to increase the pain of poverty. Melissa[iii] described in detail how she and her siblings would wait anxiously for their parent or older brother to return home in the evening, hoping that they had brought some *pancit* [noodles] or any food for the younger children to eat after feeling hungry for most of the day. The poverty of Susan's family could be argued as the main cause of

158 *Risk and violence*

trafficking, and the consequences thereof, but this would not tell the whole story. Populations that are suffering or struggling with poverty are at risk for further negative outcomes as a result of the deprivation that they are already experiencing. Being poor is inherently risky and violent due to a lack of resources, insufficient food, and little ability to construct a buffer against health or natural emergencies, but the social meaning of poverty creates further layers of risk.

In the Philippines, the family is supposed to be the ideal and safest place for women and children, but also is the locus of gender-based inequality as well as often the site of abuse. Safety is closely linked to remaining within this structure; outside of it, one is "at risk" for multiple reasons which build on each other and contribute to the experience of precarity. At the same time, the incidence of domestic and child abuse means that its risks are compounded by the difficulty and consequences of disrupting existing family and social relationships. Erica and Gabriel's stories highlight the fact that domestic violence and abuse were chronic ongoing conditions which eventually contributed to the young people leaving home, only to experience human trafficking. This is a concrete representation of the social structure in that the lives of those outside of the family network are made precarious and more easily exploitable. As such, someone alone in a new area would often be virtually excluded from organised society, as was Erica when she attempted to look for other work outside the sex industry. Social networks, based on family in the first instance, are experienced as safety and normalcy, but inherent in their production and reproduction is the idea of exclusion of those outside of the network.

The family is one place where the distinction between risk as a real probability and a social creation of what constitutes danger can be seen. Families frequently support each other financially as well as offering care and protection. However, it can be difficult to get out of a situation of domestic abuse, as many of my participants found. Almost all of my participants indicated that they either had already or intended to support their families financially. This also reflects power relations and obligations within a family network. The reluctance to prosecute traffickers, as discussed in previous chapters, demonstrates this tension between safety within and outside of existing social relationships. Social workers mentioned numerous times that where the perpetrator of child abuse or trafficking was a *barangay*[iv] leader, the family would be very unlikely to pursue a case against them. Melissa, for example, was abused by a church leader; when she told her mother, she was scolded and told never to say such a thing about him. The way that poor families would not be able to pursue a legal case against a richer or more socially powerful person also suggests unequal access to the law's potential. This relationship reflects structural violence in terms of current inequality, but also contains fragments of historic colonial relationships that were based on control and patronage by the rich and powerful to the poor and marginalised.

Risk and violence 159

Risks are thus embedded in relationships and highly gendered. Women's position in society is limited, where their prescribed role is often dependent and as such risky based on those around them. Gender-based inequality, oppression, and violence shape women's options according to the risks that it creates. Notions of risk are inextricable from notions of safety, and both are woven into the embodied practice of gender. For Susan, marrying a man she had met through sex work was risky in several ways – the financial dependence on him would make it difficult for her to leave the relationship if it did not work or turned out to be violent, the power imbalance resulting from this and his having "rescued" her, the position of her children in the new relationship; outside of this, however, she was left with few options and those were very risky. Erica, who was initially trafficked then remained in the sex industry for some time, found that financial stability also depended on her ability to win favour with men as either a boyfriend-provider or a client; until she found work with the NGO, she had few other options for survival. Joramae, who had been an underage sexual labourer, similarly, found that once she had a baby, she had few options apart from relying on her husband and father. Sexual labour in general usually falls in the same category of gender-based intimate labour that is dependent upon men for provision. Most of my research participants were women, as are the vast majority of identified trafficked persons in the Philippines, and they found that their gender limited their options in life, and that the options available came with inherent risks.

Segments of a population who live with chronic fear experience this as a day-to-day manifestation of structural violence.[11(p. 776)] An NGO in a rural area described how a boy living in poverty had climbed a neighbour's tree to steal a piece of fruit; the neighbour fired a warning shot to chase him off, but hit him instead and left him paralysed. In the Philippines, the unofficial but government-sanctioned "death squads" have operated historically and during the time I was in the field, bypassing legal bureaucracy eliminating supposed criminal groups.[12] As discussed in Chapter 2, government forces have also been known to harass rural civilian populations. Ongoing fear of physical violence is disproportionately experienced by the poorest groups in the Philippines, both from other citizens and from the state.

Structural violence not only renders certain populations invisible but also implies "the ease with which humans are capable of reducing the socially vulnerable (even those from their own class and community) into expendable non-persons, thus allowing the licence – even the duty – to kill them."[13(p. 13)] In the history of the Philippines, there are several times where certain groups of people have been considered expendable in one way or another. The Marcos dictatorship is a prime example, and records show that a majority of those killed and tortured as communist insurgents were not rebel leaders, but poor, uneducated, rural youth.[14] Paramilitary (civilian) groups further extended this violence against perceived rebels. Duterte's infamous Davao death squads are another, and their victims have often been the lowest

160   *Risk and violence*

level drug runners, rather than drug lords and those profiting, who worked because of desperation rather than criminal intent.[12] These examples illustrate how political and criminal violence are not easily separated; the fashioning of criminals, in these cases, was based on structural violence that legitimated the physical violence against some of the most marginalised and powerless young people.[13(p. 14)]

In Mindanao, the rural populations are usually considered the most vulnerable and "at risk" due to the lack of resources and dependence on subsistence agriculture. As such, they have little mitigation against the variability of the climate.[15,16] At the end of my field work, rural areas were experiencing a severe drought and the levels of hunger and severe insecurity were increasing from the already problematic situations affecting rural populations. It is not only environmental issues that are threatening traditional livelihoods. Economic development and loss of traditional subsistence resources through commercialisation, pollution, deforestation, urbanisation, market forces rendering livelihoods unsustainable, place rural populations "at risk," as in coping with ongoing conditions of hardship and suffering.

The tendency for risk to create more risk, and vulnerability to be compounding across a life path has meant that marginalised individuals tend to be equated with the risks they experience within a society. This is related to what Galtung[17] called cultural violence in referring to the form of structural violence where inequality and direct violence against certain groups were legitimised and widely accepted. Sexual labourers, for example, are a high-risk group for contracting an STI; they have also often been socially vilified and perceived to be the ones spreading, if not causing, the infections. People living in poverty are often more likely to be targeted by drug pushers as drug mules; they are also perceived to be risks to society and young drug runners have been eliminated by the so-called "death squads." The reliance on family networks also contributes to marginal individuals and groups being unable to escape their status through work opportunities. Irregular migrants in particular have been considered "at-risk" for human trafficking as a result of their individual choice to migrate irregularly[2]; the structural factors which lead people to these situations have likewise been erased for a focus on the legality of their initial migration.[18(p. 154)]

Compounding violence is evident in how people increasingly are pushed into and embody the social category of "risky" which, in practice, often means both at-risk and a risk to others. As such, narratives of victimhood and of blame are two sides of the same social process of exclusion, and compounding risk and violence. Poverty is risky: people are more likely to be hungry, exposed, sick, without protection from adverse events. Poverty is risky: people are more likely to beg, steal, be a burden on society, and act outside of safe and accepted social norms. Recognising the implication that "at-risk" youth are at risk for both experiencing and committing violence unveils that the term implies both victimhood and blame. As such, the false dichotomy between victim/perpetrator is collapsed under scrutiny

Risk and violence 161

where risk is not a future event but present violence emerging from social configurations.

Migration, any migration, domestic or international, legal or irregular, is a point of vulnerability to abuse. The comparatively low Philippine peso, very low wages locally and scarcity of jobs, particularly skilled jobs, make migration appear to be a favourable option, if not the only option, to improve a family's chances. Mariel's experience shows some of the processes which contribute to risky migration strategies, and the ways that she worked through the risks inherent to the various options available to her.

5.4 Mariel's story

Mariel's social worker took me to meet her at her home. Her neighbours stared at me, conspicuous as ever, as we walked the last part of the journey down the dirt road to her house. She and her husband had four children, and he worked in construction. They owned their home, a simple wooden building along a dirt road. Their situation was relatively stable, and they were not the poorest segment of Davao society. However, with their older children in high school, his salary was increasingly insufficient for the family's needs. "(He is a) construction worker. But we have four children. Not enough, his 500 pesos per day (~$15 NZ). It's not enough."

Mariel's parents had supported her through school, and even after her father's death her mother's job washing laundry allowed her to finish college. She married straight out of university, and was able to use her skills in a specialist field of government statistics. However, the job was contract and project based, and after a few years she found it difficult to find any work. "If the project was finished, then we stop and just wait to be called." Despite Mariel's university qualification, skills, and work experience, she has been unable to find a job in Davao after years of trying. The market for workers favours the young; a mother with four children is likely to find that the odds are against her. Time has ticked away with the older children getting closer to university and university fees to be paid.

Rita, Mariel's sister-in-law, and her family were in a different situation. The family was doing well financially, and the children's schooling was not the constant stress that it was for Mariel. Rita was one of the many overseas workers who sent home remittances to her family, dramatically changing their financial life. Rita was a domestic worker in Lebanon, and had been for a number of years. Like many other Filipinos overseas, Rita was an irregular migrant without official papers or legal working status. It was Rita who suggested that Mariel join her in Lebanon, recommending the agent that she used. Mariel found the agent, a local woman, on Facebook, who was to make all the arrangements. "They have an agreement with immigration. There is an employee in immigration, inside, who they go to."

Mariel was initially sent to Zamboanga, to go through the "back door" route by boat to Malaysia, before travelling onwards. However, in

162 *Risk and violence*

Zamboanga, Mariel was brought to a hotel where all of her documents were taken, as well as her cell phone, and she was not allowed to leave the room or contact anyone. "So then, I became nervous. I got scared." Another woman who was there with Mariel managed to escape and alert the authorities. The police and marines returned and freed a total of eighteen women who were being held at the hotel.

This was not quite the end of Mariel's ordeal. She was taken to the local women's shelter where she spent about ten days before social services were able to organise and fund her journey home. She found the experience "very difficult and sad." There she saw women who had been held for long periods, some experiencing mental illness or severe trauma, and most if not all suffering being away from their families and homes. The crowded conditions and lack of regular water supply exacerbated the pressure of forced confinement and traumatic experiences. Mariel described waking at 5:00 am to get her turn for the daily water before the pumps turned off at 8:00 am. Now, Mariel is happy to be reunited with her family, but worries that she will not be able to find a job before her oldest child reaches University. Although she feels that her family is safe in Davao, their financial situation is very insecure.

The trauma of Mariel's ordeal showed in her body, in her quiet, restrained manner, and her words which still carried pain in them. At the same time, the tenderness in her voice when she spoke about her husband and children hints at what the event must have cost her, and her family. Her youngest child hovered while we spoke, coming in and out of the room, showing me a small toy, disappearing again. Out of all the people I met, Mariel was the one for whom the residual effects of trauma were still most apparent. Departing from her family into uncertainty, being forcibly confined in unknown circumstances, followed by being kept in the women's shelter, have layered traumas into her experience of risk. Her story demonstrates the ways that trauma is not just about an experience of victimisation, but of its relation to other events, particularly the response to trauma. In Mariel's case, the response to a frightening experience of being held captive, was an even longer and more traumatic experience of essentially being held captive in the women's shelter. It extended not only the experience of being out of control, but also being depersonalised as one of many anonymous women held together without knowing each other and far from home.

Mariel's narrative presents a challenge to anti-trafficking service providers and researchers. For her, the worst part of her experience was the "rescue and rehabilitation" that she experienced in the women's shelter. This is not to cast blame on a likely under-funded and overstretched agency which is, for all else, helping women to be safe. It is to point out that victimisation and trauma are not only about the crime or event, but deeply connected with the social context including the legal and rehabilitative responses. The experience of trafficking happened when she was already in a vulnerable and liminal state of change, being in transit, away from her family, home,

Risk and violence 163

and normal routines. The decision to leave was made in the context of ongoing conditions of uncertainty. The events at the shelter added to the already layered experience of trauma, and loss of control and normality. The closeness of Philippine society is demonstrated in the experience of isolation as trauma. Mariel described a collective sense of trauma that the women were feeling individually but together, in being separated from their families, exacerbating and reflecting to each other the loneliness, shame, and uncertainty that they were each feeling.

Families would prefer to stay together, and the cost of the migration experience goes far beyond the financial factors. Migration is seen as a strategy to reduce economic risk, while at the same time, is an inherently risky experience for migrants. For Mariel and her family, risk was very much considered in financial terms; the safety of Mariel travelling alone, the risk that she would not find work, or if she did, would not be paid properly or treated well, were reckoned as less important than the financial analysis. In this case, the financial distinction between risk and uncertainty has some credence – Mariel's family evaluated the known (financial) risk of staying versus the unknown but calculated risk of going in making this decision. The uncertainties – described often in the phrase, "if it is God's will" – were not considered factors because it was impossible to know what might happen in either situation, whether Mariel remained at home or tried to migrate. This tendency to locate the risks in the future and even the outcomes of concrete plans in the unknown and unknowable – "God's will" – is one strategy for dealing with high levels of uncertainty. The present realities are highly uncertain, poverty and joblessness are all around, and calculated risks including irregular migration provide some certain action, if not certain outcomes, in response to ongoing uncertainty and experience of risk.

The timing of migration is an important part of strategic mobility. Mariel was planning to go overseas in anticipation of her oldest child attending college, after which, the daughter was intended to also work overseas to support the next children to reach tertiary study. Migration, for her, was done with a clear sense of why, when, and what was at stake. For Mariel, the risk that her children would not finish university would mean that they would be severely limited in their future prospects.

The family member already in the Middle East provided some level of security against the unknowns of finding work overseas, particularly as an undocumented worker. Migrating was a high risk decision, but made with an awareness of what was most likely going to happen if Mariel did not migrate, unless a serious change happened. However, the trafficking situation that Mariel faced was quite traumatic and took resources away from Mariel and her family. It created more risk by diminishing her capacity to work and her willingness to go overseas, and cost money for travel expenses.

In Mariel's case, the primary mitigating factor against the risk of irregular migration was the social and family network connections which supported her mobility. The same social networks are the risk mitigating factors

164 *Risk and violence*

in daily local lives, where resources are shared particularly in emergencies. In Davao and the Philippines, family and community networks form something of the financial "safety net" against risk that in New Zealand, for example, the government is expected to provide. Migrants do not leave this network, but remain deeply embedded in local relational networks, both emotionally and financially.

The government social work department that handles Mariel's case would like to press charges against the agent who tried to send Mariel overseas. When we met, as Mariel was working through her ordeal and trying to arrange counselling through the social workers, the agent was still working openly on Facebook and recruiting others. This woman had retained Mariel's passport and cell phone, and Mariel was repeatedly attempting to contact her to get them back. If she did not get her valuables by the end of the month in which I met her, she said, she would look at pressing charges. This represented an entirely financial decision, comparing the costs of going through court proceedings to the loss of these expensive items.

Mariel said she would not pursue irregular migration again. "I have already experienced it and known fear, so I would just use legal means. Even though it will take a long time." Legal migration is a long and expensive process, and without a guaranteed outcome of a stable lucrative job. There are costs involved with applying for labour migration – medical certification, transportation to the relevant offices, registration with the Overseas Workers Welfare Association (OWWA). There is also waiting involved, usually at least a few months to complete the requirements and hopefully secure a job offer. Neither of these is appealing, or often possible, for the unemployed workers who most desperately need to find a better financial option.

Irregular migration bypasses many if not all of these financial and time costs. The risks of the unknown are weighed against the costs of what is known, and prohibitive. One of the factors which influence people to keep trying for irregular migration is the fact that there are success stories. In Mariel's case, her sister-in-law had been working irregularly for many years and her family was succeeding financially through this strategy. The agent they used may in fact have been well intentioned given that Mariel's sister-in-law had had positive experiences, but the initial agent is only the first step of the process. Viewed from an external perspective, this factor is significant given that Mariel's educational level, age, employment history, and stable (though insufficient) family income make her a less likely candidate for having experienced human trafficking. Anti-trafficking workers such as those at OWWA who are already frustrated at the numbers of irregular migrants and people being exploited at home and abroad feel that people ought to know better than to take this kind of risk.

However, I wonder how influential Mariel's story will really be to her family, friends, and neighbours when compared with the success stories from the families who have managed to flourish from sending a legal or irregular migrant overseas. Stories of migrants being abused or imprisoned exist

Risk and violence 165

alongside the stories of migrants working and sending home remittances which improve the family's financial situation and future significantly. When there is no work at home that will meet the family's needs, and the costs and time required to set up legal migration are out of reach, the possibility of success through other channels can be seen as the only real option to make things better. Mariel and her family still face a significant risk to their future in that they are currently struggling, and their situation is only going to get worse unless she finds good employment. "*Wala ka kahibalo unsay mahitabo* [you do not know what will happen]" – was her philosophical and only reply when I asked about the family's future from now.

5.5 Navigating violence: choices and structure

As a point of analysis, most of my participants found themselves in an exploitative situation after deciding to leave home and pursue an opportunity, as did Mariel. The decision was not always made by the person ultimately bearing the risk of setting out, like Susan whose parents sent her to the city. In Melissa's case, she was exploited when her family sent her to work for a neighbour. Bianca is another who was explicitly sent out by her family and ended up as a trafficked migrant, and although she was a young adult, she also did not have much choice. Erica, Crystal, Jasmine, and Gabriel were all trafficked after leaving the undesirable conditions at home to pursue a job opportunity; Marcus and Jun, similarly, became underage soldiers after leaving the uncertainties of their homes. This is the point where structural violence is often manifested, in the day-to-day decision making within pressures which are not just precarious but immediately dangerous and violent to the point of shaping experiences, decisions, and reactions in real time. In the Philippines, agency does not necessarily belong to an individual alone, but to a family whose strategies and decision-making impact on the individual.[v] When considering risk in daily life, the contexts for these decisions included multiple pressures and risks which led to bearing greater risk by leaving home.

For most of my participants, the factors which led people to make a radical change in their lives and physically leave home to find work were not discrete events. I did not meet anyone who said that they had left home because of a new change or pressure – no one was seeking money for a medical treatment, fleeing a natural disaster, and few had even secured a job offer prior to leaving.[vi] A common theme in decisions to leave was that of a tipping point, where the slow, long-term dangers of little money and opportunity gave way to the fast, immediate dangers of venturing out as appearing the less risky option. Mariel, for example, was in a stable situation, but the slowly increasing financial needs of her growing children and their education eventually reached a point where taking the known opportunity – following a relative overseas – became less risky in comparison to not going. When I left the Philippines, Mariel was still struggling

166   *Risk and violence*

to find work; now in her 40s, she may indeed find that her only option is to try going abroad again. Erica took a risk in trusting a relative stranger to find her work, but this was in comparison to the options of returning to her mother to live in extreme poverty, or staying in an abusive situation. This highlights the fact that for many of my participants, taking a risk to leave their home was not just about the risk inherent to a new opportunity and the chance it would not work out. It meant *exiting* a situation that was presently unacceptable and risky. Small, daily iterations of compounding violence, which are experienced as compounding pain, reach the tipping point of becoming unbearable.

Here I particularly see the role of compounding violence in creating risk. It was the day-to-day violence of hunger, abuse, and uncertainty that built over time to create a cumulative sense of the risk of staying, and its inherent vulnerability. In these situations, the only paths my participants (or their families) saw as available to them were limited and risky in one way or another. Jun, a former underage soldier, for example, had only ever known life in the village, and living there in poverty with his siblings did not give any hope for better opportunities, only risk that they would not be able to survive. The recruiters offered him an opportunity to get an education and a career that would give him security and contribute to his family, reducing the risks they faced due to poverty and agricultural dependency. Jun did not have or know of any other options, due to his geographic location, family and social relationships, and limited education. Like Susan and many others found, there were few options and only uncertainties to choose between. Compounding violence is central to the process by which people are constrained into limited and extreme measures to offset the risk and violence that they are experiencing day by day.

However, all risk does not have the same social meaning. For Susan, choosing between sexual labour and severe hunger for herself and her children meant taking a path which increased her social marginalisation and contributed to long-term vulnerability. Negative social meanings can compound the effects in a present and future trajectory. Melissa's family, for example, found that their poverty contributed to their social marginalisation. Melissa described how their family was the poorest in the extended family which contributed to their powerlessness in these social relationships when they would be bullied and harassed by other family members. Being poor is inherently risky and violent due to a lack of resources, insufficient food, and little ability to construct a buffer against health or natural emergencies, but the social meaning of poverty creates further layers of risk. Poverty has both objective and subjective measures and definitions. Poverty is also a trajectory within a social landscape, determining the kind of paths which are open.

Structural violence compounds over time and the effects are not only cumulative but increase as a result of other violences. One of the primary ways this happens is by constraining the options that are available – cutting

Risk and violence 167

off certain options, while opening others – and so leaving the most risky options where further violence is likely. Erica and Crystal eventually chose sexual labour, although neither considered this the ideal work option, as it was available to them – while other options were not – in part because of the earlier violence in the form of sex trafficking that they had experienced. Susan's parents knew that her chances in life were limited in the village, as was the whole family's survival without other income sources. The opportunity to send her to the city to work and – hopefully – get a better education, as well as being fed and supporting the family at home, was one of only a few options available to a poor rural family. Susan's probabilities for life were shaped and limited by her rural home life and certain paths available then, but after the child labour experience, this event changed them significantly and added layers of limitation in her social interactions. Compounding violence suggests that, rather than vulnerable people "attracting" risk personally, vulnerability and multiple experiences of violence often reveal that people are already experiencing violence, and at further risk because of violence. To make sense of this in terms of evaluating risk, the starting point is recognising that marginal groups have fewer and more risky options available. This suggests a need to evaluate not only risk, but what might be considered the "normal" sense of risk "within the materiality of the lives of the poor."[19](p. 76)

Many of my participants recognised certain events or conditions which had led to their experiences of human trafficking. Gabriel and Erica both identified when their mothers left as turning points towards insecurity in their lives. Jun, Susan, Crystal, and Erica all identified a lack of education as limiting their options. Wanda, as quoted in the opening of this chapter, recognised that the prevalence of certain rural life paths is maintained by a cycle of poverty and lack of opportunities. However, Das and Das[19] have suggested that in conditions of poverty and uncertainty, people tend to blame concrete close-at-hand events, as my participants citing education and specific events. The alternative was to face the unfathomable reality that society may have fundamentally failed them, and the world that they lived in might never be the way that they imagined.

When my participants, as Mariel, could not bring themselves to speculate as to what would happen in the future, or suggested that their futures were dependent on "God's will" and as such beyond their control, they reflected the highly uncertain conditions they were facing as well as certain "traces of sociality."[19](p. 92) Historic powers, for example, have often enforced poor Filipinos' acceptance of a dependent and contingent place in the social order through violence, ideology, economic and political structures, and religious institutions.[20](pp. 26–28) Although this orientation towards dependency and benevolence (whether on a human or spiritual patron) could be read as passivity in the face of risk, it also acknowledges the fact that for my participants, risk reflected an ongoing uncertainty which was beyond individual control – or blame.

168 *Risk and violence*

At the same time, one of the meanings of so-called "risky" decisions to pursue employment or migration is in the "active risk-taking rather than passive exposure to chance."[21(p. 199)] This suggests a significant point of agency in accepting risk but choosing one's path within multiple risks. In conditions of uncertainty, the risk of human trafficking is only part of the context for the certainty of making a decision. Choosing to face new risks is choosing to acknowledge ongoing risk and compounding violence, and to bear the tension between the chosen and unchosen risks of further violence.

Moral injury is a significant source of violence within multiple forms of human trafficking and exploitation. Whether being forced to commit violence, participate in sexual activity, act submissively in domestic service or migrant labour, or bear abuse and exploitation without being able to object, the internal contradiction of morality is a significant aspect of many of my participants' stories. It suggests that the compounding effects of violence include multiple forms and sources, from the physical, to the structural, to the internal and moral struggles. Places of violence and exploitation include the risk of moral injury; moral injury compounds their effects, creating further violence and further risk, including the social blame and exclusion that frequently arise.[22(p. 1)] In contrast to the dominant trafficking narratives that link questions of morality to blame and victimhood, I argue that the pertinent question is how participants navigate their own morality, the symbolic violences of social and self-blame, and times they have been subjected to moral injury as a multi-layered form of violence.[23] For my participants, working through the internal contradictions and violences they had experienced was a significant point of agency, as will be discussed in the following chapter.

5.6 Conclusions

In applying the concept of structural violence to the idea of risk, it becomes clear that there is a distinction between the structural forces that shape people's lives and the choices that they make to navigate the world. In this chapter, I have separated the idea of risk as the evaluation and possibility of future uncertainty from the idea of "at-risk." In doing so, I have avoided neutralising past events that have contributed to the risks that my participants have faced. Each of my participants made choices within the particular risk landscape that they inhabited, shaped and constrained by the violences that they had experienced. My participants' stories demonstrate how violence is compounding to shape and limit the options available, and human trafficking has often been just one of the violences that participants experienced in their lives.

People actively make choices within the circumstances they face, even when violent, limited, or constrained. They also interpret and reinterpret their lives in ways that create meaning, and this is also a way to actively navigate risk. Local meanings can also challenge outside hierarchies of action

Risk and violence 169

in terms of people's values – "risky" migration strategies, for example, can also be expressions of agency and conscious evaluations of risk. Risk in the Philippines is understood according to local conceptions of the world and their own society, cultural landscapes of meaning that shape even the experiences of human trafficking.

One of the findings of this study was that in considering life narratives that included experiences of trafficking/exploitation, these events were often not the points of greatest victimisation or least agency. At the very least, this suggests agency in surviving multiple negative life experiences to the point where most of my participants emerged in safety and hopeful of a better future. It also suggests a pervasive risk and violence that shaped their lives and stories. Further, it suggests that participants' experiences and narrations do not fall neatly into the victim/agent categories. Resisting violence, whether physical, structural, or symbolic, and past, present, or potential, is always a place of agency. Mariel choosing to leave as a migrant against the predicted future insufficiency of the family's resources, and Susan choosing to leave after the past years of child labour were both significant acts of will and agency. The fact that neither led to the hoped-for outcomes does not diminish these moments of decision and actions in these women's lives. Agency is not fixed nor does it always increase over time; my participants' stories reveal moments of agency, and of decreasing/increasing agency, over the course of their lives as they engage with hardships, violences, successes, and opportunities.

Notes

i   *Sakit* means to hurt, to suffer, or to be ill, and many of my participants used it to describe heartache as well as physical pain.
ii   Susan referred to him as her husband even though they were not legally married; this is not uncommon as the costs of legal documentation can be off-putting for poor couples who consider themselves married.
iii To refer back to participants' stories, see the Table of Contents or chart in Chapter 1, Section 12.
iv   Municipal community within the city; a suburb, but also the smallest unit of urban governance.
v   However, in these discussions I am always aware of cases where families have overruled individuals' needs and rights for the sake of wider choices, particularly in cases of trafficking or abuse where settlements have been arranged out of court and perpetrators have not been charged.
vi   That is not to say that these things are never catalysts for travel that results in human trafficking.

References

1 Boholm, Å. (2003). The cultural nature of risk: Can there be an anthropology of uncertainty? *Ethnos, 68*(2), 159–178. https://doi.org/10.1080/0014184032000097722
2 Aradau, C. (2013). Governing mobile bodies: Human trafficking and (in)security states. In A. Cameron, J. Dickinson, & N. Smith (Eds.), *Body/state* (pp. 185–198). Ashgate.

170 *Risk and violence*

3 Bales, K. (2007). What predicts human trafficking? *International Journal of Comparative and Applied Criminal Justice, 31*(2), 269–279. https://doi.org/10.1080/01924036.2007.9678771

4 Scroggins, M. J. (2020). Poverty and the savage slot. *Diaspora, Indigenous, and Minority Education, 14*(2), 70–74. https://doi.org/10.1080/15595692.2020.1734556

5 Yea, S. (2010). Human trafficking—A geographical perspective. *Geodate, 23*(3), 2–6.

6 Denney, D. (2005). *Risk and society.* SAGE Publications.

7 Panter-Brick, C. (2014). Health, risk, and resilience: Interdisciplinary concepts and applications. *Annual Review of Anthropology, 43*(1), 431–448. https://doi.org/10.1146/annurev-anthro-102313-025944

8 Evans-Pritchard, E. (1937). *Witchcraft, oracles, and magic among the Azande* (Abridged with an introduction by Eva Gillies). Clarendon Press.

9 Douglas, M. (1966). *Purity and danger: An analysis of concepts of pollution and taboo.* Routledge.

10 Douglas, M. (2013). The risks and the risk officer. In R. Fardon (Ed.), *Cultures and crises: Understanding risk and resolution* (pp. 201–215). SAGE.

11 Vogt, W. (2013). Crossing Mexico: Structural violence and the commodification of undocumented Central American migrants. *American Ethnologist, 40*(4), 764–780. https://doi.org/10.1111/amet.12053

12 Asian Pacific Post. (2017, January 31). Duterte's war on drugs triggers global outcry. *The Asian Pacific Post.* http://asianpacificpost.com/article/7837-duterte%E2%80%99s-war-drugs-triggers-global-outcry.html

13 Scheper-Hughes, N. (2006). Dangerous and endangered youth: Social structures and determinants of violence. *Annals of the New York Academy of Sciences, 1036*(1), 13–46. https://doi.org/10.1196/annals.1330.002

14 Abinales, P. (2008). Fragments of history, silhouettes of resurgence: Student radicalism in the early years of the Marcos dictatorship. *Southeast Asian Studies, 46*(2), 175–199.

15 Levene, M., & Conversi, D. (2014). Subsistence societies, globalisation, climate change and genocide: Discourses of vulnerability and resilience. *The International Journal of Human Rights, 18*(3), 281–297. https://doi.org/10.1080/13642987.2014.914702

16 Stehr, N., & Storch, H. (2010). *Climate and society: Climate as resource, climate as risk.* World Scientific.

17 Galtung, J. (1990). Cultural violence. *Journal of Peace Research, 27*(3), 291–305. https://doi.org/10.1177/0022343390027003005

18 Schmidt, L., & Buechler, S. (2017). "I risk everything because I have already lost everything": Central American female migrants speak out on the migrant trail in Oaxaca, Mexico. *Journal of Latin American Geography, 16*(1), 139–164. https://doi.org/10.1353/lag.2017.0012

19 Das, V., & Das, R. (2007). How the body speaks: Illness and the lifeworld among the urban poor. In J. Biehl, B. Good, & A. Kleinman (Eds.), *Subjectivity: Ethnographic investigations* (pp. 66–97). University of California Press.

20 Lindio-McGovern, L. (1997). *Filipino peasant women: Exploitation and resistance.* University of Pennsylvania Press.

21 Desmond, N. (2015). Engaging with risk in non-Western settings: An editorial. *Health, Risk & Society, 17*(3–4), 196–204. https://doi.org/10.1080/13698575.2015.1086482

22 Scheper-Hughes, N., & Bourgois, P. (Eds.). (2007). *Violence in war and peace: An anthology.* Blackwell.
23 Nussey, C. (2021). 'A long way from earning': (Re)producing violence at the nexus of shame and blame. *Oxford Development Studies, 49*(1), 53–65. https://doi.org/10.1080/13600818.2020.1864311

6 Agency, sacrifice, and human trafficking in Mindanao
Conclusions

6.1 Agency and meaning

Questions around the relationships between agency and social structure in shaping people's lives have been noted as particularly relevant to understanding the experiences of risk and choice.[1-5] The interrelated, intertwined notions of structure and agency have been one of the disagreements within writing on human trafficking and labour exploitation. They have at times been presented as contradictory, or oppositional forces, and criticisms have often centred on the perceived foregrounding of one or the other. In telling these stories, I have attempted to begin to expose the social structures which leave certain options open or closed, and also shape certain ways of thinking about the self and the world, making choices, relating to others, evaluating risk. At the same time, in emphasising participants' own accounts, I have also explored the power and agency they have displayed in surviving this world, inhabiting it, embodying ways of being, whether they are challenging or reproducing social identities, actively making choices, and doing the work of endurance.[6(p. 533)]

I am wary of conceptions of agency that seek out the exceptional, the heroic, the counter-cultural, or the moments of decision and change, at the expense of the ordinary and the everyday.[7(p. 90)] Making an "extreme" or life-changing choice does not necessarily imply agency in dealing with the consequences of that decision, just as living an "expected" life does not imply a lack of agency in negotiating the challenges of life. The anti-trafficking movement has drawn on binary tropes of heroes and villains, victims and perpetrators, the innocent and the guilty. My participants are not defined in these terms, but as people navigating a particular world, life position, and set of experiences.[8] In this light, the former child soldier who is an articulate philosopher, the sexual labourer who is an innovative entrepreneur, and the formerly trafficked sexual labourer who is a social worker are not defined by particular moments of their life paths. People are not static victims but making selves over their lives and in their experiences. Considering a life that includes experiences of suffering, then, does not automatically imply victimhood or lack of agency, nor does recognising the social factors which shape the possibilities, forms, and distribution of suffering and risk.

DOI: 10.4324/9781003261049-6

Agency, sacrifice and human trafficking 173

Endurance, meaning, and daily life are points of agency that I have tried to emphasise alongside major points of change and life decision. Agency does not begin at the point of resistance against society, the pushing at the margins of normality. It is alive in the everyday, big and small, ways that people turn their past and present and context into actions and words and choices. It is evident in the person attempting to faithfully embody the values and traditions handed down to them as it is in the person attempting to escape from the traditions and worldviews they find constraining. Agency is not always making the "right" decision; in the context of human trafficking, agency cannot be defined as getting out of exploitation as opposed to victimhood while in it. Agency is not the power of the individual against the social; for a start, there can never be an agency that fully escapes the formative power of society, culture, education, family, and relationships on individual consciousness.

This is the place of anthropology, to look at not only the relationship between individuals and society, but to recognise the futility of trying to separate the two. Agency always emerges from a social and cultural standpoint – the ways we have to see the world, the language and the thoughts we use to think with, are the only ones we have. Further, conceptualising agency as an ideal and as an expression of *individual* power demands a dichotomous view of the social-individual relationship as one of control, conflict, and resistance against individual freedom. The complex experience of society and relationship cannot be reduced to these terms, nor society to a negative shackle, nor people to independent and non-social beings. Humans are social creatures, where the people, society, culture, language, and human ideas we have interacted with shape our ways of being in the world; this does not take away from the power of choice, interaction, and agency in the world. On both social and personal levels, interpreting and finding cultural meaning and coherence in the world and in experience is an expression of creativity and human agency.

My participants' lives demonstrated the temporal dimensions of agency as revealed in biography. Agency is in the present struggle for survival, the challenge of making sense of uncharted experience. Agency is in the narration of stories and memories, the making of the self in relation to one's life and one's history. Agency is in the conceptions of the future, and of the future self, and bringing hope, resilience, and strength into the present. People employ agency in working towards their imagined future conditions, self, and possible ideals. For Susan,[i] a future where her children are economically stable and successful, able to provide for themselves and for her, is her motivation and where she places her efforts. Mariel hopes for a future where something will change, and she places her efforts in surviving until a new opportunity appears – if nothing else, getting the children through school so that they can work. Both experience high levels of uncertainty when thinking about the future, but there is agency in endurance and survival despite this uncertainty.

174 *Agency, sacrifice and human trafficking*

As a former irregular migrant and a sexual labourer, both Susan and Mariel have embodied the space of blame where people are equated with the risks they experience and blamed for any negative outcomes. Although both women accept this social framing to some degree, they also point to the many factors outside of their control that shaped their decisions. This is a place of agency, in refusing to accept blame and re-narrating their own stories and identities. In doing so, they draw on cultural narratives which include conceptions guilt/innocence, force/choice, necessity, gender, and family. However, the ways that they combine, accept, and challenge these notions within their own experience is unique and expression of agency.

Agency is evident in narration and in the way that some participants cast themselves as having endured, learned, and become stronger as a result of their experiences. Times of powerlessness and lack of agency can, in fact, lead to increased agency.[8](p. 6) Ultimately, much of life – and in particular, life's hardships – is beyond human control, but choosing an interpretation of life is frequently the point of difference between victimhood and agency. Narrating stories that reflect values – sacrifice, endurance, strength out of adversity, hope, family – creates agency through finding meaning, and creates the possibility of future narration that similarly contains meaning and benefit, resilience and agency. For many – but not all – of my participants, past experiences of hardship, suffering, and exploitation had led to an increased sense of agency and personal power within the world.

6.2 Agency, sacrifice, and suffering

The idea of suffering is where the categories of sacrifice, migration, and trafficking overlap. Representations of suffering have been central to the deployment of narratives to frame exploitation and bad working conditions as trafficking. NGOs in particular have emphasised not only force or coercion, but the embodied experience of suffering and pain.[9](p. 189),10 In the Philippines, the idea of suffering as purifying has been salient in constructing trafficked women – and at times, voluntary sexual labourers – as victims rather than morally corrupt.[11] The same logic has been noted in identifying illegal migrants or sexual labourers as (innocent) trafficking victims overseas based on their experience of suffering.[11–14]

In understanding sacrifice and its role in Philippine culture, it is first imperative to note that in local usage, there is little semantic difference between the notions of sacrifice and suffering.[15](p. 55) This is true even when suffering is not explicitly linked to a specific act of sacrifice. Marcus, for example, used the term *sakripisyo* to describe the hardships he endured as a soldier, emphasising the suffering he went through. Ongoing conditions of hardship, as in migration, in sexual labour, in difficult work, in hunger, have all been conceived by my participants and other Filipinos as sacrifice.[4,16] Sacrifice is bound up with endurance, and is often about long-term suffering rather than a one-off sacrifice for a particular goal.[17] At the same time, many of my participants

Agency, sacrifice and human trafficking 175

spoke about sacrifice that gave meaning to their difficult experiences, and of sacrificing as an investment for the sake of their children's future.

The idea of sacrifice moving people to action has been an exercise in power, such as in the deployment of migrants by the State, but has also been an expression of agency – making choices, taking on an economic provider role within the family, and setting out for new opportunities. Sacrifice has also been a way to challenge power relationships – soldiers, for example, have sacrificed their lives to challenge the government over the conditions in rural areas. Although this is outside of "official" narratives on sacrifice and heroism, the former soldiers that I met conceived of their service as sacrifice for a worthy cause. Many of my participants described how being able to support their families made their sacrifices worthwhile.

Researchers working with Filipino migrants have also found a relationship between sacrifice and agency in their participants' lives.[16,18–23] Migration, they found, was a point where individual ambitions could be met while also fulfilling social obligations – self-sacrifice for the sake of the family, particularly for women.[4,22–24] Migration is a socially approved sacrifice, but Alipio[25] found that migration has also been a strategy to escape domestic family violence for possible physical and economic freedom to a greater degree. Migration has not only implied financial achievement, but new experiences and escape from conditions at home.[26] For Jasmine, for example, migration was no longer a sacrifice but a better life that she had created for herself and her son. For some of the sexual labourers I knew, the idea of sacrifice qualified their performance of socially unacceptable sexual labour for the sake of their family and led to financial autonomy. In this way, the notion of sacrifice was an expression of agency and transformation, where people drew on certain cultural values to strategically reject others.

Agency is not necessarily synonymous with exercising rights or achieving better outcomes, but is visible in the complex and strategic ways that people navigate and survive in constrained and violent conditions. Briones[4] pointed out that there is a false conflation between agency and rights – exerting agency does not directly lead to rights, and she questioned the dichotomous approach where agency is positive, and structure is negative. Researchers with Filipinos working abroad found that many of their participants overtly recognised slave like or abusive conditions, but chose to stay and did not want to return to the Philippines.[24,27–31] Despite multiple structural factors which influence and maintain the abused, indentured, and controlling working conditions, people continue to stay, to migrate, and to navigate this system. Briones[4(p. 65)] argued that this choice was not about rights but a choice between work and no work in the Philippines. People can recognise exploitation, abuse, or human trafficking in their experience and yet knowingly choose to make use of what opportunity is available, even when on a macro-level, the work can be considered exploitative.[32,33]

When considering social structure, it is easier to see the ways that structure constrains than how structure offers options and a place for agency.

176 *Agency, sacrifice and human trafficking*

In the Philippines, migration, despite the rhetoric of sacrifice and absentee mothers, does offer an approved and celebrated way for women to engage with labour and freedom – or at least the potential for it – although this freedom is contested, uneven, and partial. Bianca and Jasmine, despite their negative experiences, also had options and gained family status through their overseas work. Although Mariel's experience ended badly, choosing to pursue overseas work was a place of hope and agency. Soldiers such as Marcus also referred to sacrifice in conceptualising their armed resistance to current political and economic configurations. Agency and even resistance can exist within structure, in reinterpreting and re-enacting traditional roles, even amid violence.

Sacrifice is the concept which makes labour and suffering valuable, relational, and significant for many migrants and workers. The trope of sacrifice can make the experience of migration or domestic labour meaningful and "worth it" even in times of difficulty in support of one's family.[23] For some of my participants, once they were out of trafficking they were then free to sacrifice for their family. Other scholars have also emphasised the role of sacrifice in Filipino overseas Filipino workers' (OFWs) experiences which contributed to their well-being and resilience through enacting cultural values.[4,16(p. 29),23,25,34] The idea of sacrifice works on both a personal and social level, and is a marker of identity among OFW communities abroad as "a way to reaffirm membership in a particular community."[35] Both personal and social resources are important for the concept of resilience, and the ability to cope with and deal with stress.[16,23(p. 563)] Framing hardships as sacrifice contributes to endurance, resilience, and hope amid difficulty.

Hope and meaning that come from sacrifice can thus be a point of transformation between violence and agency. A major and common way participants expressed agency was in finding ways to help others and use their experiences as something powerful in the world, the difference between suffering alone and sacrifice being the purpose and result that emerges from sacrificial suffering. Some participants volunteered, one was training to become a social worker, and many purposely told their stories in the hope of raising awareness and showing others that there was hope. Jun held firm to a belief in possibility. He held firm to values that he saw as hope to those around him, for an equal world where all humans had access to hope. Hope is a place of agency; sacrifice thus reveals both agency and violence within my participants' lives.

6.3 Sacrifice and symbolic violence

The agency which has been evident in certain expressions of personal sacrifice has, at times been undermined by official discourse. Notions of sacrifice, particularly for women, have been invoked in government migration preparation programs which emphasise vulnerability and women's positions within families. Although women's migration has the potential to

Agency, sacrifice and human trafficking   177

challenge certain patriarchal norms and power relations through women's earnings, social practices, and narratives have continually undermined women's agency in migration.[20] The idea of sacrifice reinforces and reframes migrant motherhood as a point of still enacting this gendered ideal; it does not displace the role of mothers as caring, but demands that migration be undertaken painfully rather than with freedom and empowerment.[25,34,36] Guevarra[37,38] traced the preparation of Filipina overseas workers and noted how the state reinforced patriarchal narratives of blame, which suggest that women are vulnerable and that it is their job to manage their vulnerability. The government training programs emphasised the sacrifice that they are making as women to venture out for the sake of their families while bearing, and being blamed for, the risks of physical danger, and of moral failings such as unfaithfulness. Guevarra[37,38] argued that migration is supposed to be about empowerment, but the seminars instead reinforced submission and lack of power within the migration process. Framing Filipinas as victims has been used to further control and "protect them" in ways that do not empower.[39,40] This officially-sanctioned discourse reinforces women's lack of agency both at home and in migration.

A focus on sacrifice as providing meaning can obscure the history that has brought these conditions that must be endured, that have shaped not only material conditions but interpretations of them. A focus on resilience can also legitimise violence and suffering, presenting resilient people as "other" to the degree that their suffering and lack becomes normalised. Even in the Philippines, middle class narratives of resilience have been used to hide the ongoing issues of poverty and death, and create a social denial.[41] Talking about resilience can be a way to silence the suffering of the poor, and to de-legitimise their suffering.[42] However, that is not to deprive my participants of the agency in interpreting their world and assigning it value. The meaning, resilience and hope that come from sacrifice are real and concretely so in my participants' actions. At the same time, the role of sacrifice is intimately connected to the process of structural violence which has forced people to order their lives around suffering. Human trafficking survivors have too often been positioned just as victims, so, in discussing it, two things do need to be said: people survive human trafficking, escape, and recover from it, finding meaning and strength within their experiences, as Crystal and Jun did; people are less likely, however, to escape from the violences which led them to be trafficked in the first place.

Sacrifice is frequently made in a place of decreasing choices for survival. In Crystal's story, for example, her family's decline led to first the loss of their land, then Crystal travelling alone and with little money to take a potential opportunity, ending in human trafficking. Gabriel, similarly, left conditions of poverty and increasing family violence. We see this process of compounding violence at work in many of the narratives where the loss of stability increased to the point where my participants had to sacrifice and to leave home to pursue a new and risky opportunity, which resulted in

178　*Agency, sacrifice and human trafficking*

trafficking. At the same time, the choice within violence and the available options is also an expression of the agency of sacrifice, to choose rather than just accept risk and violences.

Ongoing conditions of suffering demand not only physical actions, but mental and emotional ways of ordering the world in order to endure and make sense of this violence. This is where we can begin to see the relationship between structural violence and sacrifice as symbolic violence. Migration, as an example which has been particularly identified as sacrifice, is not a choice to suffer, but usually a choice made in the middle of suffering, to face a different and chosen type of suffering and risk as a sacrifice. After violence has torn options, opportunities, and resources away from people, what they have left is the ability to sacrifice, to become complicit in their own destruction or exploitation for the sake of survival. In ongoing conditions of poverty and multiple violences, the way people order their lives by the logic of sacrifice reflects both violence and agency.

6.4 Summary

Human trafficking in Mindanao is a complex problem, both in terms of the multiple forms of trafficking that occur and in the social processes that relate to trafficking. Formerly trafficked persons' narratives reveal multiple factors working together to shape human trafficking, risk and vulnerability to human trafficking and other forms of exploitation, and the complexities of social life in Mindanao. In this book, I have relayed the stories of people who have experienced various types of human trafficking, as well as former migrants, abused workers, and others whose lives and stories illuminate the conditions where trafficking occurs. These people and their lives are interesting and complex, and their voices and perspectives have been central to these accounts. In the literature and discussions of human trafficking, the voices of those most directly affected are seldom heard at all except perhaps as examples of victimhood and trauma. Here, they have been presented in a different light, showing trafficking as a part of a life course where people have made choices and dealt with their experiences, as well as illuminating some of the factors which shape human trafficking. These stories show people who have navigated difficulties and constraints and managed to survive.

In approaching this topic, I have first considered individual experiences as the site where multiple and complex pressures converge in embodied experience. As such, this research is not a comprehensive or fully representative picture of human trafficking in Mindanao. However, it does present a close view of many facets of a local phenomenon in an attempt to understand the complexity of local experience, particularly from the perspective of the poor. The variety of participants that I encountered meant that the research had to respond to this complexity, and to explore the social context where so many forms of human trafficking and exploitation were affecting people. These stories also illuminate the social world they inhabit, and the

Agency, sacrifice and human trafficking   179

widespread difficulties and obstacles that people face. Individual stories and human trafficking have been considered in the light of wider social events and conditions including economics and work, the practice of migration, globalisation, and the local culture. Individual and family lives are the sites where the experience of risk including economic uncertainty, itself culturally shaped, meets social beliefs and ways of being. It is from this point of convergence that choices are made, risks are faced head on, social roles are inhabited.

The Philippines is uniquely placed to experience both the promises of globalisation to a (potentially and ideally) mobile, educated, English-speaking population, and the realities of a poor country exporting its best products and people into a world where its status is low. The global promise further obscures the so-called "dark sides" of globalisation including the inequalities that exist at every level, and the unequal distribution of rewards, costs, and harms. Human trafficking occurs in multiple situations across the Philippine social landscape, with particular risk in domestic and international migration. However, the local economic and labour conditions are also inherently risky, and create unstable and precarious conditions for workers on a continuum of abusive and exploitative situations, exacerbated by gendered/ageist employment practices which emerge from social relationships. In this book, I have explored the social context which contributes to human trafficking in Mindanao, based on first-person accounts which are contextualised in the wider society and theoretically analysed through a framework of structural, symbolic, and compounding violence. This approach has not previously been used with research specifically focussed on human trafficking, nor has Mindanao been extensively researched in terms of human trafficking. Further, anthropologists have only recently begun to explore human trafficking and adapt ethnographic approaches to this topic, and here, I also contribute to the development of methodological strategies to address the inherent challenges to research with formerly trafficked people.

The aim of this project has been to explore how human trafficking in Mindanao relates to wider social processes. I approached this aim by spending five months living in Eastern Mindanao and learning from a wide variety of local people. Specifically, during this time I talked with and interviewed people who had experienced exploitative labour, human trafficking, or trafficking-like practices; government and NGO workers from anti-trafficking and related agencies; and community members who had other relevant experiences, particularly former migrants and sexual labourers. I found that although human trafficking can represent a significant form of exploitation and abuse, most of the participants' experiences also reflected "normal" social processes, such as the vulnerability of migrants and the lack of legal protection for workers. The normality of these factors, and the degree to which they were enabled by ineffective or unhelpful social structures such as the legal system, suggest that these often-violent events were closely related to wider forms of violence. People in the Philippines face high levels of

180 *Agency, sacrifice and human trafficking*

uncertainty, and limited opportunities to escape from poverty. Human trafficking is just one of the risks and forms of violence that people navigate in trying to survive and succeed, and it is maintained by structural conditions beyond the trafficker and victims.

Human trafficking is one of the expected, possible outcomes arising from a number of related and interconnected social practices and processes. The extreme underdevelopment of rural areas and massive disparity between rural and urban areas has contributed to the vulnerability of rural youths to underage rebel recruitment, as well as other forms of trafficking and exploitation, and the ideological underpinnings of the militant backlash against the government. The overall lack of jobs, combined with women's status and position in society, has contributed to the trafficking of (mainly) women in the sex industry. The need to explore every possible job opportunity has unfortunately led to vulnerability, for women in particular, when people have been deceived and trapped into sex work. Labour trafficking emerges from similar processes related to the severe shortage of satisfactory employment. In "ordinary" work, employers often wield a great deal of power over employees, which is supported by the knowledge that workers are easily replaced by others seeking jobs. This control is extended and multiplied in situations of exploitation and human trafficking, and exacerbated by the inability of the legal system to deal with most infractions. Migration is a strategy which sidesteps the limitations of the local economy, but depends on meeting specific requirements including initial financial obligations which are already out of reach for some. For both irregular migrants, avoiding some of the costs and constraints of migration, and legal migrants, their position in international employment is often precarious and subject to external perceptions, constraints, and controls.

People navigate these multiple forms of structural violence based on culturally and socially specific narratives. From this focus, there are two aspects in particular which affect people's engagement with the global economy, their approaches to risk, and the ways that families make choices. Narratives first act as "maps" which guide choices and responses; in particular, the "culture of migration" is an example of a narrative which contributes to people's long-term planning and decision making. Narratives also always contain implicit values, which shape decisions but also provide explanations for events. In this way, narratives can also be transformative in creating personally and culturally significant meanings which can contribute to resilience amid or beyond extreme difficulties such as human trafficking. In the Philippines, the deeply held value of sacrifice contributes to both "risky" decision making and resilience; this trope, simply, can turn hardship such as difficult migration or coming through human trafficking into an expression of love.

I have explored the concepts of coercion, consent, control, and agency through my participants' experiences. I found that these were significantly affected by structural factors beyond individual choice or relationships, but

Agency, sacrifice and human trafficking 181

within this context, my participants also displayed agency in navigating and interpreting their circumstances. I have explored the idea of structural violence in the Philippines by looking specifically at rural inequality and underdevelopment (Chapter 2), labour standards in the Philippines (Chapter 3), economic issues women face in the Philippines (Chapter 3), and challenges for international migrants (Chapter 4). These areas of inquiry revealed multiple, compounding forms of indirect violence, which also affected my participants' experiences of direct violence.

I have discussed these ideas in a wider context through considering the relationships between human trafficking and various forms of violence. I first explored the global context as it is experienced in the Philippines (Chapter 4). In considering the idea of risk in the Philippines (Chapter 5), I critiqued the idea of vulnerability in terms of "at-risk" populations, arguing that this concept obscures the multiple forms of violence which are already affecting people, as well as increasing future risk. In the final chapter, I have extended the discussion of risk to consider the trope of sacrifice which is commonly invoked as part of enduring hardship. I argue that sacrifice, as trope and embodied act, can be a site of both symbolic violence and transformation where the constrained options available are strategically navigated and reinterpreted to create meaning, agency, resilience, and hope.

6.5 Implications

Scholars have questioned the value of human trafficking as a useful categorisation in law, activism, and inquiry, due particularly to the diverse regional and categorical variations. However, this study offers a model of how diverse experiences of trafficking and exploitation can be used as a focus of inquiry into a local society. Through a focus on how various types of trafficking emerge within a specific social setting, the relationships between diverse experiences become apparent through the unique local conditions which shape and constrain people's lives. At the same time, this close analysis also reveals that those whose experience aligns with definitions of human trafficking does not suggest a unity within this category, but a unity across broader definitions. Considering labour, law, economics, and labour exploitation/trafficking, for example, has been more fruitful than comparing exploited domestic workers with overseas migrants or underage soldiers.

Human trafficking is often considered a global problem, related to international migration flows. While this is in many ways true, in this book, I present an alternate perspective and demonstrate how local factors contribute to both domestic and international trafficking. The implications of this finding affect academic as well as practical approaches to human trafficking, and suggest a more integrated view that goes beyond a victim-perpetrator focus. In the Philippines, rural-urban inequality in levels of poverty, access to education, employment opportunities, and effective social infrastructures is a significant factor in the vulnerability to every type of human

182 *Agency, sacrifice and human trafficking*

trafficking in the Philippines. In urban areas, unemployment, underemployment, poverty, and unenforced employment regulations contribute to exploitation and human trafficking, and to the prevalence of migration for better conditions.

At the same time, this approach suggests a local and regional focus on the conditions that maintain exploitative systems rather than vulnerability alone. Migration laws in many destination countries, for example, enable and enforce employers' power over migrant employees. Filipino migrants are subject to these and other local laws, but their participation in such constrained conditions is also shaped by the local systems.

Human trafficking in Mindanao is an outcome and extension of unequal local situations, not separate to *normal* social processes and realities, and one manifestation of wider compounding structural violence. In this way, focusing on human trafficking has been a way to look below the surface of life in Mindanao, and to observe structural violence through a few of the sites where it spills out into other forms of violence, whether physical, emotional, financial, or other. Human trafficking has thus become a ground-level perspective from which to view local society; this approach contrasts sharply with those that focus on local society to identify possible instances of trafficking and exploitation, and the vulnerability to trafficking.

One of the challenges of ethnography and anthropology is working with people who have shared similar experiences, without being part of a single social group. This study offers one model for conducting such research with individual participants which is at the same time still grounded in a local context. It also offers an application of historical-materialist-based ethnographic research to explore the idea of structural violence as it relates to current suffering.

When considering the anti-trafficking movement and service providers, much has been written about the unreliability and exaggeration of statistics, inappropriate or exploitative violations of human rights, and the promotion of "moral panic" and "white saviour" mentalities that have characterised many efforts.[44–47] The dominant discourse and official constructions of [potential, present, and past] trafficking victims' identities, needs, victimhood, and vulnerabilities has itself been identified as symbolic violence.[48] In this book, the focus on participants' voices, biographies, contexts, and lived experience has been in part an attempt to counter this trend and write about experiences trafficking and exploitation without inflicting further violence. Beyond this, direct commentary on the anti-trafficking movement is outside the scope of this book, as is providing individual-level strategies.

Although direct action is not the focus of this work, a few general recommendations did emerge from participants' accounts. Long-term, relational support was positive for my participants who had been sexual labourers and allowed them to make their own decisions about sexual labour and how to manage their lives and economic options. For most, if not all participants, their biggest need that they identified after leaving exploitative situations

Agency, sacrifice and human trafficking   183

was a realistic and viable economic option. Migrants who had travelled to support their families wanted a safe and accessible alternative source of income, not an end to their ambitions for a better future. Former child soldiers had the same needs for economic and physical security, but they wanted more than this – they wanted security for their rural families, something that the government has never been able to provide, and, in fact, has created perpetual insecurity of land use. For rural populations, for migrants, for domestically exploited/abused workers, the conditions that they face are not exceptional but built into the structure of society. Individual-level strategies will not solve these problems, but there is still a vital role for those who support people like my participants to find agency, resources, and options in the middle of a difficult and violent world.

In 1889, the Filipino anti-colonial leader and philosopher José Rizal expressed his lament for a better world built on equality and free from exploitation:

> Humanity cannot be redeemed so long as there are oppressed peoples, so long as there are some men who live on the tears of many, so long as there are emasculated minds and blinded eyes that enable others to live like sultans who alone may enjoy beauty.[43(p. 40)]

This book has been an attempt to engage with and comprehend some of the harsh realities of global inequality as experienced in actual lives. In doing so, I join a wide variety of activists, social workers, police officers, religious clergy, communist insurgents, trafficked persons, rural farmers, homesick migrants, and even writer-poets such as José Rizal in dreaming of a better future for the people of the Philippines. For now, however, I can only return to former rebel soldier Jun's beautiful words, and ask again, "how long will we dream?"

Note

i To refer back to participants' stories, see the Table of Contents or chart in Chapter 1, Section 12.

References

1 Abu-Ali, A., & Al-Bahar, M. (2011). Understanding child survivors of human trafficking: A micro and macro level analysis. *Procedia - Social and Behavioral Sciences, 30*, 791–796. https://doi.org/10.1016/j.sbspro.2011.10.154

2 Brennan, D. (2014). Trafficking, scandal, and abuse of migrant workers in Argentina and the United States. *The ANNALS of the American Academy of Political and Social Science, 653*(1), 107–123. https://doi.org/10.1177/0002716213519239

3 Briones, L. (2009). Beyond trafficking, agency and rights: A capabilities perspective on Filipina experiences of domestic work in Paris and Hong Kong. *Wagadu, 5*, 49–72.

184 *Agency, sacrifice and human trafficking*

4 Briones, L. (2009). *Empowering migrant women: Why agency and rights are not enough.* Ashgate.

5 Poucki, S., & Bryan, N. (2014). Vulnerability to human trafficking among the Roma population in Serbia: The role of social exclusion and marginalization. *Journal of Intercultural Studies, 35*(2), 145–162. https://doi.org/10.1080/07256868. 2014.885417

6 Scheper-Hughes, N. (2009). *Death without weeping: The violence of everyday life in Brazil.* University of California Press.

7 Das, V., & Das, R. (2007). How the body speaks: Illness and the lifeworld among the urban poor. In J. Biehl, B. Good, & A. Kleinman (Eds.), *Subjectivity: Ethnographic investigations* (pp. 66–97). University of California Press.

8 Das, V., & Kleinman, A. (2001). Introduction. In V. Das, A. Kleinman, M. Lock, M. Ramphele, & P. Reynolds (Eds.), *Remaking a world: Violence, social suffering, and recovery* (pp. 1–30). University of California Press.

9 Aradau, C. (2013). Governing mobile bodies: Human trafficking and (in)security states. In A. Cameron, J. Dickinson, & N. Smith (Eds.), *Body/state* (pp. 185–198). Ashgate.

10 O'Connell Davidson, J. (2017). Editorial: The presence of the past: Lessons of history for anti-trafficking work. *Anti-Trafficking Review, 9*(2017), 1–12. https://doi.org/10.14197/atr.20121791

11 Tigno, J. (2012). Agency by proxy: Women and the human trafficking discourse in the Philippines. In W. van Schendel, L. Lyons, & M. Ford (Eds.), *Labour migration and human trafficking in Southeast Asia: Critical perspectives* (pp. 23–40). Routledge.

12 Brennan, D. (2008). Competing claims of victimhood? Foreign and domestic victims of trafficking in the United States. *Sexuality Research & Social Policy, 5*(4), 45–61. https://doi.org/10.1525/srsp.2008.5.4.45

13 Fowler, J., Che, N., & Fowler, L. (2010). Innocence lost: The rights of human trafficking victims. *Procedia - Social and Behavioral Sciences, 2*(2), 1345–1349. https://doi.org/10.1016/j.sbspro.2010.03.198

14 Samarasinghe, V. (2008). *Female sex trafficking in Asia: The resilience of patriarchy in a changing world.* Routledge.

15 Borchgrevink, A. (2003). Ideas of power in the Philippines: Amulets and sacrifice. *Cultural Dynamics, 15*(1), 41–69. https://doi.org/10.1177/a033108

16 Lamvik, G. (2012). The Filipino seafarer: A life between sacrifice and shopping. *Anthropology in Action, 19*(1), 22–31. https://doi.org/10.3167/aia.2012.190104

17 Bautista, J. (2015). Export-quality martyrs: Roman Catholicism and transnational labor in the Philippines. *Cultural Anthropology, 30*(3), 424–447. https://doi.org/10.14506/ca30.3.04

18 Lam, T., & Yeoh, B. (2016). Migrant mothers, left-behind fathers: The negotiation of gender subjectivities in Indonesia and the Philippines. *Gender, Place & Culture,* 1–14. https://doi.org/10.1080/0966369X.2016.1249349

19 McKay, D. (2007). 'Sending dollars shows feeling' – Emotions and economies in Filipino migration. *Mobilities, 2*(2), 175–194. https://doi.org/10.1080/17450100701381532

20 Parreñas, R. (2013). The gender revolution in the Philippines: Migrant mothering and social transformations. In S. Eckstein & A. Najam (Eds.), *How immigrants impact their homelands* (pp. 191–212). Duke University Press.

Agency, sacrifice and human trafficking 185

21 Tacoli, C. (1996). Migrating 'for the sake of the family'? Gender, life course and infra-household relations among Filipino migrants in Rome. *Philippine Sociological Review, 44*(1–4), 12–32.

22 Tacoli, C. (1999). International migration and the restructuring of gender asymmetries: Continuity and change among Filipino labor migrants in Rome. *International Migration Review, 33*(3). https://doi.org/10.2307/2547530

23 van der Ham, A., Ujano-Batangan, M., Ignacio, R., & Wolffers, I. (2014). Toward healthy migration: An exploratory study on the resilience of migrant domestic workers from the Philippines. *Transcultural Psychiatry, 51*(4), 545–568. https://doi.org/10.1177/1363461514539028

24 Choi, S., & Lyons, L. (2012). Gender, citizenship, and women's 'unskilled' labour: The experience of Filipino migrant nurses in Singapore. *Canadian Journal of Women and the Law, 24*(1), 1–26. https://doi.org/10.3138/cjwl.24.1.001

25 Alipio, C. (2014). Domestic violence and migration in the Philippines. *International Institute for Asian Studies Newsletter, 2014*(67), 30–31.

26 Gardiner Barber, P. (2000). Agency in Philippine women's labour migration and provisional diaspora. *Women's Studies International Forum, 23*(4), 399–411. https://doi.org/10.1016/S0277-5395(00)00104-7

27 Ayalon, L. (2009). Evaluating the working conditions and exposure to abuse of Filipino home care workers in Israel: Characteristics and clinical correlates. *International Psychogeriatrics, 21*(01), 40. https://doi.org/10.1017/S1041610208008090

28 Bernardo, A., Daganzo, M., & Ocampo, A. (2016). Abusive supervision and well-being of Filipino migrant workers in Macau: Consequences for self-esteem and heritage culture detachment. *Social Indicators Research, 2016*, 1–16. https://doi.org/10.1007/s11205-016-1446-7

29 Hilsdon, A. (2007). Transnationalism and agency in East Malaysia: Filipina migrants in the nightlife industries. *The Australian Journal of Anthropology, 18*(2), 172–193. https://doi.org/10.1111/j.1835-9310.2007.tb00087.x

30 Lopez, M. (2012). Reconstituting the affective labour of Filipinos as care workers in Japan. *Global Networks, 12*(2), 252–268. https://doi.org/10.1111/j.1471-0374.2012.00350.x

31 Ruggunan, S. (2011). The role of organised labour in preventing a 'race to the bottom' for Filipino seafarers in the global labour market. *African and Asian Studies, 10*(2), 180–208. https://doi.org/10.1163/156921011X587022

32 Pun, N. (2005). *Made in China: Women factory workers in a global workplace.* Duke University Press/Hong Kong University Press.

33 van Meeteren, M., & Hiah, J. (2020). Self-identification of victimization of labor trafficking. In J. Winterdyk & J. Jones (Eds.), *The Palgrave international handbook of human trafficking* (pp. 1605–1618). Springer International Publishing. https://doi.org/10.1007/978-3-319-63058-8

34 Magat, M. (2007). Teachers and 'new evangelizers' for their faith: Filipina domestic workers at work in Italy. *Paedagogica Historica, 43*(4), 603–624. https://doi.org/10.1080/00309230701438005

35 Mayblin, M., & Course, M. (2014). The other side of sacrifice: Introduction. *Ethnos, 79*(3), 307–319. https://doi.org/10.1080/00141844.2013.841720

36 Bautista, J. (2015). *Religion, sacrifice and transnational labor in the Philippines.* Centre for Southeast Asian Studies, Kyoto University. http://www.cseas.kyoto-u.ac.jp/2015/01/religion-sacrifice-and-transnational-labor-in-the-philippines/

186 Agency, sacrifice and human trafficking

37 Guevarra, A. (2006). Managing 'vulnerabilities' and 'empowering' migrant Filipina workers: The Philippines' overseas employment program. *Social Identities, 12*(5), 523–541. https://doi.org/10.1080/13504630600920118

38 Guevarra, A. (2010). *Marketing dreams, manufacturing heroes: The transnational labor brokering of Filipino workers*. Rutgers University Press.

39 Hwang, M. (2017). Offloaded: Women's sex work migration across the South China Sea and the gendered antitrafficking emigration policy of the Philippines. *WSQ: Women's Studies Quarterly, 45*(1–2), 131–147. https://doi.org/10.1353/wsq.2017.0017

40 Parreñas, R. (2010). The indentured mobility of migrant women: How gendered protectionist laws lead Filipina hostesses to forced sexual labor. *Journal of Workplace Rights, 15*(3), 327–339. https://doi.org/10.2190/WR.15.3-4.f

41 Ong, J. (2015). Witnessing distant and proximal suffering within a zone of danger: Lay moralities of media audiences in the Philippines. *International Communication Gazette, 77*(7), 607–621. https://doi.org/10.1177/1748048515601555

42 Bollig, M. (2014). Resilience—Analytical tool, bridging concept or development goal? Anthropological perspectives on the use of a border object. *Zeitschrift Für Ethnologie, 139*(2), 253–279.

43 Chong, A. (2020). José Rizal attacks imperialism softly: Comprehending the depths of psychological conversion and the temptations of violent solutions. In F. A. Cruz & N. M. Adiong (Eds.), *International studies in the Philippines: Mapping new frontiers in theory and practice* (pp. 34–49). Routledge.

44 Brennan, D. (2017). Fighting human trafficking today: Moral panics, zombie data, and the seduction of rescue. *Wake Forest Law Review, 52*(2017), 477–496.

45 Feingold, D. (2010). Trafficking in numbers: The social construction of human trafficking data. In P. Andreas & K. Greenhill (Eds.), *Sex, drugs, and body counts: The politics of numbers in global crime and conflict* (pp. 46–74). Cornell University Press.

46 Kaye, J., Millar, H., & O'Doherty, T. (2020). Exploring human rights in the context of enforcement-based anti-trafficking in persons responses. In J. Winterdyk & J. Jones (Eds.), *The Palgrave international handbook of human trafficking* (pp. 601–621). Springer International Publishing. https://doi.org/10.1007/978-3-319-63058-8

47 O'Brien, E. (2018). *Challenging the human trafficking narrative: Victims, villains and heroes* (1st ed.). Routledge.

48 Bearup, L. (2020). The praxis of protection: Working with—and against— human trafficking discourse. In J. Winterdyk & J. Jones (Eds.), *The Palgrave international handbook of human trafficking* (pp. 1587–1603). Springer International Publishing. https://doi.org/10.1007/978-3-319-63058-8

Index

AFP *see* Armed Forces of the Philippines (AFP)
agency 172; and children/youth 43, 104; and migration 133; and sacrifice 174; and sexual labour 104–107; and structural violence 58; and structure 172–173; and underage soldiers 53–55; vs victimhood 5, 21–22, 43, 85, 172, 174; *see also* coercion and agency
anti-trafficking 7, 13, 107–108, 133, 182
anti-trafficking law *see* law
Armed Forces of the Philippines (AFP) 41–42, 56

Brennan, D. 21, 105–106
Briones, L. 175

child *see* children
children 42; and fieldwork 12, 14; and human trafficking 42–43; and trauma 53, 56, 103–104; and violence 56, 159; *see also* sexual labour and children/youth; underage soldiers
coercion 3; and agency 54; and children/youth 43; and migrant labour 132–133; and sexual labour/trafficking 102–105; and underage soldiers 54–55, 58; *see also* human trafficking definitions
commercial sex *see* sexual labour
compounding violence 26, 59–60, 86, 106–108, 157, 160
culture of migration 135–140

Davao city 13, 70, 89
death squads 160
domestic migration 70
Douglas, M. 157
drug use 106

Duterte, R. 41–42, 141–142

emotional labour 20–21, 135, 174–176
employment law *see* law
ethics 5, 17–19; formal approval 18
ethnography 7, 22
exploitative labour s*ee* labour exploitation

family economics 70–73, 84–85, 134–136, 158
Farmer, E. 23–24, 85

Galtung, J. 24, 25, 160
Gardiner Barber, P. 139
gatekeepers 5, 15–17
gender and labour 72–74, 87–90, 106–108, 120–123
globalisation 137–142
Guevarra, A. 177

history 38, 88, 140–141; of conflict 41–42, 56–57
hope 106, 176–177
human trafficking: definitions 3, 4, 7, 28, 181; statistics 2, 7, 87, 92

illegal migration *see* irregular migration
indirect violence *see* structural violence
informal economy 71; *see also* family economics
interviews 19–20, 22–23
intimate labour 88–89, 107, 159
irregular migration 116, 119, 134, 160, 174

labour and employment statistics 71–74, 88
labour exploitation 72–75, 88, 106–107

188 Index

law: and labour 72–75, 77, 89, 91, 107; and migrant labour 120–121, 133–134
legal system *see* law
Lindio-McGovern, L. 138

Marcos, F. 41, 56, 159
migration 116; *see also* agency and migration; coercion and migrant labour; law migrant labour; risk and migration; sacrifice and migration
modern slavery *see* human trafficking
moral injury 54, 106, 107, 170

narratives 5, 9, 18, 21–22, 174–176
New People's Army (NPA) 36–37, 41–42, 52–60
NPA *see* New People's Army (NPA)

O'Connell-Davidson, J. 119

Parreñas, R. 88–89, 119
participant observation 9
poverty: definitions and statistics 39–40, 70; rural 38, 56–58; *see also* risk and poverty
precarious labour 71–74, 138

reflexivity 11–13, 19–21, 68, 116
research aim and research design 5–6
research limits 7, 10–11, 22
resilience 55–56, 78, 105–106, 134, 174, 176
risk: definition of 150–151, 157; and family 158–159; and gender 159; and migration 116–118, 161, 163–165, 177–178; and rural Mindanao 56–58, 160; and sexual labour 90–91; and vulnerability 135–136, 151, 160

sacrifice 174–178; and migration 135, 137, 176–177
Scheper-Hughes, N. 87, 159
sex trafficking *see* trafficking for sexual labour
sex work *see* sexual labour

sexual labour 87–91, 107–108; definition of 91; *see also* agency and sexual labour; coercion and sexual labour/ trafficking; trafficking for sexual labour; underage sexual labour
social suffering 24–25
Spanish colonisation 38–39, 140
the State *see* Armed Forces of the Philippines (AFP); law; structural violence and the state; symbolic violence and the state
structural violence 23–26; and gender 72–74, 88–89, 106–108, 159; and globalisation 138, 140–141; and history 37–38, 59; and labour 70–72, 83, 85–86, 107; and law; and physical violence 85, 159–160; and poverty 58, 76, 141; and the state 56–60, 72, 83, 119–123; and risk 150–151; and rural poverty 56–60
symbolic violence 37, 106, 135–136, 139–140, 174–178; and the State 119–120, 134–140, 159–160
suffering 174–176

trafficking for sexual labour 87, 90–92, 102–106; and children/youth 85, 91–92; *see also* agency and sexual labour; coercion and sexual labour/ trafficking; human trafficking definitions; labour exploitation; risk and sexual labour; underage sexual labour
trafficking of migrants 116–119, 120–122, 132–134; *see also* coercion and migrant labour; human trafficking definitions; risk and migration
trauma 53–54, 103–106

underage sexual labour 43, 91–92, 103–104, 107, 109
underage soldiers 37, 42–43, 52–53, 58
undocumented migrants *see* irregular migration

Printed in the United States
by Baker & Taylor Publisher Services